THE ART OF TRANSLATION

THE *Art* OF TRANSLATION

voices from the field

EDITED BY ROSANNA WARREN

Northeastern University Press
BOSTON

Northeastern University Press

Copyright 1989 by Rosanna Warren

Library of Congress Cataloging-in-Publication Data

The Art of Translation : voices from the field / edited by Rosanna Warren.
   p. cm.
   Contributions emerged from lectures given over the past decade in the translation seminars at Boston University.
   Includes index.
   ISBN 1-55553-048-6 (alk. paper)
   1. Literature—Translating. 2. Literature—Translations into English—History and criticism. 3. Translating and interpreting. 4. English literature—Translations from foreign languages—History and criticism. I. Warren, Rosanna.
PN241.A76 1989
418'.02—dc19   88-30699
                                              CIP

Designed by Ann Twombly

This book was composed in Trump Medieval by Grote Deutsch & Company, Inc., in Madison, Wisconsin. It was printed and bound by Hamilton Printing Company in Rensselaer, New York. The paper is Sebago Antique, an acid-free sheet.

MANUFACTURED IN THE UNITED STATES OF AMERICA
93 92 91 90 89   5 4 3 2 1

This book is affectionately dedicated to
RODOLFO CARDONA
Godfather of the Translation Seminars

Contents

Acknowledgments

I OWE a debt of gratitude to the Andrew W. Mellon Foundation, whose generosity has supported the Translation Seminars at Boston University for almost a decade. I am grateful, as well, to Katherine Jackson for her perspicacious help in editing, and to William Arrowsmith, Rodolfo Cardona, Donald Carne-Ross, Teresa Iverson, Stephen Scully, and Roger Shattuck for their criticism and encouragement. Special thanks go to Deborah Kops who has nursed this book from infancy to whatever maturity it has attained.

I gratefully acknowledge the use of the following material:

Donald Carne-Ross is indebted to Mondadori and to New Directions for permission to reprint the texts of Montale's poems "Gli orecchini" and "Meriggiare." Copyright Arnoldo Mondadori Editore 1957 and 1948 respectively. Reprinted by permission of New Directions Publishing Corporation and Mondadori Editore.

In Denis Donoghue's essay, Thomas Kinsella's translation "I Will Not Die for You" appeared first in *An Duanaire 1600–1900: Poems of the Dispossessed*, Dolmen Press, 1981.

Michael Ewans's "Aischylos; *Oresteia:* Translation and Theatrical Commentary," quoted in his essay "Aischylos: For Actors, in the Round," presents the texts of the three plays as performed in the Drama Studio at the University of Newcastle, New South Wales, in 1983.

Tony Harrison's "Phaedra Britannica" first appeared as "A Preface to Phaedra Britannica," published by Rex Collings, London, 1976. Copyright 1976 by Tony Harrison.

The excerpt from *Sweeney Astray* in Seamus Heaney's "Earning a Rhyme: Notes on Translating *Buile Suibhne*" is reprinted by permission of Farrar, Straus and Giroux, Inc. Copyright 1983 by Seamus Heaney.

Christopher Middleton's "Translation as a Species of Mime" first appeared in *Translation* 17 (Fall 1986) (Columbia University).

In A. K. Ramanujan's essay, the Tamil poems translated into English and the chart "Some Features of the Five Landscapes" are reproduced from his book *Poems of Love and War* by permission of Columbia University Press. Copyright 1985 by Columbia University Press.

Dennis Tedlock's "The Translator; or, Why the Crocodile Was Not Disillusioned" first appeared in *Translation Review* 20: 6–8 (1986).

Rosanna Warren's translation of "Ille mi par . . ." in her essay "Sappho: Translation as Elegy" first appeared in her book of poems *Each Leaf Shines Separate* (Norton, 1984). Reprinted by permission of W. W. Norton Inc.

THE ART OF TRANSLATION

Introduction

*J'ai une sorte d'habitude de m'abandonner à ces agents
du destin que l'on nomme les "Autres."*

Paul Valéry

THE PSYCHIC HEALTH of an individual resides in the
capacity to recognize and welcome the "Other." The same could be
said of civilization. Our word "idiot" comes from the Greek ἰδιώτης,
from ἴδιος, whose primary sense is of privacy, peculiarity, isolation.
A person or culture guarding its privacy to an extreme extent becomes "idiotic," even autistic, and such resistance to the foreign,
such incapacity to translate, spells its doom, like the city of Thebes
in its refusal to welcome the new yet ancient, foreign yet cognate
god Dionysus. As George Steiner suggests in chapter upon chapter
of *After Babel*, from the neurophysiological level on up through the
broadest layers of culture, translation of one kind or another guarantees our shared survival.

In speaking of a civilization, we can distinguish between contemporary and historical translation. Transferring, "carrying across" the
chasm from one language to another, is commonly thought of as a
timeless activity, and indeed it may be when the original work is
contemporary with the translator. As soon as we approach a work
of the past, however, the historical dimension yawns as a vast new
chasm to be (however tenuously) bridged. Much literary translation
faces the vertigo of the two chasms with their maze of connecting
gulches and arroyos. To describe this it might help to turn from
geology to Walter Benjamin's vitalist metaphor: "Translation is so
far removed from being the sterile equation of two dead languages
that of all literary forms it is the one charged with the special mission
of watching over the maturing process of the original language and
the birth pangs of its own."[1] It is possible, also, to consider a purely
historical process of translation within a single language, the tem-

3

poral dynamism that renders our own past foreign to us. A civilization renews itself through contact not only with the geographically and linguistically foreign but also with its own forebears estranged by time. Charles Tomlinson's essay in this book argues such a case in regard to Dryden's and Pope's translations of Chaucer. In all cases, the contemporary, the historical, and, as occurs more often and more naturally, the mixture of the two, the study of translation turns out to be a study of the way a culture interprets its own conventions and engenders its future.

The essays in this book reflect various notions of the foreign and in their diversity offer, not a comprehensive survey of contemporary translation practice, but an indication of the fecundity of the field. The contributions emerged from lectures given over the past decade in the Translation Seminars at Boston University. The project has conceptual origins in the journals *Arion* and *Delos* and in the National Translation Center at the University of Texas at Austin, a center founded by several of our authors in the late 1960s. Indeed, the foundation of the National Translation Center was prompted by the publication of one of the classic collections of witness by translators brought forth in the early days of the Austin association: *The Craft and Context of Translation*, edited by William Arrowsmith and Roger Shattuck, in 1961. That book, along with the compendious *On Translation* by Reuben Brower (1959), might have been thought to render any future collections superfluous, so masterful were the contributors. But roughly four decades have passed since those publications, and, given the recent convulsions in linguistics, philosophy, and literary theory, it seemed a propitious moment to turn once again to a sample group of translators—some of them veterans from the earlier ventures—and, interrupting them at their desks, to ask them what they were doing. Had anything changed?

Not that we asked any such literal question. And each of the contributors to this volume, of course, answers implicitly in a different way, the value of such a book being its polyphony. If we turn now to our assembled translators, the new presence we hear affecting a good number of them, and distinguishing this collection from its elders, is Walter Benjamin. Benjamin is hardly "new," but he has been widely known in the United States for only twenty years. His essay "The Task of the Translator" is so hermetic that any number of translators (not to mention poets, novelists, philosophers, and critics) can extract almost any number of readings from it and come away satisfied and nourished (or in despair). Its protean presence throughout the essays collected here—rivaled only by that of

Borges's Pierre Menard—will illustrate that point. The power of the essay resides, I think, in its fusion of the surprising, not to say the outré, with the literarily familiar: a familiarity bred especially from French Symbolism. Speaking of "the central reciprocal relationship between languages," and "the foreignness of languages" (foreign, not just to one another, but to themselves), Benjamin was articulating ideas implicitly and obscurely felt by anyone translating literature with a modicum of self-consciousness. His recommendation for supremely sophisticated awkwardness, the deliberate reproduction of the original syntax, will hardly serve most translators as a daily working practice. But like those other experiments in extremism, the Zukofskys' Catullus, where the fetish is aural fidelity, and Housman's comic "Fragment of a Greek Tragedy," Benjamin's syntactic model expresses a *state of conscience* about translation, a radical scruple which, once internalized, cannot fail to affect quotidian labor. Translation does thrive in otherness, Benjamin's glued fragments of language. Whether one regards the fragments as pointing to a lost or imminent wholeness, a mystic pre-Babel language of Truth, depends on one's susceptibility to mysticism. In spite of the diversity of approaches assembled in this volume, there seems to be a fair consensus attributing the value of a translation precisely to its celebration of otherness, whether it be political otherness, as in Klor de Alva's essay on Classical Nahuatl, or the internal linguistic otherness that Tomlinson describes within English literature. We grow by welcoming difference, not by assimilating it entirely to ourselves. Many of the essays here, accordingly, emphasize "resistance" in one way or another: the resistance of Chinese syntax to English, of Argentinian popular culture to Anglo-American culture, of the Irish lyric to the English, of Dryden to Elizabethan rhetoric.

In a fine recent essay, Antoine Berman defines translation as "the finding-and-seeking of the break in the rule [the unruly, *le non-normé*] in the maternal language, so as to insert there the foreign language and its pattern of speech [*son dire*]."[2] This difficult and paradoxical reciprocity is nowhere better illustrated than in a letter by the man who has been called the patron saint of translation, St. Jerome, author of the Vulgate. Even while recommending translation as the finding of a *comparable mode of expression*, Epistle 106 preserves the Greek within the Latin, and sets the two languages, the two "idioms," even the two words for "idiom" (ἰδιομάτα and *proprieta*) vibrating together: "*hanc esse regulam boni interpretis, ut ἰδιομάτα linguae alterius suae linguae exprimat proprieta*" (this is the rule of a good translator, that he press out [express] the ἰδιομάτα of the other language in the special manner of his own language).

In a joke that has been circulating for some years, some North American corporate executives stage a grand unveiling for a computer intended to facilitate international commerce by translating any language into any other language in the twinkling of an eye. A test is arranged: the computer is commanded to translate "Out of sight, out of mind" into Chinese. Out slip some mysterious Chinese characters. When a sinologist is finally hustled in to translate the translation, it reads, "Invisible idiot." Like the whole class of jokes to which it belongs, this one scoffs at technological hubris, but even more, it revels in the untranslatability of cultures (whose essences emerge crystallized in proverbs). Returning to the idea of the "idiotic" that launched this introduction, we might adopt the phrase "invisible idiot" to describe one conventional image of the translator: a witless mediator or scribe, whose labor is often not even mentioned in reviews of translated works. This view is changing. Not only are good translators the least "idiotic" of writers, in the root sense of least private, peculiar, self-enclosed; but they are becoming more and more visible as well. As a result of this century's commotions in linguistics and philosophy in the work of Saussure, Lévi-Strauss, Foucault, Derrida, to mention only a few, translation is seen increasingly as an activity that reflects our most radical (rooted and innovative), and radically varied, concerns. It is a model for cognition and survival. In the metamorphosis of a literary work from one language to another, we can see something like the patterns of reception and creative response to stimuli which ensure the adaptations and survival of plant and animal species, and which, on another level, ensure our own maturation and "adaptation" as individual human beings and as peoples. George Steiner's *After Babel* has done a great deal to escort translation into that larger arena, and his book is accompanied by many more and less specialized ventures, not the least of which are the testimonies of the translators themselves.

Ambitious claims have indeed been advanced for translators. Some critics and scholars, the editor of a recent anthology dedicated to translation declares, "are convinced that something has indeed happened to change our thinking about language radically, and they are determined to elaborate some of the specific and strategic consequences for translation."[3] That "something," for the editor, is the advent of Derrida and, broadly speaking, of deconstruction, which "constitutes a decisive test for thought about discourse in general and for all the usual talk about translation as the transfer of meaning from one language to another."[4] The editor goes on to note that several of the essays in his volume "render translation in the ordinary sense problematic by finding problems precisely with that ordinary sense."

Exactly what "translation in the ordinary sense" may be supposed to mean is not stated. But from both the introduction and the ensuing essays we may fairly assume it to be some simple-minded transfer of "meaning"; "traditional" translation is presumed to have been "meaning-preserving,"[5] as if up until now translators had done nothing but dump some indefinable cargo called "meaning" from one bucket to another, without ever wondering about the appropriateness of concepts of containment and transfer. Such a view of "traditional" translation betrays a certain innocence in regard to literary language and theories of literary translation (an innocence, by the way, that one can hardly attribute to that cunning magus himself, Derrida: his philosophical thought proceeds by maneuvering in language as in a literary medium). That view of "traditional" translation also betrays an offensive assumption of the superiority of current modes of critical "discourse," so enlightened by their "problematics," to all previous literary thought.

No one acquainted with literature ever believed in such a chimera as a "meaning" to be preserved apart from its dynamic embodiment in form; Walter Benjamin dispatched that sorry beast early in the pages of his essay "The Task of the Translator," because, steeped in Baudelaire and Mallarmé, he could not help finding the concept obnoxious. The dismissal of so crude a formula by Benjamin is not shocking; it is conventional literary wisdom in the best sense. To take just one of myriad examples, it is audible in Valéry's statement in his introduction to his translation of Virgil's *Eclogues*: the poet's work "consists less in seeking words for his ideas than in seeking ideas for his words and predominant rhythms."[6] The medium of the literary writer, and especially of the literary translator, was never "meaning" per se but has always been the *linguistic conditions of meaning*: tension, risk, suspicion, the perilous dance of formal language with and away from meaning.

There are translators, like Richard Sieburth and, to some extent, Rosmarie Waldrop in this volume, who have indeed found in the work of authors such as Derrida and de Man an enabling and liberating set of terms and strategies and, one could perhaps say, a new working myth. Waldrop's meditation on ruined statues as a figure for translation as mutilation in time reverberates with an intuition akin to Derridean *"différance,"* language's inevitable slippage from itself. Sieburth, who has lived long and intimately with the ghost of Benjamin, cites works of Derrida and de Man on Benjamin as "background readings" for his esssay. He insists on the provisionality and instability in the relationship between original and translation, a provisionality preserving a breathing space between the two texts and guaranteeing their evolving "afterlife" in our minds. Sieburth demonstrates with supreme tact how an approach obliquely inspired by Derrida can release to our senses some of the inherently literary power of a work.

Current criticism, of course, has turned its inquisitorial eye upon the notion of the "literary" as somehow unjustly "privileged discourse." These investigations have let some welcome light and air into the old manse; they have revealed whole rooms, a whole imaginative architecture, hitherto ignored. In this volume, for instance, the anthropological work of J. Klor de Alva and Dennis Tedlock is invaluable in suggesting the extent to which our social and political lives are permeated by language and by interpretive concerns that might traditionally have been thought of as "literary." Such boundaries are more and more difficult to maintain; they serve, more often than not, to show how literature preserves its vitality by border raids into the "unliterary." Still, as long as one finds language demoted to the status of vehicle, the old-fashioned category of the literary performs a real function, demarcating works primarily preoccupied with the artful and even amorous coaxing of the medium itself from those whose raison d'être is utilitarian, the delivery of ideas and information.

Philosophy, agog recently at the discovery that language betrays and that "meaning" is at best a fluid concept, has come rather late to appreciate the instability and dynamism which are the essence of the medium, and which a Proust, a Baudelaire, a Shakespeare, a Horace has always known and delighted in. Translation is a peculiarly specialized mode of literary composition; for translators, there never was an "ordinary sense" of translation, because the vertiginous conditions of the work do not support it. In fact, it might appear that "translation in the ordinary sense" is more useful as an easy target in a philosophical shooting gallery than as a phrase describing the real endeavors of translators.

This book joins the earlier collections of witness by practitioners, who finally must speak for themselves, and some excellent recent collections such as Edwin Honig's *The Poet's Other Voice* and *The Translator's Art: Essays in Honour of Betty Radice* edited by William Radice and Barbara Reynolds. As the problems of translation are infinite, so should be the confessions of translators. Georges Mounin concludes his monumental and, at times, highly technical survey, *Les problèmes théoriques de la traduction*, with the following clause, which consoles by its very common sense: "*. . . sans doute, la communication par la traduction n'est-elle jamais vraiment finie, ce qui signifie en même temps qu'elle n'est jamais inéxorablement impossible*"[7] (that is: . . . doubtless, communication by translation is never truly concluded, which means at the same time that it is never inexorably impossible). In terminating this prelude, I splice my language to his, his hope to mine, and make way for the performances of the translators.

NOTES

1. Walter Benjamin, "The Task of the Translator," in *Illuminations*, tr. Harry Zohn (Schocken Books, 1969; 1977), 73.

2. Antoine Berman, "*La traduction de la lettre—ou, l'auberge au lointain*," in *Les tours de Babel* (Trans-Europ-Repress, 1985), 141. The translation is mine.

3. J. G. Graham, *Difference in Translation* (Cornell University Press, 1985), 20.

4. Ibid., 19.

5. Robert J. Matthews, "What did Archimedes Mean by 'Χρυςός'?" in Graham, *Difference in Translation*, 149.

6. Paul Valéry, "Variations sur les Bucoliques de Virgile," in *Oeuvres*, vol. 1, ed. Jean Hytier (Bibliothèque de la Pleiade, Gallimard, 1957), 212. The translation is mine.

7. Georges Mounin, *Les problèmes théoriques de la traduction* (Gallimard, 1963), 279.

I

Testimonies

Earning a Rhyme: Notes on Translating Buile Suibhne

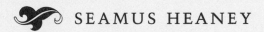 SEAMUS HEANEY

SWEENEY ASTRAY, the version of *Buile Suibhne* which appeared in 1983, was a thorough revision of work done between September 1972 and April 1973. In the summer of 1972, my family and I moved from Belfast to county Wicklow in the Republic of Ireland, where I spent the next three years working as a full-time writer. Week after week, I addressed myself with varying degrees of pleasure to D. G. O'Keefe's edition of *Buile Suibhne*, prepared, with an English crib *en face*, for the Early Irish Texts Society in 1913. What follows are some reflections on the conditions under which any Irish writer operates when he enters into the footsteps of the established translators, some of whom, like James Clarence Mangan, Samuel Ferguson, and Douglas Hyde, "sang to sweeten Ireland's wrong"; but all of whom, including Lady Charlotte Guest, Lady Augusta Gregory, Frank O'Connor, and Thomas Kinsella, sang to sustain a tradition that transcended their own personal literary ambitions. I will also say something about the actual process of working with a crib and give some examples of the changes in approach to translation which occurred between my first version and the second, published one, taken up after a period of seven years.

I

The translation of a text from the Irish language by an Irish writer who speaks English is usually to be perceived in lights other than just those of the writer's own career and impulses. The additional contexts are historical, cultural, and political, as when a Native

13

American author turns to material in one of the original languages of the North American continent. In each case, a canonical literature in English creates the acoustic within which the translation is to be heard; an overarching old colonial roof inscribed "The land was ours before we were the land's" is made to echo with some such retort as "You don't say!"

The translation of an Anglo-Saxon poem by an English writer does not have the same resonance. The invasion of England by the Normans did indeed have a powerful effect upon the language, but what occurred was a mutation rather than an obliteration. Native translations of the Old English deposits are acts of retrenchment rather than sabotage. They reinforce the English myth of continuity. They give new form to that from which the English have themselves been formed. The newness may be a disruption or countering of settled conventions, but it will not be a challenge to the deep structure. Hopkins's innovations, for example, though not strictly translations, did in fact employ an Anglo-Saxon stress in order to produce the double effect I have just outlined: they went against the grain of contemporary English verse-craft in a completely salutary way, and at the same time they went *with* an older English grain of collective memory and belonging.

When, however, John Millington Synge created a new mandarin idiom in his plays and in his prose book *The Aran Islands,* the purpose of the enterprise was very different. It may have looked the same: an attempt to revolutionize the language of English literature, one of those periodic returns to the spoken norm which Donne and Dryden and Wordsworth had initiated in their times, and which T. S. Eliot would set in motion shortly after Synge's own death. But Synge was as involved in an attempt to found a new literary tradition as he was bound within the structures of the old one. The collective memory and sense of belonging which his auditory imagination aspired to amplify were not English; on the contrary, they were what gave energy to contemporary political movements for separation from Britain, and for the restoration of Irish as the national language of Ireland. For Synge to base his style upon an otherness of usage in the absent Irish language was therefore more than a mere exoticism: it constituted solidarity with cultural and political efforts going forward in the same direction in other quarters.

The Irish Literary Revival is by now a historical phenomenon. And the Norman invasion of England, the Tudor conquest of Ireland, and English colonization of North America, all these are even more suspended and remote. Yet in Northern Ireland in the late sixties and early seventies, when the international excitements of the civil rights movement got grafted on to the political appetites of the Nationalist minority; when questions about identity and cultural difference, which were being newly plied by blacks and Native Americans in the United States, came up again urgently and violently in Northern Ireland; when the poets there—who had ignored their different religio-political origins in the name of that greater humility and flexibility which the imaginative endeavor entails—began to find themselves tugged by undercurrents of historical memory and pleas for identification with the political aims of their groups; when the whole unfinished business of the England/Ireland entanglement presented itself at a local level as a conflict of loyalties and impulses—when all this happened, historical parallels and literary precedents began to assume fresh relevance, and to offer distances and analogies which could ease the strain of the present. The poets were needy for ways in which they could honestly express the exacerbations of the local quarrel without turning that expression into just another manifestation of the aggressions and resentments which had been responsible for the quarrel in the first place.

It was under these circumstances that I began work on *Buile Suibhne,* a Middle Irish text already well known because of Flann O'Brien's hilarious incorporation of its central character into the apparatus of his *At Swim-Two-Birds*—the title itself being a literal translation of the name of a place where Sweeney has a typically eerie encounter with women. Obviously, there were several attractions in the material besides its political applicability, but since I have spoken about those things in my introduction to the published version, I will continue here on this more generalizing course. In the anxiety of those times, the abiding problem was to discover a properly literary activity which might contain a potentially public meaning; and in writing the book which would eventually appear as *Sweeney Astray,* I persuaded myself that the problem had been given at least a temporary solution.

How? Why? What had the tale of a petty king from seventh-century Ulster, cursed by a saint, transformed by the shock of battle into a demented flying creature, and doomed to an outcast's life in the trees, what had all this amalgam in verse and prose to do with me or the moment? How could a text engendered within the Gaelic order of medieval Ireland speak to a modern Ulster audience riven by divisions resulting from the final destruction of that order? The very meaning of the term "Ulster" had been forced. Originally the name of an ancient Irish province and part of a native Gaelic cosmology, it had become through plantation by the English in the 1620s and partition by them in the 1920s the name of a six-county British enclave that resisted integration with the Republic of Ireland and indulged in chronic discriminatory practices against its Irish Nationalist minority in order to maintain the status quo. What had the translation of the tale of a Celtic wild man to do with the devastations of the new wild men of the Provisional IRA?

My hope was that that book might render a Unionist audience more pervious to the notion that Ulster was Irish, without coercing them out of their cherished conviction that it was British. Also, because it reached back into a pre-colonial Ulster of monastic Christianity and Celtic kingship, I hoped the book might complicate the sense of entitlement to the land of Ulster which had developed so overbearingly in the Protestant majority, as a result of various victories and acts of settlement over the centuries. By extending the span of their historical memory into pre-British time, one might stimulate some sympathy in the Unionists for the Nationalist minority who located their lost title to sovereignty in that Gaelic dream-place.

I did not, of course, expect *Sweeney Astray* so to affect things that political conversions would break out all over Northern Ireland. I did not even think of my intention in the deliberate terms which I have just outlined. I simply wanted to offer an indigenous text that would not threaten a Unionist (after all, this was just a translation of an old tale, situated for much of the time in what is now county Antrim and county Down) and that would fortify a Nationalist (after all, this old tale tells us we belonged here always and that we still remain unextirpated). I wanted to deliver a work of imagination that could be read universally as the thing-in-itself but which would also sustain those extensions of meaning that our disastrously complicated predicament at home made both urgent and desirable.

II

First time round, I went at the work speedily and a little overbearingly. I was actually taking off from O'Keefe's parallel translation more than I was attending to the Irish itself. I was afraid that I might not finish the whole thing, so in order to forestall as far as possible the let-down of such a failure, I hurled myself at the task. My main pitch, day by day, was to keep up an animated rate of production.

I could not afford to dwell upon any single eddy of difficulty or subtlety in case it slowed me down to a discouraging rate. Consequently, the first draft was mostly in free verse, bowling along in the malleable quatrains that had become a habit in the course of writing *Wintering Out*.

First time round, I was also far more arrogant in my treatment of the verse. That is to say, I arrogated to myself the right to follow suggestions in the original, to develop a line of association out of the given elements of the Irish rather than to set down an obedient equivalent. I allowed myself to import echoes from the English literary tradition, from the Bible, to perform in metaphor what the text delivered in statement. O'Keefe, for example, gave the following direct translation of part of a typical Sweeney lament:

> Though I be as I am to-night,
> there was a time
> when my strength was not feeble
> over a land that was not bad.
>
> On splendid steeds,
> in life without sorrow,
> in my auspicious kingship
> I was a good, great king.

In 1972, however, I was in no mood to follow the drab, old-fashioned lead of this kind of thing. It became a much more jacked-up performance altogether:

> Though I am Lazarus,
> there was a time
> when I dressed in purple
> and they fed from my hand.
>
> I was a good king,
> the tide of my affairs
> was rising, the world
> was the bit in my horse's mouth.

Lowell's example was operative here. His trick of heightening the sense by adding voltage to the diction and planting new metaphors into the circuit was not lost on me. Nor was his unabashed readiness to subdue the otherness of the original to his own autobiographical neediness. I began to inflate myself and my situation into Sweeney's, to make analogies between the early medieval Ulsterman who rocketed out of the north, as a result of vehement squabbles there among the petty dynasties, and this poet from county Derry who had also come south for purposes of retreat and composure. It all contributed to a velocity that was its own reward. I cuffed the original with a brusqueness and familiarity that was not earned but that gave me immense satisfaction. I was using *Buile Suibhne* as a trampoline: I should have been showing it off, but instead it was being pressed into service to show me off.

Naturally, I did not feel this from day to day as I went baling through the stanzas. But I did have a nagging sense that the freedoms being exercised were not going to yield an integrated work. Riff by riff, it felt good, but there was no sense, as the pages piled up, of "thoughts long knitted to a single thought." I had wanted the pressure and accumulating oneness which is the reward—and justification—of a sustained writing; what I was getting was a series of lyric highs, exciting enough in themselves but not gathering force between themselves. Nevertheless, since my primary aim had become the completion of a version of the whole text, I forged ahead until that goal was achieved. Then I simply went flat, fell into a kind of post-composition tristesse. I knew that it would all have to be done over again, but I had not the stamina or the quickening relish necessary to a fresh start.

I cannot remember when I got the idea that the stanzas should be re-cast in a more hard-edged, pointed way; that they should have the definition of hedges in a winter sunset; that they should be cold, definite, and articulated; should rhyme or ring; should be tuned to a chaste, bare note; should be more constricted and ascetic; more obedient to the metrical containments and battened-down verbal procedures of the Irish itself. At any rate, it was in 1979, after my first semester at Harvard, that I suddenly started one morning to reshape stanzas from scratch, rhyming them and keeping my eyes as much to the left, on the Irish, as to the right, on O'Keefe's unnerving trot.

It was this closer inspection of the thickets of the Irish that made the second stint a different kind of engagement. Instead of the energy being generated by hurry and boldness, a certain intensity gathered through the steadier, more lexically concentrated gaze at individual words. Instead of the rhythmic principle being one of lanky, enjambed propulsion, the lines hurdling along for fear they might seize up, the unit of composition now became the quatrain itself, and the metrical pattern became more end-stopped and boxed-in.

The eight lines I quoted earlier sounded now both more literal and more limited within the stanza-shape:

Far other than to-night,
far different my plight
the times when with firm hand
I ruled over a good land.

Prospering, smiled upon,
curbing some great-steed,
I rode high, on the full tide
of good luck and kingship.

I still tried to get a self-igniting life between the words but kept them flintier and more niggardly than before. My favorite instance of the new asceticism is from section 73, where Sweeney praises the setting of a little monastery at Alternan. O'Keefe gives the place its Irish name and renders the relevant stanza as follows:

Cliff of Farannan, abode of Saints,
with many fair hazels and nuts,
swift cold water
rushing down its side.

In my original handling of this, I took fire at the possibility of making the saintliness of the place more resplendent than either the original poet or the unflashy O'Keefe would have dreamed of:

O the tabernacle of the hazel wood
on the cliff of Farannan,
and the cataract glittering
like the stem of a chalice!

Seven years later, the gilding came off and the exclamation was at least curbed:

Sainted cliff at Alternan,
nut grove, hazel wood!
Cold quick sweeps of water
fall down the cliff-side.

III

It is nine years since those lines were written, and sixteen since they were done in the freer register, so what I am giving here is a recreation of the feel of the writing experience rather than a report on the details of the procedure. Yet one does hope for a definite "feel" as one writes: It is a guarantee of the life of the thing. For in spite of the reality of all the cultural contexts and promptings that

I referred to earlier, the true anxiety and the true motivations of writing are much more inward, much more to do with freshets that start in good moments of intent concentration and hope. Literary translation—or version making or imitation or refraction or whatever one should call the linguistic carry-over that is mediated through a crib—is still an aesthetic activity. It has to do with form feeling as much as with sense giving, and unless the practitioner has the almost muscular sensation that rewards successful original composition, it is unlikely that the results of the text-labor will have life of their own.

The closer, line by line, stanza by stanza, end-stopped, obedient, literal approach finally yielded more. One had a sense of accumulation rather than of truancy—a different satisfaction, not necessarily superior but more consoling in the execution of a long piece of composition. One also had forgotten about the political extensions that were originally intended. In fact, by the time *Sweeney Astray* appeared, I had got fed up with my own mournful bondings to the "matter of Ulster" and valued more the defined otherness of *Buile Suibhne* as art. If, in the beginning, I was somewhat surprised that I had taken on the translation at all, in the end I was grateful to feel still somewhat estranged from what I had made of it. In fact, it was only after the translation had been completed for the second time and I had earned that familiarity which I had originally arrogated—it was only then that the work truly yielded itself over. The freedom and peremptoriness which I had exercised prematurely returned in a burst of confidence, and I produced the speedy poems included in *Station Island* under the general title of "Sweeney Redivivus." The identification I made previously between the green man and the rural child was admitted and even stimulated. Sweeney was unreservedly rhymed with Heaney:

Give him his due, in the end

he opened my path to a kingdom
of such scope and neuter allegiance
my emptiness reigns at its whim.
"Sweeney and the Cleric"

Translation as a Species
of Mime

 CHRISTOPHER MIDDLETON

WHAT I HAVE TO SAY here will be partly chronicle
and partly conjecture. First, I should like to say something about
the moods and places in which I have translated Robert Walser's
quite peculiar prose. Then I should like to ask some questions about
where the imagination of a translator situates an author. To conclude, I shall make some speculative remarks on mime—on translating Walser as a performance with analogies in mime.

I was introduced to Robert Walser's writings in 1954 by Ernst
Nef, at that time a student at the University of Zurich. I can not
remember if he showed me a book in the corridor outside the English
seminar, or if he knocked at the window of my Zeltweg apartment
and passed a book through the window when I opened it. Anyway
I was immediately spellbound. I was spellbound by the unliterary,
even counterliterary, character of the writing. Soon I wanted to see
how this writing would look in English, so I started to translate *Der
Spaziergang*. At the same time I ransacked antiquarian bookshops
and combed catalogues for original editions of his books, which were
hard to find, but their rarity put ginger into the search.

When the translation was finished, I wrote to Carl Seelig—
Walser's legal guardian—and he invited me to visit him. He showed
me some manuscripts, including some of the microscripts. We drank
tea and cognac. I remember how graciously he received me—and
how he called the cognac a *surrogat* for an honorarium. This was in
the spring of 1955 and Walser was still living. For me he was living
not only in his books and in the Herisau asylum, but everywhere
in Zurich and in the bony faces of young peasants I saw in the train
to Sankt Gallen one day. People on the streets, normal or eccentric,
suddenly assumed identities, all of which, however variously, I mea-

sured against my image of Robert Walser or of his characters. I thought I could perceive a *spiritus helveticus* lurking under all the orthodoxy. As a maker of mischief, my Walser was enveloping everyone in a Walserian aura. His prose was affecting me like Merlin in the Dark Ages, like Hermes in antiquity: my mind was projecting a spectacle in which all figures and events were essentially Walserian.

In 1961 and 1962 I spent some time teaching at the University of Texas at Austin. There I met another Englishman, Kim Taylor. Kim's wife, Aya, was Swiss-German. Aya read some Walser, on my suggestion, and so did Kim. In 1963, after I had returned to London, Kim wrote and asked me to translate some Walser pieces for the *Texas Quarterly*, a respectable university journal. Kim's friend Cyril Satorsky, an exuberant Polish lithographer from Cockney London, was commissioned to illustrate the translations. So it was in London that I translated *"Pierrot," "Herren und Angestellte,"* and *"Helblings Geschichte."* The room where I worked in London, like the room in Zeltweg, looked out on a street, but I did not see any Robert Walsers walking in the street, because this was in South London. Besides, I never could fathom the English or put auras around them. Even then, I managed to tear the London sky apart and provide an English basis for the astonishing, furtive, dithering, anxious, micronihilist, and somehow Laforguian Helbling.

In 1966 I returned to Austin. One evening at supper I met a lady of (I believe) Austrian descent, who happened to be an editor at the University of Texas Press. She knew of Walser's work. She said, "Why not translate *Jakob von Gunten?* We'll publish your translation." I had recently finished translating a selection of Nietzsche's letters. The idea of translating *Jakob von Gunten* excited me. (It was only later that I heard that Max Brod once said, *"Nach Nietzsche mußte Walser kommen."*) I worked on the translation during the summer of 1967, in a very small house not far from the lake. Again I was looking out of a window. This time I was seeing a green mountain laurel bush, a conical cedar tree, and a roughly built wall of stones, limestone, with singing birds, perilous insects, and deadly snakes housed among them. When I translate, I work like a maniac. So I had soon finished a rough draft of *Jakob von Gunten*. Then, in company with a friend, Ann, I traveled south through Mexico to the Yucatán. We were hoping to find a totally strange world down there. I took with me my big notebook with Walser in it. We did not find any strangeness, and it was July in the tropics down there, people begging in the streets, sweating in hammocks, pyramids, and enormous pools into which princesses had once been toppled as a translator topples into an original text. Yet—in Merida, we found a hotel where D. H. Lawrence had stayed once. I scribbled revisions into the draft while lying on a big white bed. Later, I almost got drowned inside a shoal of goldfish off the coast of Isla Mujeres, but surfaced just in time to lunch off the flesh of a barracuda, later to finish the translation of *Jakob von Gunten.*

Back in the Yucatán, in a Merida hotel, Jakob and Herr Benjamenta are still traveling in search of adventures, in search of strangeness.

After a lapse of ten years I began to receive letters from Tom Whalen, a young American writer. In the forests of Arkansas he had discovered the Walser translations, and he was now reading them excitedly with his students in Louisiana. He visited me in Austin and persuaded me, over glasses of bourbon and after several games of pool, to translate some more short prose by Walser for a little magazine which he was co-editing. Walser subsequently appeared in New Orleans, to inspire several small authors, hardly more than infants, and some of them won prizes for their inspired writings. In 1980, I believe, I began to edit *Selected Stories.* Susan Sontag had spoken about Robert Walser to my English publisher, Michael Schmidt; at that time he knew nothing of my work translating Walser, for I had never thought to mention it. So, still in Austin, still in the small house, no, by now it was twice as big, but I still worked in my dusty room among the singing birds. I translated many more short prose pieces for the new book. I was still looking through the window at bushes and stones and great gliding black swallowtail butterflies.

The question arises: When you translate a writer's work, where is the writer? Obviously he is not there, in the place where you walk around or lie or sit, wringing your hands, translating what he wrote, murmuring the words. He is not to be seen through the window. He is not in Zurich, London, the Yucatán, or River Hills (Texas). Yet, afterwards, *he has been there.* Afterwards, I say, he has been there. He has been where you translated him. The work, and the passion of translating, place him there *afterwards.* Not physically, not altogether fantastically either, but in a sense that we invoke, in all honesty, when we say that rays of feeling surround, penetrate, and situate a particular object. This work of translation, as a kind of sensitive passion, unfolds through two successive moments of *Einfühlung.* First, obviously, you enter into a relationship with the writer as a presence which pervades the original text—a presence, that is, rather than a personality. Second, from that relationship, as your translation comes into the open, the writer as a presence is released into the place in which you worked—he steps out into it, that presence.

The bond which guarantees that presence in the place is now your translation, the text you have conducted out of the original. This means that the place, too, has changed. It has become the dwelling, transitory enough, of a presence which would not otherwise have been there. If, as some suppose, the signs in writing gather momentum only to defer final signification, then the act of translating, if not the final translation, carries the movement of deferral a stage further. The translator in the act is catching what the writer threw. Even if the catch is not a complete one, the act restores to presence the writer and to that writer's signs a glow of immediacy. If the act is formally completed in the translation as text, then there is reason to think that the translation is not a copy in another idiom but a creative transcription which has ensued upon a deep assimilation of the so-called "spirit" of the original text.

Perhaps this isolation of the act from the text is merely an attempt to put a limit around a field of variables. But in proposing that such a limit is not inconceivable, I mean to propose three ideas. (1) The catching of what is thrown is almost certain to be an asymptotic movement—no finality. (2) A circuitry between the signs establishes itself and ushers into imagination a presence, which, being imaginary, is manifold. (3) We arrive here in a borderline area—or a liminal area—where a concept like "magic" passes across from discourse about the imaginative power of the original into discourse about the act of translation. The magical is a thorny issue. Possibly discourse about translation is often inhibited by cautionary ideas about a creative magic so mysteriously enshrined in the original as to be unhoped for in the translation. The caution is mandatory. Despite crass or cunning pretensions on the translator's part, no translation substitutes for its original (least of all, perhaps, the truly vital translation). On the other hand, there can be, I think, in the ongoing act of translation, in the translator psychology, if you will, a belief which exhilarates the translator, bears him up, so that he feels he might be reweaving the original spell. The notion of magical process— *katexochen* transrational—on both sides of the threshold between original and translation, is not as vain as it might often seem.

I am talking about the fertility of the spirit to which a writer may give birth in his writings. Into this fertility the translator inserts his own language roots. Latency and actuality, the imaginable to be converted and the translation text, somehow conspire. Somehow this spirit I have called "presence" fecundates places and persons, and translation can disseminate the spores, the signs, the traces, of that presence. Transformed into another language, the signs are set free to become otherwise fertile (in a different value code, which is the *proprium* of the translator's language). Becoming otherwise fertile, the converted signs modify the confines and constraints of the other language, so that English, say, may actually undergo a local change. At least, translation can re-situate its expressive range, once the Walser presence comes to life in it. This will happen as long as the other language learns to play by rules which had not been actualized in it until the dissemination occurred, had not been recognized, had only been latent. Well, but everyone acknowledges that translation negotiates intercourse, not just discourse, and that large mutations in cultural morphology may slowly occur as a result of the going-between that translation does—witness southwestern Europe during the twelfth century.

I mentioned play a moment ago. This is where Walser is eminently important to his admirers. I shall not go into particulars about Walser's ways of playfully, but also critically and often fiercely, subverting linguistic norms and behavioral codes. I shall not even explore the ways in which his "ludic" writings spring from and make hay with a defensive *Angst* which is foisted upon civilized people by their desires and, no less, by their torturers. What I shall do is offer some conjectures on mime. It seems to me that quarrels about equivalence in theory of translation, not to mention arguments about possible varieties of literary translation, are inclined to be stymied by a failure to pass from notions of imitation to notions of mime.

The manifold presence (in my case, Walser) is released into a place and comes to dwell in it. This release is negotiated by an act of translation conceived as miming which is not imitation. In practice, imitation copies appearances. Imitation reproduces the self-evident, it takes a cast of the statue, it tries to replicate. Mime, on the other hand, formalizes a profound—and rebellious—need of the central nervous system, a need of which imitation is no more than a passing shadow. The need formalized in mime is a need to become one with that which is not-self, that which is utterly beyond what self is or was. Mime actualizes a desire for union with the "other." It embodies more than contact with the other, more than inclination toward it. This is not so odd, after all. We are mimes more often than we realize, from babyhood on. Our first efforts to speak are miming, rather than imitation; you only have to watch the face of a one-year-old to see that. A passionate love-relation is perhaps the first real step toward an authentically poetic or dramatic miming. Lovers will often mime one another. Lovers hope to achieve a fullness of insight into the other person. Each dreams that the other person is a living presence, not a mere skin-coated bundle of nervous and bodily reactions. (And so many loves founder because they are, at root, narcissistic.) Love is what makes the other person seem like a spirit who makes life happen, who inaugurates life. The beloved person means the beginning or the refreshing of life. Think what festive inaugurations they are, the moments that lovers enjoy. If the love is reciprocated, this miming for insight is countermimed. With imitation there is no such intense reciprocity. There is less *Einsicht*, as one might say in German, there is *Zweischt* and *Vielsicht* instead, and these go on multiplying, never completing the clean mimetic circuit, only augmenting—as in Kafka—the labyrinth of *Angst*. This does not imply that the clean mimetic circuit of reciprocity is less than catastrophic. Bland lovers can be boring ones. It does imply that the mime's ecstatic self-surrender, by which a naked insight into the other is achieved, is not part of the experience of imitation.

In the field of representations occupied by mime and imitation, the interval between them may be no more than a hair's breadth, or it may be greater. Both are, inescapably, modes of representation. Yet with imitation you recognize the original through its representation and judge whether the imitation is good or poor by measuring it against the original. The original is what you are reminded of. With mime, certain traces of the original may be implied in the act, but the act itself is originative. If the act is powerfully originative, the traces may be reduced to a mere ghostly scaffolding.

This, I realize, is an as yet insufficiently considered distinction. To suggest the scope of it, rather than grappling with Aristotle and his heirs, I shall furnish a small but extreme instance. At lunch in a leafy arbor on a hillside near Itschnach east of Zurich in 1956, one of my fellow guests was a deaf-mute, in his early twenties, an engaging and high-spirited person. He had learned to simulate Swiss-German speech patterns, several, and despite the oddity of his sounds he was able to get by, even amusingly so. After lunch, urged by our hostess and other guests, he stood on the terrace tiles and showed us how a hatted middle-aged man might trundle to his place of work. The showing was, to some extent, an imitation of something quite commonplace—but it differed in kind from the simulation audible in his speech. The performance had an outline and distinctness that set it apart, it was sui generis. It projected an image that surpassed mere impersonation. It had a quiddity that was all its own. The energy blocked on the level of speech had been conducted into another area, that of the deaf-mute's motor-muscular system. His act of miming, with its intense empathetic hyperbole, set *this* hatted man's trundling altogether apart. The act condensed all rigmaroles, revised and reframed all routines, to project a creation as singularly "inscaped" as anything by Chaplin or Marceau.

What does a mime do? He imitates, yes, but not the actions, gestures, idiosyncrasies of one individual, isolable, human or animal subject. Rather, he takes possession of a total structure by bringing countless small and subtle perceptions into an imaginative configuration. This distinction in effect subordinates all imitation, subordinates it to a spellbinding, independent, and creative action. That action has an air of being its own principle, and of being positive, as opposed to derived or secondary as an imitation is. And surely it is the "absolute" aesthetic and the coherent style of his performance that distinguishes a creative mime. So imitation is only his sketch. What's more, once his synthesis is varied enough, profound enough, he distances himself from the integral image he has created. Next, out of the aura provided by the distance achieved, he leaps into life with a performed "total structure." Technically, the breathing matters most—and the breathing is a matter most intimate. With the breathing, an essential image springs into the mime's whole body and actively occupies it as a breath of life. For a translator, an essential image springs into his language to animate it, often as a voice or grouping of voices. A translator's body-mind is, after all, his language. Voice—character and quality—is altogether crucial in literary translation and not only in poems. What is language, when all is said and done, without voice?

Two more thoughts. (1) For a mime, the key to his performance is the rhythm of his breathing (as for a dancer). The rhythm of his breathing is the ghostly system through which his essential image is channeled, to become the dynamic of his gestures, his individual body articulated as motion. For the translator, this breathing is the syntax which makes the words ring true. Without the right syntax, even the rightest words can lack appropriate bonding. (2) The mime seems to exaggerate. In motion or motionless, his body projects the dynamic of his image in hyperbolic ways. Why this hyperbole? Does expressive language have to be exorbitant, as Gottfried Benn once proposed? Does hyperbole, as Mallarmé conjectured, track the true oddity or profile of a spirit which would otherwise choose to remain mute? I cannot say. But I do know that in the sacred miming dances of central and south India, this hyperbolic expression is required,

required by the myth which is danced and by the veteran dance instructors.

Even the tiniest children, learning the temple dances, are disciplined to quell their mortal pride and to express humbly—in hyperbole—the satisfactions of divine desire, *Ananda*. Without the exaggerated gestures, without the hyperbolic facial expressions, the myth would remain indistinct, and so would the gods that the myth invokes. The god being danced does move as humans do, but his movements and gestures are made doubly distinct. The double distinctness projects all the distance the god preserves in the very midst of his dancing immediacy. The distance sustains, it would seem, the numinous. It is precisely the distance of the numinous that calls for the hyperbolic gestures, which make, as it were, the points and edges of the numinous perceptible under and through its aura, like the peaks of a mountain range (to adapt Walter Benjamin's description of aura). One might also suppose that the distance has to be sustained in order that it should absorb the shock—the mortal danger—that divinity would otherwise present.

There are relations, I think, between mime so conceived and the task of translation. There is at least a workable analogy here. As the mime performs hyperbolically the distant god, so too does the translator perform the presence he divines in the original text. The dancing mime's breath is matched by the translator's syntax—syntax, the non-apparent part of language, as Mallarmé said. As for hyperbole, it comes into play as the translator raises into profile the animating impulse, the speech-as-play in Walser's case, which fashions the text. Sometimes one has to lift up this impulse, having sensed it fathoms down, higher than Walser might perhaps himself have done, but with tact. Why? Because Walser like any writer was unaware of himself as a spirit (or "god" in the Indian analogy), let alone as a presence. He was self-aware in quite another way—as an incorrigible, fragmentary, impecunious, mischievous, or forlorn person. Here, presumably, is a domain of high risk. The translator responds to a spirit. Believing that he perceives it, he performs it. He thinks and laughs and wrestles with a spirit as language. Moreover, in translating Robert Walser, a very trickster, an architect of liminalities, you have to be keenly mindful of the iridescent switchings of his language-gestures—one moment subverting stereotypes, and the next embracing them, though coyly, or fiercely; one moment distant, and the next point blank.

This spirit, this manifold configuration in all its mobility, which the translator tries to mime, is of course not identical with the spirit he performs, or hopes to voice. Precisely that discrepancy is the area of risk which provokes the translator as mime to grapple with the manifold, now insightfully, now blindly. A translation can only achieve so much, no more, of a manifold spirit which persistently disseminates itself. The spirit a translator hopes to have voiced is never more than one that has been there and probably got away. It is fugitive, it is afterward. "Anyway," as Vladimir Holan put it in his poem "A Night with Hamlet,"

> . . . that is the moment
> when you are still expecting guests
> and they're already here, for they came earlier.

From *"Little Painted Lips"*
to Heartbreak Tango

 SUZANNE JILL LEVINE

> *Peut-être . . . le métier du traducteur est plus subtil,*
> *plus civilisé que celui d'écrivain: le traducteur vient*
> *evidemment après l'écrivain. La traduction est une étape*
> *plus avancée.*
>
> Jorge Luis Borges

Translation: A Creative and Critical Act

TRANSLATING LITERARY PROSE has received much less attention than poetry, no doubt because of the "notion that a novel is . . . a simpler structure than a poem and consequently easier to translate."[1] But the formal and linguistic complexity of twentieth-century fiction belies this notion. While the virtue of translators has traditionally been their invisibility—scribes scribbling in the back room, serving the house of Literature—exploring the prose translator's role as creative writer and as literary critic can illuminate the interpretation of texts in unique ways. For translation is only the most concrete form of the interpretive act performed by *all* readers, scholars, and teachers of foreign literatures. Translations "and translation practices are *observational facts*"; the description of these facts is not only essential but prior to any possible theory.[2] I hope to show how a selective and self-referential inquisition by a prose translator can provide useful insights for translation studies, but also how such an inquiry can serve as a model of self-questioning for all interpreters.

A Poetics of Translation

"TRANSLATION" PRIVILEGES "ORIGINAL"

In 1932 Jorge Luis Borges questioned, in an essay whose title could be translated as "Some Versions of Homer," the privileged

30

status of the original *Odyssey* and *Iliad*. Which interpretation of the original is the "original"? he asked, speculating that only a Greek from the tenth century B.C. (according to Borges) might be able to tell us. Borges prefigured here Michel Foucault's challenge to the concept of authorship: What is an author? How can we determine intentionality? The only real difference between original and translation—Borges playfully specified—is that the translator's referent is a *visible* text against which the translation can be judged; the original escapes this scrutiny (and mistrust) because its referent is unspoken, perhaps forgotten, and probably embarrassingly banal.[3]

This meditation on translation contains the subversive seed of Borges's poetics of "reading as writing" which he articulated further in 1939 in his amusing parable "Pierre Menard, Author of Don Quixote": here Cervantes' canonical masterpiece becomes a tentative web of propositions that change with each new historical act of reading. Each successive interpretation (i.e., reading, rewriting, translating) of a text enriches and ensures the original's survival anew. Every work enters into a dialogue with other texts, and with a context; texts are *relationships* which of necessity evolve in other contexts.

Borges has shown us, time and again, how literary works already give us the theoretical models through which we may interpret them. In "Some Versions of Homer" and "Pierre Menard" we see the foreshadowings of reader-response and reception theories. We also see not only the thin line between originals and their interpretations but the both parallel and complementary nature of these interpretations, that is, the related activities of translation, parody, and literary criticism.

"Pierre Menard" is a parody of the laborious bibliographical homage an obscure French provincial writer pays to his mentor Pierre Menard, an obscure French symbolist whose most fantastic project is his attempt to rewrite *Don Quixote* word-for-word in Spanish, the language of Cervantes. We can imagine that both "Frenchmen" are thin disguises for Argentine literati, living in the colonies under the cultural imperialism of Paris, France. Our vertigo upon reading this *ficcion* is infinite. To begin with, *Don Quixote*—often labeled the first modern novel—was born both as a parody (of the chivalresque novel) and a "translation": within its fictional world, the narrator insinuates that the "original" is a found manuscript which had been written by an Arab, suspiciously named Cide Hamete Benengeli (Sir Eggplant). That a modern French writer would attempt to recreate (without plagiarizing) a seventeenth-century Spanish classic, and that an Argentine writer, Borges, would attempt to write Menard's disciple's homage produces a *mise en abîme*. Menard's faithful rendition of a sentence from the *Quixote* turns out to be as different as a parody, that is, an imitation with a critical difference. The same Spanish phrase becomes an affectation and takes on different, even opposite meanings, reinscribed in another linguistic and historical context. Borges's Spanish "rendition" of a supposed French original (the invented disciple's homage to the invented mentor) is both a "translation" and a parody (about the parody/translation of a parody/translation) which makes us puzzle over the status of an ever-elusive original text and language. Borges conflates the modes of parody (satirical imitation) and translation (imitation in another language) in "Pierre Menard" and also shows how they function as literary criticism with one important difference: both translations and parodies attempt to reiterate the discourse of the original; the critical essay exploits other discursive and rhetorical strategies.

WORK-IN-PROGRESS

Borges has proposed, essentially, a more tentative view of the original, as one of many possible versions. James Joyce, collaborative translator of his own writing into Italian, was thinking along similar lines when he chose to call his originals "work-in-progress," which he continued to complete in the next stage, translation. In recreating passages of *Finnegans Wake* he elaborated, in this Romance language which he loved for its earthy musicality, on aspects of the original which became even more explicit in Italian. That is, he took advantage of Italian—and his relationship to Italian—to create a more slangy version, and different double, even triple, puns.[4]

Translation as (Sub)version

Polyglot authors like Borges, Joyce, Pound, Beckett, and Nabokov have, of course, an authority to recreate, to "subvert" the original—particularly their own originals—that most translators do not command. They offer a model, however, of what literary translation needs to be: (trans)creation. Having collaborated with several Latin American fiction writers (among them Guillermo Cabrera Infante, Julio Cortázar, Carlos Fuentes, and Manuel Puig), I have been able to observe the symbiotic, and even parasitic, relationship between translation and original composition.

Far from the traditional view of translators as servile, nameless scribes, we might consider the literary translator a subversive scribe, and not only because translations are betrayals in the traditional *traduttore traditore* sense. An effective translation is often a "(sub)version," a latent version, "underneath," implied in the original, which becomes explicit. This view corresponds perhaps to Walter Benjamin's mystical vision of the hidden harmony between distant languages which poetic translation seeks to integrate. "Subversion" is used with a certain irony here, of course, mainly to subvert our traditional positivistic view of translation, to help us view translation's guilty subversiveness in the light of the original's *"traicion"* of realities and referents. But "subverting" particularly qualifies the translating of innovative writers like Severo Sarduy, Cabrera Infante, and Manuel Puig since it continues the mode of their originals. Their originals are already proposed as translations of texts, traditions, realities, touching upon the gaps between word and sense. The "author" has been dethroned in their writing, and as self-translators they are self-subverters.

Writers/Translators

Cabrera Infante, Puig, and Sarduy form a generation which blossomed in the 1960s. Their work continues the avant-garde spirit of an earlier generation that included Borges, Cortázar, and Lezama Lima but breaks new ground particularly in exploring popular forms, in interpreting the modernist tradition with a more authentically Latin American, or better, Argentine/Cuban idiom.

Cabrera Infante, in his novel *Tres tristes tigres* (*Three Trapped Tigers*, 1971), is perhaps the first to make "Cuban" into a literary language, a language consisting of slang, wordplays, and dislocutions, a Spanish enriched by a specific regional culture but also by many cultural and literary references. "The Death of Trotsky as described by various Cuban writers, years later—or before"—a chapter of this vast and fragmentary *roman comique*—satirizes history as interpreted, or as interpretation, through the both affectionate and savage parody of Cuban writers. But Petronius' *Satyricon* (of which Cabrera Infante has called *TTT* a "failed translation"), *Alice in Wonderland*, and Hollywood movies of the 1940s and 1950s also form part of the book's rich intertext. Manuel Puig's work can be considered in some ways more "pop," less literary in a traditional sense, reproducing and analyzing popular or mass culture and the

Argentine language within the sophisticated, stylized parodic structures of novels such as *Betrayed by Rita Hayworth* and *Kiss of the Spider Woman*, which was translated into a successful Hollywood film.

For brevity's sake I would like to retrace the process of translating Puig's second novel, *Boquitas pintadas* (literally Little Painted Mouths or Lips), which became *Heartbreak Tango* in English.[5] My purpose is to show how translation functions as (1) a continuation of the creative process; (2) a critical act which cannot and does not replace but rather complements the original, illuminating its strategies. Another issue which transcends the purely literary will also surface: that is, how do contextual constraints influence the production of translations? What aspects of Spanish American texts are or are not accessible to the American English reader? How do cultures/languages/literatures "read" the texts produced by other cultures?[6]

Boquitas pintadas:
Parody or Nostalgic Requiem?

In *Boquitas pintadas* Puig continues to reconstruct the provincial world of his childhood in a small town on the Argentine pampas, a labor begun in his first novel, *Betrayed by Rita Hayworth*. But whereas the first book was explicitly autobiographical, a sort of bildungsroman, *Boquitas* performs a broader socio-historical task. In presenting the intertwining lives of several characters from different social castes, Puig attempts to understand, to analyze—empathetically—the demise of provincial middle class values in Argentina, and particularly the petrified sexual roles in a traditional, repressive society. *Boquitas* is in a way an elegy on this past, specifically the 1930s and 1940s, as the frilly title, lyrics from an old song, suggests. But the book has consistently been described as a parody. It imitates the form of the soap opera or serial romance novel—framing the melodramatic plot involving tragic love affairs and triangles—and an ironic, satirical effect is produced by Puig's mimicry of his characters' speech and his reproduction of outdated cultural artifacts.

Puig describes his "intentions" as follows:

> When I wrote this novel, I was very interested in working with the language of the characters, because the way they spoke tells more about

them than anything the author could explain. Most of the characters in the book are first generation Argentines, of Italian or Spanish parents, most of them peasants who hadn't been able to give their children any cultural heritage. Their traditions were peasants' or underdogs' traditions, but they wanted to suppress or forget them. Much the same happened with immigrants who came to the United States. This meant that the children of these people had no models of conduct at home, and, least of all, no models of speech. They therefore had to invent a language of their own, using the culture they had at hand. All they had were the popular songs of the era, the subtitles of films, and stories in women's magazines. These models were not the best, but they were the only ones available to the lower middle class in small pampas towns. Mainly they were unrealistic and romantic. The language was overblown and was meant to impress quickly. That's why the tango is so truculent: because it had to make an impression on an audience lacking any subtlety. The characters in my book, based on the people of that era, try to use the language of *passion*, and they even think they act passionately, too.[7]

What Puig sets out to demonstrate is the gap between the language his characters use to communicate, to fantasize about their lives, and the harsh, calculating reality of their existence. To produce this effect for his reader, Puig recreated their language with mimetic accuracy so that the reader would hear it, at the same time establishing ironic distance between language and "reality" which the reader would also perceive.

But Puig is quick to balk at the label "parody":

> I think it is misleading. I'm often embarrassed when someone says to me: "You mock the way poor people speak." That isn't my intention, and I'm sorry if it comes out that way. The point is that the ordinary speech of these people is already a parody. All I do is record their imitation. (p. 35)

Puig is in a way both right and wrong, as Lucille Kerr has shown in her study *Suspended Fictions: Reading Novels by Manuel Puig.*[8] A prime instance of the reader's "suspension" by Puig's undermining of author(ity) involves a continuous "shifting" between parody, the critical imitation of a model, and stylization, "pure" non-judgmental imitation. Distinguishing parody and stylization is problematic, however: Russian "post-formalist" Mikhail Bakhtin ultimately saw the two as overlapping. Parody (particularly in the carnivalesque role it plays in Latin American fiction) reflects both critical and "cannibalizing" stylized difference.

What Puig does is not mere "burlesque imitation"; but, in the

strictly formal sense, *Boquitas is* a parody, a work that imitates a
conventional genre with the effect (here I distinguish effect and
intention) of imposing a critical difference, of producing a double
message involving both praise (elegy) and criticism (mockery).
Boquitas unmasks the false or exaggerated sentimentality of the
tango and the glamorized images of Hollywood, adopted by Argentine
cinema, which reify his characters' behavior, as well as the clichés
and the alienated journalistic, bureaucratic forms of everyday communication.

But the praise is also there: Puig takes the refuse of popular
culture—song lyrics, advertisements, sensationalist journalism—
and recycles it; in this sense he is the artist as *bricoleur*, taking old
material and creating something new, giving "used parts a second
life."[9] *Bricoleur*, in Lévi-Strauss's sense of the primitive tinkerer,
but more precisely in Adorno's use of the term to qualify, for example,
the composer Gustav Mahler, who scandalized (in his time) bourgeois
esthetics by taking folkloric material and using it in new ways that
resisted "passive listening."[10] The same applies to Puig: his books
are entertainments, but for active readers. An apparent "praise" of
popular forms involves also a criticism of "bourgeois esthetics."
Puig's writing reevaluates "bad taste," provokes the reader to enjoy
and not suppress it as "good taste" has done.[11] Puig questions the
category of "kitsch" since that word presupposes something shame-
ful, a judgmental distance, and claims to *seek* the poetry in bad
taste.[12] He also challenges, by suspending our interpretation, and by
blurring the boundaries between art and "trash," the "theoretical
categories, critical positions, and cultural systems through which
we both receive and perceive works of literature" (Kerr, p. 16).

Again, his empathetic reappraisal is also parody—which often
transcends mockery and becomes sympathy. Citing Bakhtin again:
"Another's word, having been at an earlier stage internally persuasive, mounts a resistance to [the ironic stylizing of parody] and frequently begins to sound with no parodic overtones at all."[13] Through
the process of reading *Boquitas pintadas* we, the readers, grow to
empathize with the characters despite their corny clichés, or maybe
even because of the way they speak. They are all Don Quixotes,
aspiring to what they are not, to what they cannot have. The borrowed words they unconsciously "parody" are ultimately "authentic"—or at least the only language to which they have access. As
readers, we are no longer laughing at their absurdity but rather crying
with their predicament, which is, at a more sophisticated level
perhaps, our own.

The Tango: Authentically Argentinian or Mendacious Myth?

An awareness of a book's intended effect on its original reader is obviously necessary in order for us to understand the difficulties of repeating that effect. The author's intentions, overdetermined by her or his own context, may or may not be verifiable, or even relevant, but the translator—like all interpreters—has to decide, within a given context, what function she or he is trying to fulfill. In *Boquitas*, how to recreate in English the parodical effect that spoken Argentine has upon its reader? It is hard to imagine how I would have translated *Boquitas* without Puig's collaboration and knowledge of United States mass culture, precisely because another and yet a very Argentinian book had to be written. I would like to examine here the main impasse, which involves the translation of the title: How to reproduce in translation the flavor, the function of the tango lyrics in the original version? The translation of the title—those key words which direct our reading of the text to follow—can give us an emblematic view of the critical and creative strategies involved in translating the whole text.

While, as in his novel *Betrayed by Rita Hayworth*, imported films (or domestic films modeled after the Hollywood imports) continue to be an influential medium upon the characters of *Boquitas* (at one point a female character fantasizes that her greatest desire is for Robert Taylor to enter her bedroom), in *Boquitas* the tango, an authentic indigenous form—and a dominant manifestation of popular Argentine culture during the 1930s and 1940s—appropriately takes the foreground.

As one Argentine critic remarked,

> the artificiality of those films, the way in which they make the viewer participate in their conventions, is similar to the structure of the tangos by Alfred Le Pera, tangos that we cannot help but imagine being sung by Carlos Gardel, the legendary tango singer and star of musical pictures, who interpreted the tragic tango lyrics with a sarcastic and oblique voice.[14]

Gardel's irony doubtless reflects the sexual battle that the tango engages, between the male's erotic domination in the actual dance and the content of the lyrics which speak of betrayal perpetrated—when the song is sung by a man—by the woman.

In the original *Boquitas* quotations of tango lyrics appear as epigraphs at the head of every episode, phrases that immediately touch the Argentine reader by invoking a well-known melody and evoking thus a mood or a theme. Again, the tango usually stresses the dark side of love: seduction and abandonment, betrayal, the death of a lover. Here is a list of the first four epigraphs, accompanied by their "translations" that is, substitutions:

Boquitas pintadas

Heartbreak Tango

"*Era . . . para mi la vida en-*
tera. . . ."
(She was my whole life.)
                    Alfred Le Pera

The shadows on the dance floor,
this tango brings sad memories to
                                    mind,
let us dance and think no more
    while my satin dress
    like a tear shines.
        (H. Manzi's tango, "His Voice")

"*Charlemos, la tarde es*
triste. . . ."
(Let's talk, it's a sad afternoon.)

As long as you can smile, success
can be yours.
        (radio commercial for toothpaste,
                    Buenos Aires 1947)

"*Deliciosas criaturas perfumadas,*
quiero el beso de sus boquitas pin-
tadas. . . ."
(Delicious perfumed creatures, I
want a kiss from your painted
lips. . . .
                    Alfred Le Pera

She fought with the fury of a
tigress for her man! He treated her
rough—and she loved it!
        (ad for *Red Dust*, starring Jean Harlow
                    and Clark Gable)

". . . *sus ojos azules muy*
grandes se abrieron. . . ."
(her eyes of blue did open wide)
                    Alfred Le Pera

My obsession, heartbreak tango,
plunged my soul to deepest sin
as the music of that tango
set my poor heart all a-spin.
        (Roldan's "Blame That Tango")

These familiar quotations metaphorically introduce the characters, plot, and/or narrative form of each chapter. The Spanish-speaking but particularly the Argentine reader—whose feelings have been awakened by a musical memory—immediately captures the intonation of these words, what is implied between the said and the unsaid. Their exaggerated "bad taste" and the popular singer Gardel's sarcastic interpretations add a self-reflexive dimension, a distancing effect heightened by the novel's historicity. Their function as both nostalgic and ironic counterpoint is "heard" by the Argentine reader, but for the American reader, for example, a literal translation of poetic clichés like "She/he was my whole life" rings hollow. It could be a line from a popular song, but the specific tone, the contact between the speaker and the listener, is lost.

The tango "means" something else anyway outside of the "River Plate" (as the British nicknamed the region); for Europeans and North Americans, Latin American dance music has always had a stylized *Latin* connotation, whereas in Argentina the tango is as homespun as blues and jazz are in the United States. But it would have been absurd to substitute Billie Holiday's singing for Libertad Lamarque's, or Cole Porter's lyrics for Alfred Le Pera's. The original culture would have been completely erased by such a drastic transposition; the translation would have been an imitation, in the spirit of Lowell's Baudelaire. And American popular music, according to Puig's representations of Argentina of the 1930s and 1940s, did not invade the popular consciousness and media as significantly as the Hollywood cinema and consumer-oriented advertising.

The solution we finally came up with was to translate some tango lyrics that were essential to the plot, but to substitute at least half of the epigraph quotation with either taglines from Hollywood films or Argentine radio commercials (originally based, most probably, on Madison Avenue inventions). That is, artifacts relevant to the original context but which rang a funny, familiar, exaggerated bell for American readers. The *Red Dust* tagline, for example, glamorizes sexism, machismo, and feminine submissiveness: an appropriate epigraph to episode 3, which introduces main male lead Juan Carlos, with whom women are always falling fatally in love. In "real life" we discover he is an insecure lout, and Mabel, his favorite girlfriend, also introduced in this episode, accepts an archetypal submissive role in appearance but is in reality a tough and calculating woman.

These substitutions added a new dimension of interpretation, or more precisely, they emphasized certain elements in the text which had been more implied than explicit. For example, the highlighted advertisements underscore Puig's implicit comment on how our thoughts and behavior are mediated by commercial imagery. They also stress his intent, in writing the books he writes, to show how the popular media have broken down the traditional distinction between consumerism and art. And by placing Hollywood movies on an equal plane with Argentine tangos (the *Red Dust* quotation is one of several movie epigraphs), it would appear that the translation suggests perhaps an equivalence between the cultural role of Hollywood productions—produced in an "atmosphere of un-reality for a passive audience . . . [and] the role of Argentine music rooted in a popular past and enjoying popular participation in the present."[15]

Making this equation could be dangerous, and subversive.

That is, if Puig's works call our attention to the alienating effects of North American cultural imperialism, is not this criticism mitigated in translation by the foregrounding of United States culture at the expense of "indigenous" Latin American cultural phenomena?

The answer to this question can be both yes and no. Yes, the "target" culture does to a certain extent censor the ideology of the source text; an ideological subversion does occur by the mere fact of rewriting—appropriating—these books in American English. Translation is a form of conquest, as Pound, in Nietzschean spirit, has shown us. But the other side of the coin is that, if the reader cannot recognize the book's parodical effect, its ideology is suppressed even more radically.

More to the point here is that both original and translation have placed both the sentimental tango and the glamorous Hollywood movies in a critical perspective. We first have to understand—as the Argentine reader does—what Puig is saying about the tango and its supposed authenticity, or more specifically, the middle class's relationship to a popular form which arose out of the "lower depths." Like jazz, the tango was accepted by its middle class milieu only after it had been canonized in Paris, the fashion center and cultural capital of the world (in the nineteenth—and a good part of the twentieth—century). But in the process of passing from the *barrio Sur* and the brothels, the tango had undergone a "translation." What had been originally considered obscene (couples bumping and grinding in a tight embrace) had become, as Borges put it, "*melancólico . . . lánguido . . . nostálgico.*"[16]

While Puig articulates his characters' values in authentic Argentine terms, he is showing—through ironic juxtapositions—how these "original" terms are, in a way, false ones, translations, particularly for the upwardly mobile middle class. As he says: "The characters in my book . . . try to use the language of passion, and they even think they act passionately, too." Only the working class characters, in Puig's view, wholeheartedly adhere to the tango's melodrama. It was precisely the tangos echoing in the thoughts of the main working class female character, the maidservant Fanny, which somehow had to be "faithfully" translated.[17] In episode 11 Fanny is listening to tangos on the radio as she scrubs the floors in the house of middle class Mabel; as she hums the tangos, she reflects on the stages of her love affair with Pancho the bricklayer which the different tangos evoke: illusion—seduction—abandonment—revenge.

But let us examine further the issue of "false" values. The artificiality of the supposedly authentic gives us a clue to the motivation behind the apparently lighthearted title, *Boquitas pintadas:* these words are not tango lyrics but, treasonously, from a foxtrot titled "Blondes of New York." "Rubias de New York" was a very popular song in the 1930s, sung of course by the legendary Gardel in an Argentine movie called *Tango on Broadway*—a movie which, for Argentines, glamorized the tango and their star in a Hollywood context. One could almost say that the foxtrot lyrics "Boquitas pintadas" emblematize the tango's displacement.

But what are the roots of Argentine culture? The Mexican Carlos Fuentes quoted the following *boutade* in an essay on the new Spanish American novel (1969): "The Mexicans descended from the Aztecs, the Peruvians from the Incas, and the Argentinians from the boat." A burlesque reduction of course, but such indeed was the cradle of the quintessential Gardel—the illegitimate son of a Frenchwoman from Toulouse. Gardel's foxtrot on Broadway can be read not only as the tango's betrayal but as a confirmation of Argentina's imported origins.

Expanding the Context

Hence, the translation of *Boquitas pintadas*, though foreshadowing the movies more than the original, continues the critical act begun in the original: exposing the tango's lies by juxtaposing them with the false values of a foreign popular (or mass media) culture, by reproducing these diverse artifacts in an "analytic" ironic context. Again, to understand how *Boquitas* became *Heartbreak Tango*, the reader has to be conscious of the necessary transformations a text undergoes in a different context, how inter- and contextual relationships change. The translator-as-critic writes in a necessarily expanded context, and must take into consideration (1) the reception of the work in other cultures, and his/her own function as mediator between past and present, between one culture and another; and (2) the relationship of the work to the author's entire opus—in Puig's case, the significance of Hollywood mythology throughout his writing.

Regarding our first consideration—the reception of the work in another culture—as an interpreter of Latin American literature for North American readers, I had to be cognizant of the fact that the "collective memory" shared by Puig's readers outside of Argentina is not the tango but the mythology of Hollywood. Even the more widely distributed edition published in Spain underwent changes to make the book accessible in the way it had been for Argentine readers. For certain epigraphs complete stanzas [see above list] from the tangos were quoted—the one-liners would not have been familiar enough. As in the American English edition, some of Le Pera's tangos were replaced by Homero Manzi's, which, as Puig noted, told stories with more concrete imagery. An example of Manzi's are the translated lyrics in the epigraph to episode 1—more vivid to an American reader than a literal translation of the original tango quotation. But even in the Spanish (Spain) edition the lyrics could not work as *musically* (i.e., subliminally, implicitly) signifying, as in the original; but they had to, at least as they do in the English translation, serve an *explicit thematic* function.

Translation, though it necessarily practices the rift between sign and meaning, finally seeks to (re)unite signs with meanings. Even though the translated epigraphs strayed—semantically and formally—away from the originals, they reinstated meaning in a broader sense, transmitting their *function,* the semantic and/or formal relationship between the head (epigraph) and the body of the episode.

Now to another consideration: the author's original and its relationship to his textual universe. In a discussion of the status of self-translation in the works of Samuel Beckett, it has been observed that the original is no longer necessarily the first work but rather the "sum total of textual material constituted by all the early drafts."[18] Although Beckett is a unique case, this observation applies to some extent to writers like Puig and Cabrera Infante who collaborate extensively on the translations of their work, and who even write in English.

Puig's "found objects"—taken from popular mass culture—cover a broad range of textual artifacts, some of which appear quoted in his originals. The fact that in the epigraph to episode 1, one tango can replace another, reminds us not so much of translation's inadequacy as of the provisional, makeshift nature of the original. Or as Borges tentatively remarked in his essay on the versions of Homer, "The concept of a definitive text pertains either to fatigue or to religion." The interchangeability of certain artifacts (tango for tango, movie tagline for tango) indicates that what matters here is not the unicity, the monolithic value of a quoted text but rather the relationship between texts, a relationship that changes according to the milieu of reception. Just as many tangos (and their texts) are not but could have been incorporated into the original *Boquitas*.

Remote but Intelligible

This all goes back to what was said earlier about the novelist as a *bricoleur*: he does not invent but rather finds words which resonate in the ear of the reader. In order for the translation to be a dialogue between writer and reader as it is in the original, the translator too must become a tinkerer. Again, the translator concretizes the historical act that all writers/readers/interpreters perform as mediators.

If the translated title was somehow to "fulfill" the original title's function, it had to register in the ear of its reader, to suggest nostalgia for a past era, to satirize sentimentality in popular culture, and to anchor the book in its Argentine, or at least Latin American, frame of reference. As is often the case with titles—originals and translations—*Heartbreak Tango* did not come to us until the last minute, when I had finished the translation. As mentioned earlier, necessity—that of translating lyrics essential to the plot—was the mother of our invention:

Maldito Tango	*Blame That Tango*
". . . en un taller feliz yo trabajaba, nunca sentí deseos de bailar . . ."	I was happy in the sweatshop, felt no need to dance at all . . .
". . . hasta que un joven que a mi me enamoraba	till the day a gallant wooer came to take me to the hall . . .
llevome un día con él para tanguear . . ."	
"fue mi obsesión el tango de aquel día,	My obsession, heartbreak tango
en que mi alma con ansias se rindió,	plunged my soul to deepest sin
pues al bailar sentí en el corazón que una dulce ilusión nació . . ."	as the music of that tango set my poor heart all a-spin
". . . la culpa fue de aquel maldito tango,	I will always blame that tango
que mi galan enseñome a bailar,	and the wooer with his wiles
y que despues hundiéndome en el fango,	once he'd made my heart break
me dio a entender que me iba a abandonar . . ."	all he told me was good-by

The words "Heartbreak Tango" are lyrics from our translation of "Maldito Tango"—the tango cited in the original episode 11 which brings to Fanny's mind what happened between herself and the bricklayer who seduced and abandoned her. The translation was a *bricoleur*'s find. That is, though the unique tango rhythm is lost—in which the stress of each line falls characteristically at the end, a dark downward motion—at least our translation parodied the mechanical rhyming, and told its story in comically heavy-handed language. Since the "Cursed Tango" was to blame for this tale of seduction, I translated the title of it (literally "That Damn Tango") as "Blame That Tango," a Hollywood resonance inspired in "Put the Blame on Mame," but also evoking (and this choice, as almost always, occurred intuitively) a syncopated Latin-like rhythm, as in "Hold That Tiger." Our associations here were not random but, on the contrary, relevant to Puig's world: "Put the Blame on Mame" invokes the image of that treasonous *femme fatale* icon of Puig's first novel, Rita Hayworth, who sings and dances this number in *Gilda*, a 1940s film noir (which Puig quoted in his following novel, *The Buenos Aires Affair*).

This translated song helped reconstruct an appropriate context. It characterized the era, the very "Latin" frame of reference, and a principal theme of the book—disillusionment. We decided to quote different stanzas from it in two epigraphs (4 and 9) to prepare the reader for its appearance in episode 11. It would become an (almost) familiar motif—like *boquitas pintadas*—which would epitomize the book for the reader. Seeking symmetry perhaps, we chose lyrics from "Blame That Tango," the words "Heartbreak Tango." "Heartbreak" resonates with United States Country and Western associations, Elvis Presley's "Heartbreak Hotel," wrong period but a similar corny effect.

The creative aspects of this tinkering are probably self-evident, but it is perhaps necessary to underscore the critical implications. We chose to foreground—to be a critic is to choose, to distinguish—a song in the book which, though it had been quoted only once, in our interpretation was a potential key, an internally persuasive text. Again, what was implied became explicit in translation.

Donald Keene once observed that when translating obscure, or culturally bound, allusions, the translator should produce an effect that is remote but intelligible.[19] *Heartbreak Tango*, with "tango" in the title, and the particular details of everyday Argentine life in every page of the text, marks its cultural difference, remaining a "remote" book despite the fact that Puig's humor is made "intelligible." *Heartbreak Tango* attempts to perform, like *Boquitas*, a critical task, exhibiting the false and real values of popular culture in Argentina by reproducing these textual ruins in an analytic context. The translation responds not only to the author's context—which includes the web of cinematic references woven throughout Puig's writing—but, most urgently, to its potential reader.

NOTES

1. Susan Basnett-McGuire, *Translation Studies* (London & New York: Methuen, 1980), 109.

2. See Gideon Toury, *In Search of a Theory of Translation* (Jerusalem: Porter Institute, 1980), 80–81.

3. See *"Las versiones homéricas," Discusión* (Buenos Aires: Emecé Editores, 1964), 112.

4. See Jacqueline Risset, "Joyce Translates Joyce," *Comparative Literature: An Annual Journal*, ed. E. S. Shaffer (New York & London: Cambridge University Press, 1984), 6–11.

5. *Boquitas pintadas* (Buenos Aires: Editorial Sudamericana, 1968); *Heartbreak Tango*, tr. Suzanne Jill Levine (New York: E. P. Dutton, 1973). "Painted" suggests painted "woman of the street"—a student recently observed—which would have introduced a misleading note!

6. Umberto Eco speaks of telling the process in his *Postscript to the Name of the Rose*: "Telling how you wrote something does not mean proving it is 'well' written. Poe said that the effect of the work is one thing and the knowledge of the process is another. . . . Sometimes the most illuminating pages on the artistic process have been written by minor artists, who achieved modest effects but knew how to ponder their own processes." (*Postscript*, tr. William Weaver [San Diego: Harcourt Brace Jovanovich, 1984, 11–12]).

7. S. J. Levine, "Author and Translator: An Interview with Manuel Puig," *Translation* (New York: Columbia University Press, 1974), 34.

8. Lucille Kerr, *Suspended Fictions: Reading Novels by Manuel Puig* (Urbana: University of Illinois Press, 1987).

9. T. Adorno, "The Fetish Character in Music and Regression of Listening," *The Essential Frankfurt Reader* (New York: Continuum Publishing, 1980), 298.

10. Cf. Claude Lévi-Strauss, *The Savage Mind* (Chicago: University of Chicago Press, 1966), and the above-cited Adorno.

11. Puig has an exquisite precedent in Baudelaire, who celebrated the aristocratic pleasure of displeasing.

12. Danubio Torres Fierro, "Manuel Puig," *Memoria Plural: Entrevistas a escritores latinoamericanos* (Buenos Aires: Editorial Sudamericana, 1986), 208.

13. Mikhail Bakhtin, "Discourse in the Novel," *The Dialogical Imagi-*

nation: Four Essays, tr. Caryl Emerson and Michael Holquist, ed. Michael Holquist (Austin: University of Texas Press, 1981), 348.

14. Alicia Borinsky, "Castration: Artifices: Notes on the Writing of Manual Puig," *Georgia Review* 29, no. 1 (spring 1975): 106.

15. Judith Weiss, "Dynamic Correlations in *Heartbreak Tango*," *Latin American Literary Review* (fall-winter 1974), 139.

16. H. Rebora, ed., *Granada/Tango*, (Granada: La Tertulia, 1982), 74.

17. "Fanny" is my translation of the character's original nickname, La Raba, literally "chicken tail," identifying an "outstanding" part of her anatomy.

18. Brian T. Fitch, "The Status of Self-Translation," *Texte* 4 (Toronto, 1985): 118.

19. See "The Translation of Japanese Culture," *Landscapes & Portraits: Appreciations of Japanese Culture* (Tokyo & Palo Alto: Kodansha International Ltd., 1971), 322–29.

On Translating a Tamil Poem

 A. K. RAMANUJAN

I

HOW DOES ONE TRANSLATE a poem from another time, another culture, another language? The poems I translate from Tamil were written two thousand years ago in a corner of South India, in a Dravidian language relatively untouched by the other classical language of India, Sanskrit. Of the literatures of the world at that time, Sanskrit in India, Greek and Latin in Europe, Hebrew in the Middle East, and Chinese in the Far East were Tamil's contemporaries. Over two thousand Tamil poems of different lengths, by over four hundred poets, arranged in nine anthologies, have survived the vagaries of politics and wars; changes of taste and religion; the crumbling of palm leaves; the errors and poverty of scribes; the ravages of insects, heat, cold, water, and fire.

The subject of this paper is not the fascinating external history of this literature, but translation, the transport of poems from classical Tamil to modern English; the hazards, the damages in transit, the secret paths, and the lucky bypasses.

The chief difficulty of translation is its impossibility. Frost once even identified poetry as that which is lost in translation. Once we accept that as a premise of this art, we can proceed to practice it, or learn (endlessly) to do so. As often as not, this love, like other loves, seems to be begotten by Despair upon Impossibility, in Mar-

---

This paper uses examples and materials from my other work, especially from *The Interior Landscape* (Indiana University Press, 1967) and *Poems of Love and War* (Columbia University Press, 1985). For further details and a body of translations from classical Tamil poetry, the reader is referred to these books and the afterwords in these books.

vell's phrase. Let me try to define this "impossibility" a little more precisely.

Here is a poem from an early Tamil anthology, *Aiṅkuṟunūṟu* 203, in modern Tamil script.[1]

அன்னுய் வாழிவேண் டன்2னநம் படப்பைத்
தேன்மயங்கு பாலினு மினிய வவர்நாட்
டுவலைக் கூவற் கீழ
மானுண் டெஞ்சிய கலிழி நீரே.

Transcribed in a phonemic Roman script, it looks like this:

annāy vāḻivēṇ ṭannainam paṭappait
tēṉmayaṅku pāliṉu miṉiya vavarnāṭ
ṭuvalaik kūvar kīla
māṉuṇ ṭeñciya kalili nīrē

How shall we divide up and translate this poem? What are the units of translation? We may begin with the sounds. We find at once that the sound system of Tamil is very different from English. For instance, Old Tamil has six nasal consonants: a labial, a dental, an alveolar, a retroflex, a palatal, and a velar—m, n, ṉ, ṇ, ñ, ṅ—three of which are not distinctive in English. How shall we translate a six-way system into a three-way English system (m, n, ṅ)? Tamil has long and short vowels, but English (or most English dialects) have diphthongs and glides. Tamil has double consonants that occur in English only across phrases like "ho*t t*in" and "si*t t*ight." Such features are well illustrated by the above poem in Tamil. Tamil has no initial consonant clusters, but English abounds in them: "*sch*ool, *scr*atch, *spl*ash, *str*ike," etc. English words may end in stops as in "*cut, cup, tuck,*" etc.; Tamil words do not. When we add up these myriad systemic differences, we cannot escape the fact that phonologies are systems unto themselves (even as grammatical, syntactic, lexical, semantic systems too are, as we shall see). Any unit we pick is defined by its relations to other units. So it is impossible to translate the phonology of one language into that of another—even in a related, culturally neighboring, language. We can map one system on to another, but never reproduce it. A poem is identical only with itself—if that. If we try and even partially succeed in mimicking the sounds, we may lose everything else, the syntax, the meanings, the poem itself, as in this delightful example of a French phonological translation of an English nursery rhyme:

Humpty Dumpty	Un petit d'un petit
Sat on a wall	S'étonne aux Halles
Humpty Dumpty	Un petit d'un petit
Had a great fall	Ah! degrés te fallent
And all the king's horses	Indolent qui ne sort cesse
And all the king's men	Indolent qui ne se mène
Couldn't put Humpty Dumpty	Qu'importe un petit d'un petit
Together again.	Tout Gai de Reguennes.

Sometimes it is said that we should translate metrical systems. Meter is a second-order organization of the sound system of a language, and partakes of all the above problems and some more. At readings someone in the audience always asks, "Did you translate the meter?" as if it is possible to do so. Tamil meter depends on the presence of long vowels and double consonants, and on closed and open syllables defined by such vowels and consonants. For instance, in the first word of the above poem, *annāy*, the first syllable is heavy because it is closed (an-), the second is heavy because it has a long vowel (-nāy). There is nothing comparable in English to this way of counting feet and combinations (marked in the text above by spaces). Even if we take familiar devices like rhyme, they do not have the same values in different languages. English has a long tradition of end-rhymes—but Tamil has a long tradition of second syllable consonant-rhymes. In the above poem the first, second, and fourth lines have n as the second consonant in the line-initial words *annāy*, *tēn*, and *mān*. End-rhymes in Tamil are a *modern* innovation, just as second syllable rhymes in English would be considered quite experimental. The tradition of one poetry would be the innovation of another.

Let us look at the grammar briefly. If we separate and display the meaningful units of the above poem, we see the following.

annāy vāli vēṇṭ(u) annai[A]/ nam paṭappai-t-
tēn - mayaṅku - pāl - iṉum iniya[B]/ (v)avar nāṭ-
ṭ(u) uvalai-k-kūval - kīla
mān - uṇṭ(u) - eñciya kalili nīrē[C]/

The translation,[2] piece by piece, would be:

mother, may [you]- live, desire [to listen], mother,[A]/ our garden -
honey - mixed - with - milk - than sweet[er][B]/ [is] his land's,
[in-] leaf - holes - low,
animals - having - drunk - [and-] leftover, muddied water[C]/

In my English rendering it becomes the following:

What She Said

> *to her girl friend, when she returned*
> *from the hills*

Bless you, friend. Listen.
  Sweeter than milk
  mixed with honey from our gardens

  is the leftover water in his land,

  low in the waterholes
  covered with leaves

and muddied by animals.

Kapilar, Aiṅkuṟunūṟu 203

One can see right away that Tamil has no copula verbs for equational sentences in the present tense, as in English, e.g., "Tom *is* a teacher"; no degrees of comparison in adjectives as in English, e.g., "sweet, sweeter, sweetest"; no articles like "a, an, the"; and so on. Tamil expresses the semantic equivalents of these grammatical devices by various other means. Grammars constrain what can be said directly and what can be left unsaid. An English friend of mine with a French wife, with whom he spoke French at home, used to complain half-jokingly that he could never tell his wife, "I went out with a friend for a drink last night," without having to specify the gender of the friend. The constraints of French require you to choose a gender for every noun, but English does not. The lies and ambiguities of one language are not those of another.

Evans-Pritchard, the anthropologist, used to say: If you translate all the European arguments for atheism into Azande, they would come out as arguments for God in Azande. Such observations certainly disabuse us of the commonly held notion of "literal" translation. We know now that no translation can be "literal," or "word for word." That is where the impossibility lies. The only possible translation is a "free" one.

When we attend to syntax, we see that Tamil syntax is mostly left-branching. English syntax is, by and large, rightward. Even a date like "the 19th of June, 1988," when translated into Tamil, would look like "1988, June, 19." A phrase like

A   B   C   D   E
The man who came from Michigan

would be "Michigan–from come–past tense–who man":

E D C B A
micigan-ilirundu vand-a manidan.

The Tamil sentence is the mirror image of the English one: what is
A B C D E in the one would be (by and large) E D C B A in Tamil. This
would also be true of many other Indian languages. Postpositions
instead of prepositions, adjectival clauses before nominal phrases,
verbs at the end rather than in the middle of sentences—these characterize Tamil, and not only Tamil. (Turkish, Japanese, and Welsh are
also left-branching languages). The American English style of *Time*
magazine, affected by German, Yiddish, or whatever affects *Time*,
leans toward the left-branching—in Alexander Woollcott's parody,
"Backward run the sentences till boggles the mind."

Not that English does not have left-branching possibilities, but
they are a bit abnormal, as Woollcott suggests. There are writers
who prefer to use them for special effects. Hopkins and Dylan
Thomas used those possibilities stunningly:

> Never until the mankind making,
> Bird beast and flower
> Fathering and all humbling darkness
> Tells with silence the last light breaking
> And the still hour
> Is come of the sea tumbling in harness
>
> . . . .
>
> Shall I let pray the shadow of a sound
>   Dylan Thomas, "A Refusal to Mourn the
>   Death, by Fire, of a Child in London"[3]

Remember, both were Welshmen, and Welsh is a left-branching
language. But, in Hopkins's and Thomas's poetry the leftward syntax
is employed for special poetic effects—it alternates with other, more
"normal," types of English sentences. In Tamil poetry the leftward
syntax is not eccentric, literary, or offbeat, but part of everyday
"natural" speech. One could not use Dylanese to translate Tamil,
even though many of the above phrases from Thomas can be translated comfortably with the same word order in Tamil. What is everyday in one language must be translated by what is everyday in the
"target" language also, and what is eccentric must find equally eccentric equivalents.

If poetry is made out of, among other things, "the best words in
the best order," and the best orders of the two languages are the
mirror images of each other, what is a translator to do? Many of my
devices (e.g., indentation, spacing) and compromises are made in

order to mimic closely the syntactic suspense of the original, without, I hope, estranging the English. Frequently the poems unify their rich and diverse patterns by using a single, long, marvelously managed sentence. I try to make my translation imitate a similar management, even in the relatively simple examples cited here.

The most obvious parts of language cited frequently for their utter untranslatability are the lexicon and the semantics of words. For lexicons are culture-specific. Terms for fauna, flora, caste distinctions, kinship systems, body parts, even the words that denote numbers, are culturally loaded. Words are enmeshed in other words—in collocations, in what can go with what ("a blue moon, a red letter day, a white elephant, purple prose"). Words participate in sets, in contrasts, in mutual recallings. "Red" is part of a paradigm of colors like green, yellow, etc., with which it contrasts. It is also part of a paradigm of near-terms or hyponyms, "scarlet, crimson, pink, rosy," etc. These collocations and paradigms make for metonymies and metaphors, multiple contextual meanings, clusters special to each language, quite untranslatable into another language like Tamil. Even when the elements of a system may be similar in two languages, like father, mother, brother, mother-in-law, etc., in kinship, the system of relations (say, who can be a mother-in-law, who can by law or custom marry whom) and the feelings traditionally encouraged about each relative (e.g., through mother-in-law jokes, stepmother tales, incest taboos) are all culturally sensitive and therefore part of the expressive repertoire of poets and novelists.

Add to this the entire poetic tradition, its rhetoric, the ordering of different genres with different functions in the culture, which, by its system of differences, distinguishes this particular poem, "What She Said," from all others. Tamil classical poetry would call the poem an "interior," or *akam* poem, a poem about love and its different phases. Contrasted to it are "exterior" or *puṟam* poems, which are usually public poems about war, society, the poverty of poets, the death of heroes, and so on. Here is an example:[4]

A Young Warrior
O heart
sorrowing
for this lad

once scared of a stick
lifted in mock anger
when he refused
a drink of milk,

> now
> not content with killing
> war elephants
> with spotted trunks,
>
> this son
> of the strong man who fell yesterday
>
> seems unaware of the arrow
> in his wound,
>
> his head of hair is plumed
> like a horse's,
>
> he has fallen
> on his shield,
>
> his beard still soft.
>
>   Poṉmuṭiyār, *Puṟanāṉūṟu* 310

Now, the classical Tamil poetic tradition uses an entire taxonomy, a classification of reality, as part of its stock-in-trade. The five landscapes of the Tamil area, characterized by hills, seashores, agricultural areas, wastelands, and pastoral fields, each with its forms of life, both natural and cultural, trees, animals, tribes, customs, arts and instruments—all these become part of the symbolic code for the poetry. Every landscape, with all its contents, is associated with a mood or phase of love or war. The landscapes provide the signifiers. The five real landscapes of Tamil poetry become, through this system, the interior landscapes of Tamil poetry. And each landscape or mood is also associated with a time of day and a season. Each landscape, along with its mood and the genre of poetry built around it, is usually named after a tree or flower of that region. For instance, the first poem we cited is a *kuriñci* poem— *kuriñci* is a plant that grows six thousand to eight thousand feet above sea level—representing the mountains, the night, the season of dew, the mood of first love, and the lovers' first secret sexual union. In the war poems the same landscape is the scene for another kind of clandestine action: a night attack on a fort set in the hills.

The love poems and war poems are somewhat similarly classified (though the war poems use the landscape differently and less strictly). So when we move from one to the other we are struck by the associations across them, forming a web not only of *akam* and *puṟam* genres, but also of the five landscapes with all their contents signifying moods, and the themes and motifs of love and war. The following charts[5] summarize the taxonomy.

Chart 1. Tamil "Correspondences"

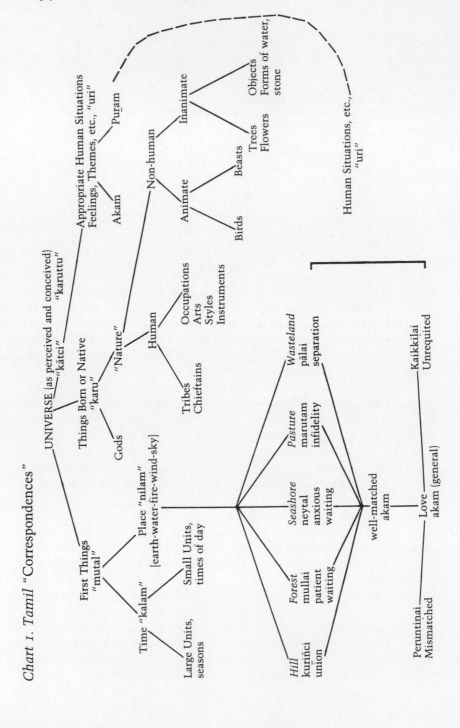

Chart 2. Some Features of the Five Landscapes[5]

	Lovers' union	Patient waiting, domesticity	Lover's unfaithfulness, "sulking scenes"	Anxiety in love, separation	Elopement, hardship, separation from lover or parents
Characteristic flower (name of region and poetic genre)	*kuriñci*	*mullai* (jasmine)	*marutam* (queen's-flower)	*neytal* (blue lily)	*pālai* (desert tree)
Landscape	mountains	forest, pasture	countryside, agricultural lowland	seashore	wasteland (mountain or forest parched by summer)
Time	night	late evening	morning	nightfall	midday
Season	cool season, season of morning dew	rainy season	all seasons	all seasons	season of evening dew, summer
Bird	peacock, parrot	sparrow, jungle hen	stork, heron	seagull	dove, eagle
Beast (including fish, reptile, etc.)	monkey, elephant, horse, bull	deer	buffalo freshwater fish	crocodile shark	fatigued elephant, tiger, or wolf lizard
Tree or plant	jackfruit, bamboo, *vēṅkai* (kino)	*koṉṟai* (cassia)	mango	*pūṉṉai* (laurel)	*ōmai* (toothbrush tree), cactus
Water	waterfall	rivers	pool	wells	waterless wells, stagnant water
Occupation or people	hill tribes, guarding millet harvest, gathering honey	plowman	pastoral occupations	selling fish and salt, fisherfolk	wayfarers, bandits

This is not an exhaustive list; only a few of the elements that appear frequently in the poems are given here. The Tamil names of gods, heroes, clans, musical instruments, and kinds of food have been omitted.

Love and war become metaphors for one another, enmesh one another, in poems[6] like "A Young Warrior" (pages 52–53) and the following:

What Her Mother Said
If a calving cow
chewed up her purslane creeper
growing near the house,

She'd throw the ball to the ground,
push away the doll,
and beat herself on her pretty tummy,
my little girl,
who knows now how to do things.

With a look tender as a doe's,
she'd refuse the milk
mixed with honey
her foster-mother and I would bring,
she'd sob and cry.

                                Yet today,
trusting the lies
of a blackbeard man
she's gone
through the wilderness, laughing,
they say,
showing her white teeth
like new buds on a palm tree.
                      Anon., *Naṟṟiṇai* 179

In the following poem,[7] the same evergreen tree, *nocci*, entwines the two themes of love and war in an ironic juxtaposition. A wreath of *nocci* is worn by warriors in war poems; a *nocci* leafskirt is given by a lover to his woman in love poems.

A Leaf in Love and War
The chaste trees, dark-clustered,
blend with the land
that knows no dryness;
the colors on the leaves
mob the eyes.

    We've seen those leaves
    on jeweled women,
    on their mounds
    of love.

Now the chaste wreath lies slashed
on the ground, so changed, so mixed
with blood, the vulture snatches it
with its beak,
thinking it raw meat.

> We see this too
> just because a young man
> in love with war
> wore it for glory.
>> Veṛipāṭiya Kāmakkaṇṇiyār,
>> *Puṛanāṇūṛu* 271

Thus a language within a language becomes the second language of Tamil poetry. Not only Tamil, but the landscapes and all their contents, the system of genres, themes, and allusions, become the language of this poetry. Like ordinary language, this art-language too makes possible (in Wilhelm Humboldt's phrase) "an infinite use of finite means." When one translates, one is translating not only Tamil, its phonology, grammar, and semantics, but this entire intertextual web, this intricate yet lucid second language of landscapes which holds together natural forms with cultural ones in a code, a grammar, a rhetoric, and a poetics.

II

I would now like to take a closer look at the original of "What She Said," and my translation. (See pages 49–50.)

The word *annāy* (in spoken Tamil, *ammā*), literally "mother," is a familiar term of address for any woman, here a "girl friend." So I have translated it as "friend," to make clear that the poem is not addressed to a mother (as some other poems are) but to a girl friend.

Note the long, crucial, left-branching phrase in Tamil: ". . . *his land's/(in-) leaf-holes low/animals-having-drunk-(and)-leftover, mud-died water*" (in a piece-by-piece translation). In my English, it becomes "the leftover water in his land,/low in the waterholes/covered with leaves/and muddied by animals."

I have omitted their "drinking," as it is suggested by "waterhole" in English. I had to expand "the leaf (covered) holes" in Tamil to "waterholes covered with leaves," making explicit what is understood in the original.

My phrase order in English tries to preserve the order and syntax of themes, not of single words: (1) his land's water, followed by (2) leaf-covered waterholes, and by (3) muddied by animals. I still could not bring the word "sweeter" (*iniya*) into the middle of the poem as the original does. That word "iniya" is the fulcrum (in the original) which balances the two phrases, the one about milk and honey, and the one about the muddied water. It weighs the speaker's entire childhood's milk and honey against the sexual pleasure of the leaf-covered waterholes muddied by animals. The presence of nineteen nasals in the Tamil poem foregrounds the n̲ in this central word *iniya*—quite untranslatably. Since it is such an important word for the poem's themes, I put it at the head of the sentence in my translation, preferring the inversion (which I usually avoid) to the weaker placing of "sweeter than" in the middle of the poem. The latter choice would have also forced me to invert the order of themes in English: "the muddied water is sweeter than the milk and honey." That would have forfeited the syntactic suspense, the drama of the ending: "muddied by animals." To enact this *effect* of balancing and weighing, I also arranged the lines and spaces symmetrically so that "is the leftover water in the land" is the midmost line set off by spaces.

The poem is a *kuriñci* piece, about the lovers' first union, set in the hillside landscape. My title ("What she said to her girl friend, when she returned from the hills") summarizes the whole context (speaker, listener, occasion) from the old colophon that accompanies the poem. The poem speaks of the innocent young woman's discovery of sex, in the hills, with her man. The leaf-covered waterholes that animals muddy with their eager thirst become a tangible way of talking about sex. The contrast between the safe, "cultured," garden of milk and honey (with overtones in English of the *Song of Songs*) and the wilder "natural" hills with their animals guzzling at the waterholes is also a progression for the virginal speaker. It is a movement from culture to nature, also from innocence to experience, preferring the excited muddy water of adult eroticism to childhood's milk and honey. This progression is lost if we do not preserve the order of themes so naturally carried by the left-branching syntax of Tamil.

More could be said about it from the point of view of the old commentaries. For instance, the commentaries summarize the mood (*meyppāṭu* which, significantly, means, "bodily state") and the purpose of the poem. The mood here, they say, is one of "great wonder" (*perumitam*); the purpose is "to speak of life's goodness" (*vāl̲kkai nalam kūrutal*).

Now, this poem on lovers' first union is part of a series of ten with different speakers, moods, and purposes. I shall cite only the very next poem[9] in the series:

What She Said,
  her lover within earshot

Tell me:
how is it then
that women gather
like hill goddesses

and stare at me
wherever I go,
and say
"She's good, she's so good,"

  and I,
  no good at all for my man
  from the country of the hills?

The mood in this companion poem is "sadness" (*alukai*, "weeping"); the purpose is to "persuade the lover to marry her." So, the poem's "mood," as here, may have ulterior ends, adding a twist to the texture. As the title (summarized from the colophons) suggests, the poem is often addressed to one person but meant for someone else within earshot, as in a joint family. Such poetry is "overheard" by us as well as by the personae that people the poems.

Thus poem follows poem, with the same paradigm of personae, details of landscape (hillside, in these ten), often the same phrases, but playing a different tune on the same strings, making a different figure, evoking a different mood within the same theme. The ten poems together make for a complex, psychologically nuanced, progressive enactment of a given conventional situation. Like Indian music, architecture, and much else in Indian culture, these poems develop a mood, a situation, a dwelling, a mode or *rāga*, by original recombinations, placements, and repetitions of a given set of motifs.

Furthermore, these ten poems in this anthology, *Aiṅkuṟunūru*, are part of a hundred on the theme of *kuriñci* (lover's union) by a single great poet, Kapilar. Indeed, even in other *akam* anthologies, he wrote about no other landscape. And he is not the only poet to have written about it. All the poems of a landscape share the same set of images and themes, but use them to make truly individual designs and meanings. Now the five landscapes of *akam* ("interior" love poems) define each other. All the *akam* poems, in turn, contrast with *puram* ("exterior") poems, though they share the landscapes. The love poems get parodied, subverted, and played with in comic

poems and poems about poems. In a few centuries, both the love
poems and the war poems provide models and motifs for religious
poems. Gods like Krishna are both lovers and warriors. Human love
as well as human politics and conflict become metaphors for man's
relations with the divine. The relations of lover and beloved, poet
and patron, bard and hero, get transposed, or translated if you will,
to poet-saint and god.

Thus any single poem is part of a set, a family of sets, a landscape
(one of five), a genre (*akam, puram*, comic, or religious). The intertextuality is concentric, a pattern of memberships as well as neigh-
borhoods, of likenesses and unlikenesses. Somehow a translator has
to translate each poem in ways that suggest these interests, dialogues,
and networks. St. John Perse, in his *Birds*, has an ambiguous story
about a Mongolian conqueror who heard a strange bird sing in a
foreign land and wanted to take that song home. In order to transport
that song, he had to become

> taker of a bird in its nest, and of the nest in its tree, who brought back
> with bird and nest and song the whole natal tree itself, torn from its
> place with its multitude of roots, its ball of earth and its border of soil,
> a remnant of home territory evoking a field, a province, a country, and
> an empire. . . .[10]

III

If attempting a translation means attempting such an impossibly
intricate task, foredoomed to failure, what makes it possible at all?
At least four things, maybe even four articles of faith, help the translator.

1. *Universals.* If there were no universals in which languages
participate and of which all particular languages were selections and
combinations, no language learning, translation, comparative
studies, or cross-cultural understanding of even the most meager
kind would be possible. If such universals did not exist, as Voltaire
said of God, we would have had to invent them. They are at least
the basic explanatory fictions of both linguistics and the study of
literature. Universals of structure, in both signifiers (e.g., sound systems, grammar, semantics, rhetoric, and poetics) and the signifieds
(e.g., what poems are about, like love, war, and what they mean
within and across cultures), are necessary fictions, the indispensable
"as ifs" of our fallible enterprise.

2. *Interiorized contexts.* However culture-specific the details of a poem are, poems like the ones I have been discussing interiorize the entire culture. Indeed, we know about the culture of the ancient Tamils only through a careful study of these poems. Later colophons and commentaries explore and explicate this knowledge carried by the poems, setting them in context, using them to make lexicons, and charting the fauna and flora of landscapes. The diagrams and charts given above are based on the earliest grammar of Tamil, *Tolkāppiyam*, the oldest parts of which are perhaps as old as the third century A.D. Such grammars draw on the poems themselves and codify their dramatis personae, an alphabet of themes, a set of situations that define where who may say what to whom, a list of favored figures of thought and figures of speech, and so on. When one translates a classical Tamil poem, one is translating also this kind of intertextual web, the meaning-making web of colophons and commentaries that surround and contextualize the poem. Even when we disagree with them, they give us the terms in which we construct the argument against them. There is no illusion here of "the poem itself."

3. *Systematicity.* The systematicity of such bodies of poetry, the way figures, genres, personae, etc., intermesh, in a master-code, is a great help in entering this intricate yet lucid world of words. One translates not single poems but bodies of poetry that create and contain their original world. Even if one chooses not to translate all the poems, one chooses poems that cluster together, that illuminate one another, so that allusions, contrasts, and collective designs are suggested. One's selection then becomes a metonymy for their world, re-presenting it. Here intertextuality is not the problem, but the solution. One learns one's lessons here not only from the Tamil arrangements but from Yeats, Blake, and Baudelaire, who all used arrangement as a poetic device.

4. *Structural mimicry.* Yet, against all this background, the work of translating single poems in their particularity is the chief work of the translator. In this task, I believe, the structures of individual poems, the unique figures they make out of all the given codes of their language, rhetoric, and poetics, become the points of entry. The poetry and the significance reside in these figures and structures as much as in the untranslatable verbal textures. So one attempts a structural mimicry, to translate relations, not items—not single words, but phrases, sequences, sentences; not metrical units, but rhythms; not morphology, but syntactic patterns.

To translate is to "metaphor," to "carry across." Translations are transpositions, reenactments, interpretations. Some elements of the original cannot be transposed at all. One can often convey a sense of the original rhythm, but not the language-bound meter; one can mimic levels of diction, but not the actual sound of the original words. Textures are harder (maybe impossible) to translate than structures, linear order more difficult than syntax, lines more difficult than larger patterns. Poetry is made at all these levels—and so is translation. That is why nothing less than a poem can translate another.

Yet "anything goes" will not do. The translation must not only re-present, but represent, the original. One walks a tightrope between the To-language and the From-language, in a double loyalty. A translator is an "artist on oath." Sometimes one may succeed only in re-presenting a poem, not in closely representing it. At such times one draws consolation from parables like the following: A Chinese emperor ordered a tunnel to be bored through a great mountain. The engineers decided that the best and quickest way to do it would be to begin work on both sides of the mountain, after precise measurements. If the measurements are precise enough, the two tunnels will meet in the middle, making a single one. "But, what happens if they don't meet?" asked the emperor. The counselors, in their wisdom, answered, "If they don't meet, we will have two tunnels instead of one." So too, if the representation in another language is not close enough, but still succeeds in "carrying" the poem in some sense, we will have two poems instead of one.

NOTES

1. Ramanujan 1985, 203.

2. Ibid., 10.

3. Dylan Thomas, *Collected Poems* (New York: New Directions, 1939–53), 112.

4. Ramanujan 1985, 165. For further details of akam/puṟam genres and their implications, see ibid., afterword.

5. Ibid., 242.

6. Ibid., 65, 165.

7. Ibid., 186.

8. The words "waterholes" and "animals" could have been in the singular. For, in Tamil, neuter words may omit the plural marker. The word for "animal" here is māṉ, which also means "a deer." The grammar of such Tamil words makes them both general and specific, not either the one or the other. In this case, I preferred the generality of the English plurals in my translation, losing the teeter-totter of the Tamil singular/plural.

9. Ibid., 10.

10. St. John Perse, *Birds*, tr. R. Fitzgerald (New York: Pantheon Books, 1965), 40.

Fortunata and Jacinta:
A Polyphonic Novel

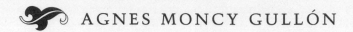 AGNES MONCY GULLÓN

"POLYPHONIC" is one of the relatively few big words in this study. They are few because their use implies theorizing, and in discussing literary translation it seems more helpful to explore specific artistic examples. Some technical terminology will be useful at first, though, to contextualize the kind of object we are concerned with—a polyphonic novel. Let us consider the nature of the polyphony we find in Galdós's novel.

More than one voice shares the narrative speaking space in *Fortunata y Jacinta*. Galdós deliberately assigns the telling of his tale (or "Two Stories of Married Women," as the subtitle defines it) not to one individual character but to a number of them. The translator's sense of identity with the central narrator, or author's "second self," is an important relationship, one that guides subsequent associations forged with the minor voices in the text. In other novels by Galdós the narrator is a simpler figure, but in this, his masterpiece,[1] the central narrator is in charge of many kinds of language; he conducts an orchestra of voices whose diversity impresses. And the translator must reflect that variety, be able somehow to regain the multivocal texture in English.

Four points which I shall deal with in a general way will reveal the frame within which the translator works. The first is: What kind of communication scheme must be set up in English to deliver this text? The question involves two realms, the public and the private. In the public, there is a book known for its author, the work itself, and the reader. The translator does not even exist. Using communication theory, we may say that there is a sender, a message (the book), and a receiver. So it appears that there is a three-part scheme to reproduce. But working as translators, we know very well that

64

the situation is far more complicated. In English we find that the author or sender continues to exist, of course, but he is not known by most English-speaking readers. (I am referring to this particular case, not to those of authors who pose no recognition problem.) In trying to present a "new" author to an audience, the translator appears in his place, acquiring temporarily a more authorial position than is actually possessed. In English, then, the original sender is not perceived yet as such, because of a lack of familiarity, and the message, or book, is an altered object, just as the category "reader" relates to an alien culture, one which becomes, with the reincarnation of the work, the target culture.

At first glance such distinctions may seem obvious, and perhaps they are. But when you are working within a changed context, producing the English text, the distinctions imply numerous decisions. Both communication schemes are operative, for the translator is passively absorbing the features of the first while actively determining the features of the second. This way of considering the act of translation belongs to the theory of communication.

Turning now to J. R. Firth's theory, in *Papers in Linguistics: 1934–35* (London, 1957), as interpreted by Don Kiraly in a lecture given in the Department of Linguistics at the University of Illinois in February 1987, we could depict the translator's position in the reculturization process as follows:

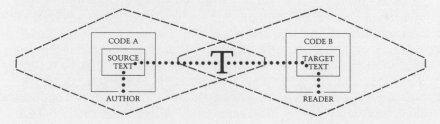

Kiraly's interpretation corrects the long-held notion that the translator inhabits a limbo between the original (text A) and the new version (text B). As the diagram shows, the translator creates a third context or situation in the overlapping area between the two spheres outlined, which represent the two cultures and languages involved. Vladimir Nabokov's use of overlapping disks to represent the meanings (coincidental versus divergent) of a word in source and target languages shows that certain connotations match, whereas others do not. The scheme is emblematic of the translator's place between the two contexts of situation, the original work's versus the translation's. The translator must invent the totality of that overlap, and in so doing he or she becomes the key figure in the production of the new work: the author disappears from center view, and with him go his original readers. In their place, analogous figures take shape.

In addition to these transformations of the figures who occupy the scheme, there is a private exchange between author and translator. This, unfortunately, cannot be shown in a sketch. Too many tiny perceptions and reflections succeed one another as their minds meet, as the original gives way to the new version. Schematization is not possible because each new set of individuals makes possible a new relationship (e.g., Galdós with translator A, translator B, etc.). What can be said, though, is that the translator eventually must *become* the author. This may sound a bit dramatic, but it is no more than what already takes place in a good reader's mind. As Virginia Woolf advises in her essay "How to Read a Book" (*Collected Essays*), "try to become the author." Why? To receive fully all the text has to offer. Our literary experience, our affinity with the text in question, and our verbal skills all influence our ability to live this exciting component of literary translation. The becoming, or imitation, is naturally limited to our imitation of the writer projected in the text, not to our capture of the human being behind the authorial voice and stance.

To approximate the stance of Galdós, a very imposing author whom I soon realized I must somehow become, I decided to start by following his work method. I had read that Galdós worked methodically, writing several pages a day, and that he was careful not to interrupt his continuous contact with the evolving imaginary world. Revising the previous day's pages first, he continued writing, then stopped after several hours work. In three years he completed the four-volume novel. Many years ago in Texas, where I did the first draft, I imitated his pace: I would revise the previous day's work, translate for several hours, put the manuscript away, do other things, and return the next morning for the same routine. This continuous renovation of the imaginary world kept the process steady. Whether or not it was the best way, I do not know, but it was in any event a very pleasant one. By giving the project priority, my own life's rhythm became secondary to it, and this helped, I think, that private exchange that was so vital to happen. There were stages in the process, and here I might recall George Steiner's clear condensation of the process as explained in his book *After Babel*. Briefly, he delineates four: (1) knowledge of the author's times, (2) familiarization with the sphere of sensibility within which the author wrote (so as to make correct stylistic choices, in accord with the author's temperament), (3) decoding of the original text, and (4) encoding, which can occur only after one has deciphered meanings and found cultural equivalents. The recoded, or encoded, work is then elaborated and should end up inserted in the new cultural context. With this explanation we see the translator getting to know the times, culture, language, and temperament of the author and target culture as a gradual recreative process.

I am not sure it is possible to divide the process into a fixed number of stages, because the demands of different texts vary. Robert Bly has written an essay on the eight stages necessary for translating poetry (a German poem), and he makes a convincing case for that number. I tend to think the number may be arbitrary, variable from one translator to the next, from one literary situation to the next, and even changeable in the course of translating a single work, because of the progress from stage 1 to stage 2, etc. The value of these outlines is to alert us to what may occur, thereby orienting us to what is occurring.

Another point—what kind of art are we trying to recreate?— suggests that we need an artistic stance in order to produce a comparable object in the target language. A literary translator, as opposed to a non-literary translator, must want to create a novel; not to write one's own, perhaps, but to bring to a new readership a new work of art, taking on the role of producing the novel which the original's author might have written had he or she written in our language. The question seemed overwhelming at the outset: I, a graduate student at the time, channel a Spanish saga into English literature? Seeing the results now as a compact block on the table, the book in English, makes it easy to forget how unsure I felt when I started. I had only read the novel quickly when Keith Botsford, then director of the National Translation Center in Austin (where I was a Spanish consultant), suggested that I translate it. When I commented on the idea to a friend in the classics department at the University of Texas, Professor Donald Carne-Ross, his response was: "That's like trying to cross the Atlantic in a rowboat." Unaware of the complexity of the projected task, though, I simply jumped in and started rowing. Almost twenty years later it was done. Or as done as I could make it. As we all know, no translation is ever finished. But that is another issue.

So the art I proposed to translate was very complex. The late professor Stephen Gilman of Harvard University has called this novel "the most complex universe between two covers of a book." In many senses. Let us examine the language now, and leave other issues for other occasions. Giving a short external definition of *Fortunata and Jacinta,* we could say that it is a late nineteenth-century realist novel in the European tradition. Set in Madrid, it is virtually *the* novel of Madrid. It came after several cycles of novels written by Galdós, whose creative experience had already encompassed theater, translation, essays, historical novels (almost forty), and journalism. His contact with Victorian realists such as Dickens was valuable, as was his knowledge of Balzac and Dostoevsky.

Turning to more technical questions now, we may say that like a number of European realist novels, *Fortunata and Jacinta* is polyphonic. The term was coined by the Russian critic Mikhail Bakhtin in 1929 in his study of Dostoevsky's poetics. Bakhtin used the term to describe any novel written from a pluralistic narrative perspective: one that admits, together with the one distinguishable as the author's, the perspectives of some of the work's characters. The novel so conceived is determined not only by the narrator's or implicit author's set of values, but also by those of the characters whose voices join in the telling of the tale. So it is the novel as a merry collision—clashes, harmonies, combinations, contradictions—the coexistence, without hierarchization, of different voices and their corresponding value systems. It goes without saying that a novel so written is rich in its stylistic texture: it admits all the verbal and tonal idiosyncracies its speakers bring to its pages, and Galdós was a master at concerting these peculiarities.

He was writing at a time that was favorable to this kind of art. Spanish literature was in what Bakhtin would call a heteroglossic situation. To understand what he means, we should recall that Bakhtin divides language into moments of awareness in time. There was originally, he says, a monoglossic situation: the moment when the native language was assumed supreme. Out of that state came the heteroglossic, or moment when a society or culture recognized different levels of discursive expression, believing that the native language existed equally on these different levels of discourse. From that state came polyglossia: today's situation. A native language has as integral parts, parts from other languages. In other words, not only intralingual features are considered constitutive; interlingual ones are as well. The exchange among languages is mutually animating, affecting the mental life in each culture. When a society is highly aware of the existence of other languages, something starts to happen: the others begin to fuse gradually with the native.

Galdós was writing not in a polyglossic, but rather a heteroglossic moment. It was considered normal, then, to admit into literary language different kinds of descriptions and speech habits, or imitation of earlier literary models of both. Naturalism, the literary movement that began in France, had started to examine areas of man's being in a semi-medical way, exploring human characteristics according to environment and heredity. In literature, speech became important: the medium of expression of a literary character being words, it followed that inclusion of a character's own peculiar speech was essential in order to present him as he was.

Aesthetically, *Fortunata and Jacinta* is a realist-naturalist work, a reflection of reality in an urban setting; heavily populated in fiction too, the world shown in the novel requires that its sounds and sights be transmitted accurately. This brings us to another point: how is the linguistic complexity organized? The narrator is the key figure. Curiously enough, I did not realize this until ten years after translating the novel. In revising the first draft (which had lain untouched for ten years), I realized that the mass of paper I had before me was like a cassette in a tape recorder: all there intact, but not plugged in. Everything was there, but I had to get it going, give it the energy it lacked. What did I have to do to get it going? And then it occurred to me that the text needed a voice, a kind of thread that would start on the first page and flow to the very last, into the final word. From the first sound to the last, there had to be some kind of unity in all that incredible variety. And the unity, or unifier, was the narrator. He was the one who was telling us the "Two Stories of Married Women." He was fitting together the voices belonging to those stories as well as telling it all to us from without. To find the narrator's voice, I was forced to analyze, as translator, when the narrator was present in the text and when not. And that is when translating became fascinating. A lot of the drudgery was over with—not being able to find a certain term in English, not understanding exactly what kind of lace, or custom, or kitchen measurement, or exclamation was to be rendered in modern American English; frustration from not finding an equivalent even after doing the research; or a food—how a certain food tasted, and how it looked at the marketplace, on the table. . . . Getting beyond all that, into the sound of the text, I now had a new challenge: judging which speaker was operative in the text and how, at given moments. It seemed wise to heighten the contrasts, to profile distinctly in English those narrative entries and exits. Such emphasis was not intended to alter the texture of the original, only to highlight the shifting narrative focus enough so that the English reader would be sensitive to the comings and goings of the main narrator, who controls the story lines.

In studying the text anew, I found that the narrator was not particularly easy to pin down; sometimes he was there chatting away in the midst of a scene, but he would imperceptibly vanish, dissolving into a character's voice. This was due to his strategy for directing the story: he had a habit (the art) of guiding the action toward a person who would be watching things, then he would want to add some remark of his own about what was happening. He was behind the person who was telling something his or her way, and then he would come in a little closer to speak up himself, and sometimes he would then go off on a tangent with a typical nineteenth-century omniscient narrative intrusion. He was being a Narrator, and also a character-narrator. We may be reminded, in describing him, of Wayne C. Booth's classifications in *The Rhetoric of Fiction*. Galdós's main narrator is pretty reliable, as Booth would say, but he is not always reliable in the same sense. Sometimes he is reliable as a character (i.e., he tells the truth; it is not a detective story meant to throw us off the track). As the main narrator, he is reliable in that he upholds his values, but we have to accept the prejudices and limitations implied by the upholding of any one system over another. As a character, he belongs to a certain social class (middle class); has certain tastes, especially in the amorous area (lower class women); he has a certain age (Galdós's own, about forty-three); he comes from a certain place (Spain); and so on. Translating him, one must somehow take on those attributes. In order to speak like him I had to be like him, become him. And this individual had other facets, too: those of a genius. He blended into the literary judgment passer, philosopher, knower of mankind whose wonderful vision of others' souls and hearts allowed him to make highly perceptive and often humorous statements about life and human conduct. It was important to distinguish when one was speaking, i.e., the omniscient narrator blessed with these gifts, and when the other, the narrator-character, Juanito's bourgeois friend.

I

What I propose to do now is to trace the entries and exits from the text of this narrative entity so that we may see what kinds of things the translator has to do in order to reproduce his techniques. In volume 1, in the chapter called "The Honeymoon," we find a sample of how the narrator accompanies the two protagonists Jacinta and Juanito Santa Cruz on their lyrical trip through southern Spain. It seems as if the narrator is having a pretty nice time too, being carried along on the wings of the train in their light emotions, seeing it all through their eyes. The bride's innocence, aiding Juanito's escape from his troubled relationship with Fortunata, contributes to the airy background and the immediacy of the talk. The passage reads as follows:

> Quite late the next day, they went to the cathedral. Jacinta already knew several terms of endearment that she hadn't used yet, except in the discreet vagueness of her own mind, which was still reluctant to reveal itself. She was not embarrassed to say that she idolized him—yes, that was the word, precisely—or to ask him over and over if it was true that she had become his idol and would continue to be forever and ever. And the one whose turn it was to answer the question that had become as frequent as blinking would say, "Yeth," lisping to make the word sound childish. Juanito had taught her this "Yeth" that night, just as he had taught her to say "D'ya *luv* me?" in a special way along with other silly childishness, all in the most serious of tones. Right there in the cathedral, when the sexton who was showing them a chapel or a cloistered treasure took his eyes off them for a minute, the newlyweds snatched the opportunity to steal a few kisses in front of the holy altars or behind the reclining statue on a sepulcher. Juanito was a rascal, greedy and bold. These profanities scared Jacinta, but she consented and tolerated them, turning her thoughts to God and trusting in Him, the source of all love, to disregard them with His proverbial indulgence. (P. 54)

We can see in this paragraph that the person who holds the reins of the story is the narrator; it is he who describes what they see, what they feel, inserting a few phrases of theirs. He shares with them the focalization of the events: using his own words, he incorporates observations and perceptions of his characters'. Several sentences in, he switches to the wife's perspective when he writes, "She was not embarrassed to say. . . ." We can faintly hear the wife in his language, thanks to his use of the indirect style, which leads into the free indirect several sentences down. Another sentence is noticeable for its technique too: "Juanito was a rascal. . . ." This thought comes from Jacinta, not the narrator, who looks down on Juanito, and hardly shares the bride's awe of him.

In telling the story the main narrator uses a language that is flexible enough to incorporate into his descriptive mode enough dramatization and material from the characters to make it rich.

There is an intimate scene in which he, the narrator, is present, invisibly almost, but closely identified with them in their visit to the cathedral. The following paragraph on that page corresponds more closely to the omniscient narrator, the implicit author overviewing the scene:

> Everything made them happy. Contemplating an artistic marvel excited them, and out of pure enthusiasm they laughed, just as they did at any minor annoyance. If the food was bad, they laughed; if the carriage taking them to the Cartuja hit all the potholes in the road, they laughed; if the sexton at the Huelgas church told them absurd stories, like the one about the abbess who wore a miter and ruled all the priests, they laughed. Everything Jacinta said, even the most solemn comment, seemed incredibly funny to Juanito. And no matter what he said, his wife burst out laughing. The colorful street slang that Santa Cruz came out with every now and then was what she liked best, and she repeated some of it, trying to memorize it. When not too gross, these expressions are fairly amusing, being caricatures of language. (P. 54)

Evidence that one voice and set of judgments belong solely to the narrator comes in the last sentence, when the observations on language signal to the reader that Jacinta could not have such wide knowledge of language as to classify certain expressions as deftly as the narrator can. And the third paragraph, similarly, corresponds to the narrator: they experience the ecstasy, whereas he reflects on it:

> Time doesn't exist for lovers and people in ecstasy. Neither Jacinta nor her husband kept track of the fleeting hours. She, especially, had to think for a moment whether it was the third or fourth day of this blissful existence. Yet even though it cannot gauge the passing of the days very well, love aspires to dominate time, like everything else, and when it triumphs over the present, it longs to own the past, or at least to inquire into its events and see if they are favorable. (P. 54)

The tonal change—from happy, playful, lyrical tones to more serious ones—has been effected. Toward the end of the paragraph, though, Jacinta seems to join in with the narrator: "There shouldn't be any secrets between husband and wife." Then he adds: "This is the first law laid down by curiosity before it gains the status of inquisitor." Ironic humor begins to surge from the text at this point.

As a split develops between the newlyweds, the split caused by her curiosity and jealousy on one hand and his evasiveness on the other, the narrator's language registers the split. In the next few passages there is no longer the cozy trio of newlyweds and intimate narrator. Instead, there is a reporting that registers their distancing:

"As Jacinta called her husband 'Baby' (which he taught her to do), when she asked him the first question, he couldn't help but feel a bit annoyed." Description, but notice in the next sentence how there is a refocalization to accommodate Juanito's point of view: "They were walking along one of the poplar-lined avenues in Burgos, a straight and indefatigable stretch, like a path through a nightmare." The comparison—"street" equals "path"—belongs to Juanito, who does not want to be questioned about his affair with Fortunata. Continuing:

> His reply was affectionate but evasive. All he could tell his "Baby" was: mere flirtations, nonsense! Things boys will do. A man's education nowadays wasn't complete if he didn't deal with people from all classes, have a look at all the possible ways there are to live, have a taste of every passion. Just to educate himself. It wasn't a question of love, because as for love—and <u>he</u> knew what he was talking about—he had never known what it was until he had been smitten by the woman who was already his wife. (P. 55)

He becomes sanctimonious, glib. He is of course rationalizing his past relationship, and in an attempt to forget it he casts it in less flattering terms than before. Voices flash in and out of this charged scene almost like birds, the narrator guiding the characters' questioning and confessing, going through it with them. So in what is essentially descriptive narrative discourse we see that it is possible to describe his prose as flexible, for it admits several focalizations without losing its own style. A look at other samples now should prepare our attempt to characterize the narrative prose more fully.

In the next passage the narrator differentiates his style from that of other speakers in the text. He, Juanito, and Jacinta share a colloquial style which the passages examined so far indicate: members of the bourgeoisie, they speak as such, their different ages notwithstanding. In the next passage Juanito recalls (to his wife) episodes of his life as Fortunata's lover. His intention is to depict it in a negative way so as to camouflage his bad conscience. If he can show that world to his wife in its most disgusting, offensive light, he reasons, his conduct may be condoned. The strategy in this use of language is to convey other characters as worse than they are, put them down with derogatory descriptive language. Juanito tells Jacinta how he left:

> "That kind of life wasn't possible. Admit it. I was so fed up I couldn't stand it. Pitusa became hateful to me, just like the disgusting words they used. One day I said, 'I'll be back,' and I never went back. As

Villalonga put it, 'Make a clean break.' My conscience bothered me though, as if a fine thread in it were tugging at me to be back there. I snipped it. Then Fortunata started to pursue me. I had to play hide and seek. She'd be in one place and I'd be in another. Oh, I was as slippery as an eel. She wasn't going to catch me, no sir. The last one of the bunch I saw was Izquierdo. I met him one day on the staircase, going up to my house. He threatened me. He said Pitusa had 'gotten big,' five months along . . . five months! I shrugged my shoulders. He made a few remarks, I made a few remarks, he made a few, then I swung at him and crash! Izquierdo fell down a whole flight of stairs at once . . . another blow and crash! down the next flight, head over heels. . . ."

He was visibly disturbed as he told this. He remained seated on the floor, legs extended, one arm resting on the seat of the chair. Jacinta was trembling. She felt a deathly cold, and her teeth were chattering. She remained standing in the middle of the room like a statue, contemplating the incredibly pitiful figure that her husband made, not daring to ask him anything or request that he clarify any of the strange parts of what he was revealing to her. (Pp. 74–75)

Juanito's drunken confession causes the mutually exclusive worlds to merge, their dissonance combining with his bad feelings and his wife's disturbance. The narrator's job through it all is twofold: to tell us how the honeymoon is going, what it is like, and to relay interior narrations that bring Fortunata's world into the Santa Cruzes'. Juanito's story about Fortunata involves other speakers who are from outside the intimate circle composed of Juanito, Jacinta, and the narrator. New voices, like rough threads, are woven into the finer, more familiar ones, and their dramatic differences engender new reactions. Jacinta, especially, is resistant; the vulgar expressions recalled by her husband after drinking, and indeed, even his drunken state, are things she avoids mentioning the next day.

Of technical interest to translators is the fact that the artistic value of the text rests on the presence of the various speakers, each well delineated. If they fail to reappear in English, the novel is less vivid, less itself. This first example has been the most complex. I hoped to hint at the kind of listening necessary when translating a polyphonic novel, and also the structuring around the narrative voice, which lends unity.

II

The next three samples are simpler. The second, showing us a social, public context for speech, is also a good example of Galdós's humor.

The narrator gives the floor to the characters, and the scene is a bunch of kids playing outside the tenement house Guillermina is visiting. The latter, called "the saint," or "the founder," is a friend of Jacinta's; she is building an orphanage, and knows the neighborhood very well. The passage, also from volume 1, reads as follows:

> They contemplated the ladies silently and with extreme excitement, secretly enjoying the surprise and terror that their frightful looks produced in such refined, delicate ladies. One of the little ones tried to clutch at Jacinta's coat, but longlegs began to scream at them:
> "Get outta here, go away, you dirty little pigs! You're getting these ladies dirty with your paws."
> "God above! . . . They look like cannibals. Don't touch us. It's not your fault, it's your mothers' for letting you do such things. . . . And if I'm not mistaken, these two loafers are your brothers, child."
> The two alluded to smiled, showing their milk-white teeth and redder-than-cherry lips in the surrounding blackness; they replied that they were, nodding their savage heads. They were beginning to feel ashamed and didn't know what to do. At that very moment a big woman came out of the nearest door, and, grabbing one of the besmeared little girls, she pulled up her petticoats and began to give her such a beating on the appropriate spot that it could be heard from the first patio. In no time another furious mother appeared, one who looked more like a wolf than a woman, and she got started on another of the devils, slapping at his dirt, with no fear of dirtying herself too. "You little savages, stinkers, look what you've done!" And more irritated mothers poured out. What a scene! Soon there were tears streaming over the tar, and their grief blackened. "I'm going to kill you, you big rascal, thief. . . ." "It's the blasted varnish that Señá Nicanora uses. Holy Jesus, Señá Nicanora, why do ya let these youngsters . . . ?"
> One of the noisiest of the women calmed down when she saw the two ladies—Señora Ido del Sagrario, whose face had smudges and stains of that same tar the Caribbeans use, and hands that were entirely black. She was a bit abashed by the visit: "Please come in, ladies . . . I'm an awful mess." (Pp. 138–39)

So much for the ladies' arrival on the scene, whose graphic depiction prepares the reader for the interior, which the narrator will presently paint: the poverty-stricken dwelling he ironically calls "Ido's mansion." In there, careful description leads to a central point: the figure of Ido's weary wife, Nicanora (an admirable verbal portrait, typical of the kind we find in most Galdosian novels), and an explanation of the character's activity:

> But what stirred both ladies' curiosity most was a large drawing board in the middle of the room, taking up almost all the empty space; it was

a table set up on benches, like the kind document writers use, and on top were quires of fine writing paper. On one side the stacked quires contained compact white reams; on the other, those same reams with newly painted black borders became mourning paper.

Ido spread out the unfolded sheets of paper on the drawing board. A girl (probably Rosita) counted the sheets that were already "in mourning" and made the quires. Nicanora asked the ladies for permission to continue her work. She was an aged rather than old woman, and it was plainly evident that she had never been beautiful. At one time she must have been well rounded, but now her sagging body was wrinkled and bumpy, like an empty shepherd's pouch. In fact, you couldn't tell what was breast and what was belly on her. Her face was snoutish and disagreeable. If it expressed anything, it was a very bad temper and an acrid disposition; but in this, her face, like so many others, was deceiving. Nicanora was a miserable woman, kinder than she was intelligent, worn out by the trials of life, which for her had been a battle with neither victories nor rest. All she had left was patience. Facing adversity so long must have given her that drawn-out snout which considerably uglified her. The "Venus de Medici" had sickly red eyelids deprived of eyelashes and, since they were always damp, people said that "she cried for her father with one eye and for her mother with the other." (Pp. 139–40)

Using this material, the author indulges in various kinds of humor: black humor, puns, juxtapositions, malapropisms. The scene is another mixed focalization; this time, the perspectives are Jacinta's, Guillermina's, Nicanora's, Ido's, and the narrator's:

Jacinta didn't know whom to pity more, Nicanora for being what she was, or her husband for believing that she was Venus when he got "electrified." Ido was very inhibited in the presence of the two ladies. When the chair that Doña Guillermina had sat in so often began to squeak in protest, announcing that it would perhaps collapse, Don José ran out to look for another in the neighborhood. Rosita was graceful, but decayed and chlorotic, greenish-colored. Her hairdo was what one noticed first: ringlets that had been teased and stiffened with quantities of lacquer.

"But what are you up to with that paint, woman?" Guillermina asked Nicanora.

"It's my work; it's *mourning.*"

"It's *morning!*" said Ido, smirking, very satisfied at having the opportunity to crack his joke, which was as old as the hills and had been used on many a previous occasion.

"The things he says!" said Guillermina, miffed by his joke.

"Be quiet, stop saying stupid things," Nicanora instructed him. "I'm in the mourning business; I paint mourning paper. When I don't have something else to do, I bring home a few reams and turn them into mourning paper, as the ladies can see. The salesman pays a *real* a ream. I pay for the dye, and working all day long, I make six or seven *reales*. But times are bad, and there's not much 'dyeing' to be done. All of us are out of a job because naturally, either not many people are dying, or they're not announcing it. José," she said to her husband, making him tremble, "what are you doing with your mouth hanging open? Start the dissembling." (P. 140)

Each of these passages from the second sampling illustrates how realist portraiture is combined with comedy of various kinds, constituting in their entirety the specifically Galdosian effect.

III

Deformity as found in extravagantly incorrect speech also interested Galdós. In the third sample of discourse (also from volume 1), we hear such language from Izquierdo, a friend of Ido's. An occasional use of italics, a practice Galdós copied from Balzac—who uses them persistently for the Baron de Nucingen in *Splendeurs et Misères des Courtisanes*—indicates deviational features. A rash of obscenities, verbal eccentricities, malapropisms, political allusions, quirky expressions. . . . Izquierdo's speech falls into an extreme category, and Galdós again handles the material masterfully. I found it extremely hard to translate such speech. The conversation takes place in a tavern, as the two men sit down to lunch:

> Izquierdo must have had to catch up on his hunger, because when he saw the steaks his eyes pounced on them as if to say: "Charge!" And without so much as a reply to his friend, who was talking, he viciously attacked them. And Ido began to gulp down big pieces without even chewing them. For a while they were silent. Izquierdo broke the silence by loudly banging his knife-handle on the table and saying:
> "Fuck the Republic! It's a lot of *garbage!*"
> Ido assented by nodding his head.
> "Republickins, ha! You're a stew of chopped lungs is what *you* are, ya bunch of smart alecks. You're worst than slavish, worse than *mod*-irates!" added Izquierdo, wildly exalted. "Not give *me* a job—*me*, the endivid'al that worked the hardest for the Republickins in this fuckin' country. . . . It's just like they say: 'Give 'em the milk of human kindness and. . . .' Oh, Señor Martos, Señor Figueras, Señor Pi—try to tell *me* you don't know poor ole Izquierdo, just because you don't like my clothes. Ha! Before, when Izquierdo had enflince in the Inclusa district, and when Bicerra came around to see 'im with that bit about

going into the streets, *then* . . . Fuck it! So we've lost our prestige and we don't have any money. But if we get back up there again, I swear to those stuff shirts, we'll have a real 'yection'!"

Ido kept commiserating with him, although he didn't understand the bit about the "yection," nor could anyone have understood it. For Izquierdo, the word implied a bloody collision, a row or something of the sort. He drank glass after glass without its going to its head, which had a notable capacity.

"'Cause look, maestro, what gets 'em is that I was there *pers*nally in Cartagena. And damn it, I say it's to my credit. Only us *real* libbrals was there. And lemme tell you somethin' else, namesake: all I've done all my life is spill my blood for fuckin' liberty. In '54 whaddid I do?—throw myself at the barricades like a decent endivid'al. They can ask poor old Don Pascual Muñoz who's dead now, bless 'im; the guy that had the hardware store, the Marqués de Casa-Muñoz's father; he had more pull than anybody in these parts, and you know what he said to me? Said: 'Plato, friend, give me your hand.' So then I go to the Palace with Don Pascual himself, and he goes up to talk to the queen, and pretty soon he comes down with the paper with the queen's signachure. Wow! That really let them modirates have it. And Don Pascual tole me to put a white handkachiff at the end of a stick and go first sayin': 'Cease fire, cease fire!'

"In '56 I was a militia lootnint and Genrul O'Donnell got scared a me, and when he talked to the troops he said, says, 'If there's nobody that can get me Izquierdo, then we haven't done a damned thing.' In '66, when there was the artillery thing, me and my buddy Socorro were shootin' from the corner of Leganitos Street. In '68, when things really blew up, I was on guard at the bank so they wouldn't rob it, and lemme tell *you*, if some goddam robber so much as shown his face around there, I'd of suicided 'im. . . . So then it gets to be time for the payoff, and they make Pucheta a guard at the Casa del Campo, and Mochilo at the Pardo—and they give *me* a kick in the pants. And all I wanted was a lil' job, carryin' the mail somewheres, and pfft! Then I go see Bicerra, and do you think he knows me? Not on your life! I tell him I'm Izquierdo, my nickname's Plato, and he shakes his head. It's just like they say: they forget about the fuckin' step as soon as they've climbed up it." (Pp. 148–49)

Mimicry of this speech requires a good ear and a previous hearing of its counterpart in your native language. And what can be especially hard is to use words you normally exclude from your vocabulary, because you have to overcome your own resistance. But your own vocabulary is irrelevant, of course. What you have to do is change roles, become the character if you want to project him convincingly in English. This aspect of the art we may call translator as actor, and it complements others, such as translator as critic, or poet, or thinker.

The passage of butchered speech shows how the author is as capable of destroying language as he is of constructing it. Equal pleasures, perhaps, for the writer is more interested in playing than in moralizing or correcting. By contorting the Spanish language to fit the imaginary speaker, the author brings him alive on the page. The force of Izquierdo's tirade cannot be underestimated or dismissed as comic relief only; it has the structural function of giving us a defamiliarized view of Spanish history. What starts out as a conversation between friends turns into a tyrannical monologue as Izquierdo drinks more wine and gets carried away with his own cursing. Some of the features of his speech as captured by Galdós include neologisms ("I'd of suicided 'im"), use of the dramatic present, grammatical errors ("I'd of" instead of "I would've"), phonetic destruction (as indicated by the intentional misspellings in my translation). In the original—and I recommend Francisco Caudet's critical edition (Cátedra, 1983)—these pages are heavily footnoted. Difficulty exists for the Spanish reader too. If I have footnoted only a minimum, it is because there is already a wealth of new material to learn in English (mostly cultural and historical). Shifting the emphasis to the notes, while good instructionally, would have made it excessively slow reading, and perhaps the flow of the story would have been interrupted too many times to make its reading enjoyable. And I have sought in my version to preserve the airy, familiar tone of the original. Had there been cumbersome footnotes, the text in English might have become didactic rather than remain entertaining as Galdós intended.

Izquierdo's talk, fraught with political references, functions more as character expression and comic relief than as description of the events mentioned. Also, it ties in with the main story line, as we see at the end of the second paragraph, when he says to Ido:

> I was so hungry. Oh, namesake, if I hadn't a had the luck to run inta my niece Fortunata there, I wouldn't a been here to tell the story. She helped me out. She's a good girl, and with the money she gave me, I hopped the fuckin' train for Madrid."
>
> "So then," said Ido, tired of the incoherent story and grotesque vocabulary, "You took in that adorable child."
>
> Ido was hunting for a novel on that garrulous page of contemporary history, but Izquierdo, having a shrewder mind, scorned the novel and resumed his serious history. (P. 150)

As the reader is led back to the main story, the narrator depicts Izquierdo's listener, Ido, as someone "hunting for a novel," someone who is tired of "the incoherent story." Clearly, we are dealing with a story within a story, metaliterature, a substance found repeatedly in *Fortunata y Jacinta*.

Fortunata's being mentioned in the midst of this monologue is effective artistically because we can suddenly hear the verbal medium within which she has grown up, and which she tries to escape during her relationship with Juanito. She thinks that he will not marry her because she speaks in a funny way and comes from a poor home. So when we hear such a torrent of words erupting out of Izquierdo all full of warts and moles, we get a sense of what assailed her ears as she was growing up. Indirectly, then, his speech helps us to understand her character: it fills in part of the network of her family relations that is left out of the main narration.

Notice how emphatically section 6 starts. Izquierdo's repetitions are almost like a coda: "He said ''cause they're *mod*irates' at least six times, raising his voice gradually; the last cry could have been heard from the Toledo Gates" (P. 151). The narrator has stepped back into the story, relating the exclamations to a more general context, that of his own remarks on these two characters who he again views from afar (or above). The rash of incredible malapropisms, obscenities, etc., is over, having been contained in a dialogue, and the narrator resumes his work of advancing the story. With this there is a switch back to the usual slower pace of his storytelling, and the normal style we associate with his words. We have witnessed the destruction of language, then abruptly, suspension and return to the norm.

IV

Turning now to the last sample of discourse, we could identify this one as technical language, and more specifically, as pharmaceutical. Until checking, I thought that the terms should be called pharmacological, but after consulting a pharmacologist, I understood the difference: industrial use—i.e., manufacture and sales—of medicines is pharmaceutical, whereas medical study and prescription of the same is pharmacological. In the excerpt we are about to consider, the chemical substances are used as materials in a business; the scene is a pharmacy, where the characters are talking about medicines and about how these substances could help them make a bundle.

Technical language in general is wonderfully precise in Galdós. Other types include the fabric trade, import and export business (especially the Chinese shawl business), architecture, foods—from the marketplace to the table, in various households—cafés, bullfighting, convents, shops. . . . In short, urban life of the Victorian period is fully recreated, transmitted accurately because the author has observed his subjects closely and learned the proper terms for naming and interrelating the components of his culture.

The sample containing pharmaceutical terms comes from volume 4 and is set in the pharmacy where one of the main characters, Maximiliano Rubín, works for Segismundo Ballester:

> Segismundo Ballester (the pharmacist in charge of Samaniego's pharmacy) had frequent arguments with Maxi over the awful mistakes the latter made. He finally had to forbid him to prepare any strong medicines on his own. "Now look, son, if you're going to mix up the alcoholates with tinctures, let's call it quits! This flask is the alcohol for scurvy and this is the aconite tincture. Take another look at the prescription; read it carefully. If you don't improve, we'll simply have to tell Doña Casta to close down the business."
>
> And with these words, uttered in a rather harsh, teacherly way, Ballester appropriated whatever was in his subordinate's hands. Then, sniffing the mixture Maxi had concocted, he asked angrily: "What the devil did you put in this? Either this is valerian or I've lost my sense of smell. I knew it—you're just not well today. Why not go home? I can get along better by myself. Take care, now, and here—take this laxative on an empty stomach. Then at mealtimes and bedtime take one of these hydrogenated iron pills with extract of wormwood. With this heat it's wise to watch your intake; not overdo it, you know? And above all, go out and walk. Don't read so much." (P. 619)

Maxi, whose lapses into his dream world are frequent, makes some mistakes as he mixes the medicines and succeeds in enraging his boss, who is a kindly fellow. Ballester is fatherly with the orphaned Rubín and prescribes a cure for his malaise. That is when we notice it is not the present, the 1980s; instead of a couple of aspirin, hydrogenated iron pills are recommended. And the reader is reminded suddenly of the temporal distance between the text and today. It was a temptation to modernize in the translation, but the original remedies had to be respected; otherwise, they would not fit in with the rest of Ballester's pharmacy.

Galdós admits differing degrees of technicality in the mention of medicines. On the next page there is a scene at Maxi's house. His aunt, Doña Lupe, does not speak with the same degree of precision as her nephew or Ballester. Aunt and nephew are talking about how to earn money with a new formula or something:

> "Aunt, don't think I haven't considered it too. Yesterday it occurred to me that you could add a solution of iron to all sorts of medicines. I think I could come up with a new formula."
>
> "Look, son, these things are done either on a big scale or not at all. If you're going to invent something, make it a panacea, something that will cure everything, absolutely everything, that you can sell in any form—liquid, pills, tablets, capsules, syrup, plasters, and even special cigars. With all the drugs that you and Ballester have in there, aren't there three or four that could mix well and be good for everyone? It really hurts me to see you with a fortune at arm's length and you not even reaching for it. Look at Dr. Perpiña on Cañizares Street. He's made a bundle from that syrup . . . what's it called? Something like—"
>
> "Refined lacto-phosphate of lime," said Maxi. "As for panaceas, pharmacological ethics don't permit them."
>
> "What a fool! What do pharmacological ethics have to do with this? See? You're proving I'm right: you'll never be anything but poor. You're just like that simpleton Ballester; he gave me that business about 'ethics' the other day. Doesn't experience teach you two anything? And poor old Samaniego didn't leave his family any capital because he had the same dumb streak you have. Humph! In his time almost anything you bought at a pharmacy had to be mixed while you waited. Casta was exasperated, of course. She's hoping, too, that you and Ballester will come up with something to give the business a name and fill the registers with cash. A fine pair she's got running her business. . . ." (Pp. 620–21)

The terms are sketchy in the aunt's mind and exact in the nephew's, since he is a scrupulous pharmacy student. Later on, when Fortunata enters the conversation, the simplest reference of all becomes appropriate: "Rather timidly, Fortunata ventured that her husband should stop taking pills and make up his mind to go to San Sebastián for medicinal baths" (p. 621). For her, treatment is just pills.

It is curious to watch how the same thing must be renamed according to who is speaking, so that the characters' speech habits will serve to portray them accurately. While it is easy to take for granted the renamings, it is not so easy to achieve them as Galdós does, effortlessly, as if each mind were actually independent and free of its creator's own verbal limitations.

We have looked at only a few samples, so I cannot pretend to go beyond that material, but because it embraces considerable (and typical) diversity, it should be possible to select significant features. Galdós's art includes something which is common in most narrations: competent description of events, states, and characters. And then again, it includes something not quite so common: narrative identification with various perspectives; the narrator ably takes on the speech mannerisms of others. Also typical are the occasional omniscient intrusions, a nineteenth-century feature. This trait is often combined with humor, and the result is specifically Galdosian. Indirect mimicry, by the use of the free indirect style, is one of the trickier features because it is not always clear how much of the language corresponds to the narrator himself, and how much to the character whose view or thought is being evoked in words or a style we tend to identify with that character. The snatch of alien speech in the narrator's own is sometimes dramatic (as when the narrator recalls a picturesque expression of, say, Ido's), but at other times it is harder to detect because of the similarities between the speakers (as for example the narrator and Feijoo, the protagonist of volume 3).

Catching the presence or absence of other voices in the narrator's discourse allows the translator to reproduce the tonal and verbal nuances that make Galdós's narrative prose delicious in the original; sustaining the consequent effect was perhaps the most challenging problem in translating *Fortunata y Jacinta.* the narrator is the permanent connector of the many voices and verbal peculiarities in the text.

Portraiture is another significant part of Galdós's narrative art in all his novels. Destruction of language, as previously commented on, is a sign of the writer's ability to play with language, to let his pen fly through worlds of otherness and return to his individual style unscathed. Somewhat related are the technical terms, excursions into specialized areas of knowledge, that fill in the background of this chatty novel.

So much, then, for Galdós's variegated language. My purpose has been to see how the parts fit, in hopes of shedding a few rays on one of the more difficult aspects of translating this author.

NOTE

1. I take "masterpiece" to mean Galdós's most finished and complex work as Spain's greatest nineteenth-century realist document. For a curious discussion of the concept of a literary masterpiece, see the *New York Times*, May 29, 1988, section 4, p. 18, "Ideas and Trends," for an article summarizing the conclusions reached by comparativists at a recent symposium at Princeton.

On the Translation of
Chinese Poetry

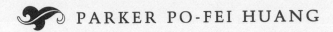 PARKER PO-FEI HUANG

THE FOLLOWING is a simple classical poem written by Wang Chih-huan (A.D. 688–742), a Chinese poet in the T'ang dynasty (A.D. 618–905). Beside each character in the poem a word-by-word dictionary annotation is given.

climb crane bird tower	登鶴雀樓
white sun close mountain end of	白日依山盡
Yellow River enter sea flow	黃河入海流
attempt exhaust thousand *li*[1] eye	欲窮千里目
again ascend one flight tower	更上一層樓

Translation:

> The sun is setting
>   behind the mountain;
> Yellow River flows on
>   into the sea.
> Desiring to envision
>   the remote distance,
> I climb
>   another storey
>   of the tower.

Before we get into the discussion of problems in translating Chinese poetry into English, let me point out two factors which frequently puzzle the translator at the outset: (1) Who is the actor in the poem? (2) When is the action taken?

These questions are not easy to answer. Witter Bynner in 1920 translated the last two lines of the above poem as follows:

But you widen your view three hundred miles
By going up one flight of stairs.

84

Innes Herdan in 1981 translated them into:

> Desiring to scan
> the thousand miles vista
> I climb another storey
> of the pagoda.

Now, who is supposed to be the actor? The second question seems even more puzzling. A subsequent example, "Still Night Thoughts," will illustrate where the problem is.

Before we put such questions to rest, I think we should, first, know what the Chinese language is and how it is used as a medium for poetic expression. Chinese is written with characters rather than with an alphabet. The characters have been traditionally classified according to six graphic principles. Here are the four more important ones governing the composition of characters.[2]

1. *Imitating the form.* Characters of this kind may also be described as simple pictograms. The ancient form of such characters as those for "sun" (⊙ ancient form, 日 modern form), "moon" (ꓷ, 月), "mountain" (屮屮, 山), "water" (沕, 水), "field" (田, 田), "tree, wood" (木, 木), "bamboo" (竹竹, 竹), "gourd, melon" (瓜, 瓜), "man" (㐧, 人), "child, seed" (子, 子), "mouth" (▽, 口), and others bear some resemblance to the objects represented.

2. *Pointing at the thing.* Characters of this classification may also be called simple ideograms. Some examples of a simple ideogram are the characters 一 (one), 二 (two), 三 (three), 上 (above, top, summit), and 下 (low surface, bottom). Simple ideograms can also be composed by adding strokes to a character which already has a separate meaning of its own. For instance, the character which means "tree top" (朱) is written by adding a stroke to the top of the character of "tree" (木). Similarly, the word for "root" (本) is written by adding a stroke to the bottom of the character for "tree."

3. *Understanding the meaning; or, composite ideogram.* For example, the character meaning "bright" (明) is simply a combination of the characters for "moon" (月) and "window" (囧), or "moon" and "sun" according to other etymologists.

4. *Harmonizing the sound—the phonogram.* Phonograms are composite characters (i.e., characters made up of two or more recognizable component characters). One component of the phonogram indicates the meaning, while the other component of the phonogram suggests the word's phonetic value. Thus it is possible for a reader to make an educated guess as to the sound and the meaning of the

radical (such as "flower" 花 : ⁺⁺ the grass radical, plus 化 the phonetic) to a character he has never seen before.

The Chinese character is unique, in both a visual sense and an auditory sense. In terms of sound, as a syllable, a character not only represents a combination of consonant and vowel, but it also carries a tonal value. The meaning of any syllable in Chinese may be changed by altering its tone. Here is a simple story to illustrate this. A Chinese boy and his mother were walking down a narrow path when they encountered a horse, which was blocking their way. The mother tried to shove the horse away, but the horse just stood there and did not move. Finally the mother became quite angry and yelled loudly. The boy could not tell what his mother was really saying, and he asked: "mama ma ma ma." This translates as: "Mother, are you scolding the horse?"[3]

Chinese is an uninflected language, and it is not burdened with cases, genders, moods, and tenses. Chinese words are not bound by "parts of speech." The same word can be used as a noun, verb, adjective, adverb, etc. This high degree of freedom is fully employed in literary prose, and even more so in classical poetry.

After the appearance of the first Chinese anthology, *The Book of Poetry*, a collection of poems written between the twelfth and sixteenth centuries B.C., Chinese poetry developed into three major genres. They are *shih* (or verse), *ts'u* (or lyric meters), and *ch'u* (or dramatic verse).

Shih, the traditional verse, is always written in a rather regulated form. The regularity and variation in the number of characters, in addition to the variation in tone, play a significant role in Chinese versification. The four tones are used to contrast with each other for auditory effect. The four-character (syllable) form is mostly used in poems collected in *The Book of Poetry*. In the Han dynasty (206 B.C.–A.D. 219), the five-syllable form was created. Later the five-syllable and seven-syllable eight-line regulated verses and the five-syllable and seven-syllable four-line "cut-shorts" came into being.[4] These verse forms flourished in the T'ang dynasty (618–905).

Ts'u, or lyric meters, became popular during the Sung dynasty (960–1278). It is a verse form written in lines of varying length. It varies from one to eleven or more characters. *Ts'u* is more pliable and adaptable to musical requirements than the *shih*.

Ts'u and *ch'u* are similar in form. They differ mainly in their purpose and representation. *Ts'u* is written to express the poet's own feelings and observations, while *ch'u* is a sequence of songs written to utter the sentiments of a certain character in a play. While *ts'u* was the most popular verse form in the Sung dynasty, *ch'u* and its variations were very popular through the Yuan dynasty (1206–1341) and the Ming dynasty (1368–1628).

My discussion here is limited to *shih*, the traditional classical verse, because it is the mainstream of Chinese poetical work. I leave out the modern colloquial poetry, since it is, in many aspects, influenced by Western poetry.

With this cursory knowledge of the Chinese language, we may now begin to comprehend how a Chinese poet, with the given syntactical freedom and poetic license, is able to achieve what he is pursuing. By omitting the subject in a poem, he creates a sense of universality—the missing subject can be identified with anyone; with a verb left out, images can be vividly presented with the use of an uninflected verb, and the immediacy of experience and the sense of timelessness are quintessentially enhanced. It is quite amazing that by using merely twenty or twenty-eight characters such as the "cut-short" form, the poet can compress the essence of a scene, a mood, a whole experience, even an inspiring message into an entity. The poem of Wang Chih-huan cited above could serve as an excellent illustration.

Li Po (701–762), one of the two greatest poets in China,[5] has written a good number of best-loved poems. One of these has been well learned by Chinese children at an early age so that they may chant it along with nursery rhymes. The poem is "Still Night Thoughts."

still	*night*	*thoughts*			靜夜思
bed	front	bright	moon	light	牀前明月光
doubt	to be	ground	above	frost	疑是地上霜
raise	head	look	bright	moon	舉頭望明月
low	head	think	old	country	低頭思故鄉

In comparing seven different translations of the poem which I have come across in half a century or so, I find them to have missed either the beauty of simplicity or the direct appealing effect of the original.

Given the word-by-word translation of the poem, it would be natural to translate it as follows.

Still Night Thoughts

The moonlight in front of my bed,
Could it be the frost on the ground?
Raising my head, I look at the bright moon,
Bending my head, I think of my old home.

Let us see how the other translators deal with the first two lines:

> I wake, and moonbeams
> play around my bed
> glittering like hoar-frost
> to my wondering eyes.
> (Herbert A. Giles)

> As by my bed
> the moon did beam
> It seemed as if with frost the earth were spread.
> (John Turner)

> In front of my bed there is bright moonlight.
> I think there must be hoar-frost on the ground.
> (Soame Jenyns)

> I saw the moonlight before my couch,
> And wondered if it were not the frost on the ground.
> (Shigeyoshi Obata)

> So bright a gleam on the foot of my bed,
> Could there have been a frost already?
> (Witter Bynner)

> Moonlight in front of my bed,
> I took it for the frost on the ground.
> (Burton Watson)

> The bright moon shone before my bed,
> I wonder
> was it frost upon the ground?
> (Innes Herdan)

First, I think Mr. Giles and Mr. Turner are too eager to make their translations into perfect English poems. They have brought in superfluous words like "play around," "glittering," "wondering" (Giles) and "with frost the earth were spread" (Turner). Second, it is permissible and even admirable to ignore the Chinese syntax by moving the imagery of the moon to the leading position in the sentence, as several of the translators did; but introducing the first person verbs "I wake" (Giles) and "I saw" (Obata) weakens the appealing and subtle effect of universality so important to this poem. Third, use of the past tense to indicate when the action is taken completely loses the sense of immediacy.

In judging translations of Chinese poetry, we can assemble a variety of pragmatic criteria, such as the respect displayed for the poem's original verbal economy, its "universality" of reference, and its immediacy. But these standards or touchstones will remain pragmatic, and will vary from translator to translator since each has his own way to "interpret" and his own right to "recreate." One can merely say how a translator might have emphasized a certain aspect of the poem and overlooked the others. For instance, on the problem of dealing with rhythm and rhyme, Arthur Waley has said in his *Translations from the Chinese:*

> One or two questions which readers are bound to ask. Is it [Chinese poetry] really at all like our poetry? Does it scan; does it rhyme? The answer to their questions is that Chinese traditional poetry is very similar to ours. Its lines have fixed syllables and rhyme is obligatory.

But when he decided not to use rhyme in his translation, he gave a rather weak explanation:

> Most of the poems in this book are either in lines of five syllables or in lines of seven syllables all the way through. In the English, so far as possible, a stress represents each syllable; so that a Chinese reader will easily recognize the meter of the original. I have not used rhyme, because what is really, in the long run, of most interest to American readers is what the poems say; and if one uses rhyme, it is impossible not to sacrifice sense to sound.[6]

John A. Turner says in his preface to a collection of his translations that rhyme is an important element in Chinese traditional poetry. He intended "to make the translation of a poem to read like a poem itself." He carried this point further by saying: "In an attempt to preserve the singing [I assume he means singing and chanting] or musical quality in Chinese, I regularly employ rhyme." And he also says:

> I do not comply with the modern fashion of putting Chinese verse into line by line prose, or into unmeasured sprung rhythm, which is the same thing. Besides, I believe that poetry cannot really be translated into prose. The translation of a poem into prose, which is merely verbally accurate, is not itself a poem and remains a crib. It misses the point and soul and reason of a poem, its specific beauty.[7]

In discussing one of the difficulties of translating the sound-pattern from Chinese into English, James J. Y. Liu says:

> As for rhyme, I formerly advocated reproducing the original rhyme schemes in translation of Chinese poetry, and tried to put this in practice, with unfortunate results, for which I have been criticized by several reviewers. I now realize the virtual impossibility of keeping the rhymes without damage to the meaning, and no longer wish to insist on the use of rhymes. Thus two of the most important elements of Chinese versification, tone-pattern and rhyme, have to go.

As a matter of fact, besides the differences mentioned, there are still other things which are impossible to convey in any translation. First let me ask a simple question: Could an English reader of "Still Night Thoughts," which is so beloved by Chinese, be as deeply touched by these twenty simple characters as Chinese are? I believe not. The reason is: The Chinese way of thinking of the moon is different from the Western way. The moon, as an image, is closely associated with Chinese life. A full moon symbolizes a perfect home life, or a happy family reunion; a waning moon, destitution or separation. Besides, the thinking about nature, time, history, leisure, nostalgia, and the feeling of love and life are not the same.[8] These Chinese concepts should all be under consideration in translation, but such a demand is hardly satisfactorily met by any of the translations of Li Po's "Still Night Thoughts."

Ezra Pound was called by T. S. Eliot "the inventor of Chinese poetry for our time." Pound's career as a translator of Chinese poetry was launched in 1915 when he published *Cathay*, a booklet containing his translation of poems from *The Book of Poetry*. Before Pound there were some English translations of these poems already in existence. James Legge, a missionary in China, published his complete translation of 305 poems in *The Book of Poetry* in Hong Kong in 1861. In the preface of the new edition issued in 1892, while he was the professor of Chinese at Oxford, he writes:

> The author [James Legge himself] thought indeed at one time of recasting the whole version in a terser and more pretentious style. He determined, however, on reflection to let it stand as it first occurred to him, his objects having always been faithful to the original Chinese rather than grace of composition. Not that he is indifferent to the value of an elegant and idiomatic rendering in the language of the translation, and he hopes that he was able to combine in a certain degree correctness of interpretation and acceptableness of style.

It was Legge's translation that inspired Helen Waddell to render some of Legge's poems into lyrics. They were published under the name of *Lyrics from the Chinese* (Houghton Mifflin, 1915). In her preface she quoted James Legge's words: "Anyone who is willing to undertake the labor . . . to present the piece in a faithful metrical version" is welcome.

Pound's translations in *Cathay* are merely based on the theory put forth by Ernest Fenollosa in his article "The Chinese Character as a Medium for Poetry." Fenollosa says in his article:

My subject is poetry, not language, yet the roots of poetry are in language. In the study of a language so alien in form to ours as is Chinese in its written character, it is necessary to inquire how these universal elements of form which constitute poetics can derive appropriate nutriment.

And he furthers his statement:

It is clear that these three joints, or words [man sees horse], are only three phonetic symbols, which stand for the three terms of a natural process. But we could quite as easily denote these three stages of our thought by symbols equally arbitrary, *which had no basis in sound* for example, by three Chinese characters:

人　見　馬　　Man Sees Horse

If we all knew *what division* of this mental horse-picture each of these signs stood for, we could communicate continuous thought to one another as easily by drawing them as by speaking words. We habitually employ the visible language of gesture in much this same manner.

But Chinese notation is something much more than arbitrary symbols. It is based upon a vivid shorthand picture of the operations of nature. In the algebraic figure and in the spoken word there is no natural connection between thing and sign: all depends upon sheer convention. But the Chinese method follows natural suggestion. First stands the man on his two legs. Second, his eye moves through space: a bold figure represented by running legs under an eye, a modified picture of an eye, a modified picture of running legs, but unforgettable once you have seen it. Third stands the horse on his four legs.

The thought-picture is not only called up by these signs as well as by words, but far more vividly and concretely. Legs belong to all three characters: they are *alive.* The group holds something of the quality of a continuous moving picture.[9]

As I have said above, a Chinese character is absolutely not like what Fenollosa has described. The "vivid shorthand picture" is only one of the forms created under the six graphic principles. To project the idea that "the Chinese notation is something more than arbitrary symbols" and is "based upon a vivid shorthand picture of the operations of nature" is preposterous. It is fair to say, in the present day, that no one would ever believe this to be an adequate presentation of the nature of the Chinese language, not to mention that it is an erroneous approach to the understanding and appreciation of Chinese poetry.

In the introduction to the new version of Pound's translation of *Shih-ching: The Classic Anthology Defined by Confucius* (Cambridge: Harvard University Press, 1954), we are told on p. xiii: "The first poem of that slim volume (*Cathay*) is actually Ode 167 (of the 305 poems); the appreciable difference between the present version is understandable because in the earlier version Pound was at the mercy of Ernest Fenollosa's notes."

On the back of this Harvard edition we find I. A. Richards's comment on Pound's new translation:

> Great cultures start in great poetry and here are the seeds of one of the greatest. They have been thought untranslatable in poetry. Nevertheless here is Mr. Pound at his best:—on sky and earth and most that haunts between, from sounds caught in the heart's pang and on to thought's possession of the mind at peace.

Comparing the new translation to the old one, I, for one, am elated that Mr. Pound has irrevocably cast away the misleading theory of Fenollosa for his guide.

Below are translations of a section of the poem "East Gate" from *The Book of Poetry* by two scholars—James Legge and Bernard Karlgren—and two poets, Helen Waddell and Ezra Pound. It is interesting to see what craft each employs to render this ancient Chinese poem into English.

The She King—Ch'uh k'e tung mun.

茹匪如出綦匪如出
愿我荼其巾我雲其出
○思○闍○思○東其
聊且雖闍聊存雖門東
可○則○樂○則○門
與縞如有我縞如有
娛衣荼女員衣雲女
　○　　○　　○　　○

I went out at the east gate,
Where the girls were in clouds.
Although they are like clouds,
It is not on them that my thoughts rest.
She in the thin white silk, and the grey coiffure,—
She is my joy!

(James Legge)

I go out at the East gate;
there are girls (numerous) like a cloud;
but although they are like a cloud,
they are not those in whom my thoughts rest;
(she with) the white-silk robe and with the
    black-mottled grey kerchief,
she will rejoice me.

(Bernard Kalgren)

I went out at the Eastern Gate,
   I saw the girls in clouds,
Like clouds they were, and soft and bright,
   But in the crowds
I thought on the maid who is my light,
Down-dropping, soft as the grey twilight;
    She is my mate.
(Helen Waddell)

At the great gate to the East
Mix crowds
be girls like clouds
who cloud not my thought in the least.
        Gray scarf and a plain silk gown
        I take delight in one alone.
(Ezra Pound)

In Pound's translation the simplicity of language, the clarity of style, and his powers of transmitting the poetics in the original poem to a new organic unity have given birth to a unique creation. Someone who can read Chinese may be aware that Pound has ignored the Chinese versification, such as the metrical structure, the rhythm and rhyme scheme, etc.; nevertheless, the translation is excellent poetry, and a distinguished model of free verse in English. So distinguished is it that I believe Mr. Pound would be more appropriately honored and remembered as a founder of the free verse style in English poetry, than as an "inventor," as T. S. Eliot put it, or translator of Chinese poetry.

As we know, poetry from different cultures, different forms, different aesthetics, can bring us a sense of the breadth and range of poetry in the world. Since James Legge's first translations of *The Book of Poetry* into English, a century has already elapsed. The times demand adequate translation of Chinese poetry into English. The number of sinologists who can both read and speak Chinese has been increasing, and so is the number of students who are interested in studying Chinese literature and Chinese poetry. Translations of Chinese poetry into English have grown in noticeable numbers since the 1950s.

It is obvious that as long as Chinese is learned in the English-speaking world, as long as the study of comparative literature must include Chinese works for consideration, the curiosity and interest in knowing Chinese poetry better will ensure that translations will always be in demand.

The serious studies of the art of Chinese poetry conducted by the late James J. Y. Liu and Wai-lim Yip are remarkable contributions to the understanding of Chinese poetry. They opened the door upon a world that has for a long time been an enigma to Westerners.[10] *Sunflower Splendor: Three Thousand Years of Chinese Poetry, A Comprehensive Anthology of Chinese Poetry*, co-edited by Wu-chi Liu and Irving Yucheng Lo (Doubleday Anchor original, 1975), includes more than fifty translators' work in a praiseworthy achievement.

To conclude the discussion I will add my humble translations of some poems in classical form I have written recently, to show the difficulties a translator encounters. There are brief explanations for the three poems to illustrate what I mean. I think it may amuse you to see how someone who is supposed to know the original work so well still fumbles along in frustration.

Mountain in Distance
There is nothing
and there is

Brush dipped with
a little ink
or almost with none

A picture of
distant mountain
is spiritually painted.
  (Parker Po-fei Huang)

山色有無中
無中竟是有
識有便知無
天地闃無朕
捉筆入畫圖

Mountain hue being non-being amid
non-being amid actually is being
know being then know non-being
heaven earth quiet no sign/incipient
grasp pen enter picture map/picture

I could translate this poem literally as well in the following form:

In the non-being actually there is being,
Recognizing being then know non-being.
The heavens and earth quietly show no sign,
(I) snatch a pen and turn the mountain hue into a picture.

But in doing so, I lose the intensity of a poem. The words "being" and "non-being" are used in *Tao Te Ching*, a book presumably written by Lao Tzu, a philosopher, who lived around the sixth century

B.C. This book is one of the major underlying influences in Chinese thought and culture. I took the idea for my poem from the following lines in its opening chapter:

> Therefore, constantly based on non-being,
> One will have insight into its subtlety;
> Constantly based on being,
> One will have insight into its potentiality.
>   (Paul J. Liu)[11]

This philosophical concept could rather easily be intuited by a Chinese reader, but would entirely elude an English reader.

When I started to translate this poem, I did not want the imagery "mountain hue" to diffuse the theme; also, I needed the word "spiritually," which is not in the Chinese poem, to manifest the connection between man and nature. As for the title, if I had rendered it into English literally, it would have provided a misleading introduction to the poem.

Naive Anxiety
The laughter of the
spring sun; the ice cracking
on the lake; the hills
are beautiful
after a light snow;
the buds on each bough
ask anxiously: What distance
did the swallows cover
on their return flight?
        (Parker Po-fei Huang)

燕枝雪春
鳥頭後陽春
歸蓓青笑問
來蕾山裂
第頻最一
幾相好湖
程問晴冰

spring ask

spring yang/sun smile crack one lake ice
snow after green mountain extreme good clear
branch head flower bud frequent mutually ask
swallow bird return come number which stage

I break the first two lines—both are complete sentences—to create the cadence for the sake of the culminating effect. The direct translation of the first line ought to be: "spring *smiles* (as a transitive verb, I do not think there is such a case in English) crack a whole lake frozen with ice."

Watching the Fish

A fish
being with other fish
it is so lively

I watch and watch
feeling silly

All of a sudden
my mind is stricken
on this piece of paper
there's a poem
　(Parker Po-fei Huang)

紙 偶 我 魚
上 然 觀 樂 觀
故 觸 我 魚 魚
留 妙 我 魚
詩 思 痴 樂

look fish

fish　happy　fish　fish　happy
I　look　I/me　I/me　silly
accidental　so　touch　mysterious　thought
paper　on　therefore　keep　poem

I just do not know how to make the three "fish" words in the first line and the three *I*s in the second function in English as I would like them to. Could anyone enlighten me?

NOTES

1. A Chinese measure of length reckoned at 360 paces, or about 1,890 feet in English measure.

2. Besides the four listed, the other two are "mutually defining" and "borrowing," which modern scholars consider to be extended uses of already existing characters and not the formation of new ones.

3. The first tone is indicated by a macron ˉ, the second tone by an acute accent ´, the third tone by a haček ˇ, the fourth tone by a grave accent ˋ, and the fifth is neutral without a marking. So this question asked by the boy is: Māma mà mǎ ma? (Mother scold horse, eh?)

4. For the complete sound pattern, see James J. Y. Liu, *The Art of Chinese Poetry* (Chicago: University of Chicago Press, 1961), 22–27, and Wai-lim Yip, *Chinese Poetry: Major Modes and Genres* (Berkeley: University of California Press, 1976), 228–30.

5. The other poet is Tu Fu (712–770). Li's work is loved for its splendid language, vividness, and originality of thought, while Tu Fu is admired for his brilliant technique and his transcendent power to overcome the misery of life.

6. Arthur Waley, preface to *Translations from the Chinese* (New York: Alfred A. Knopf, 1941), 1.

7. *A Golden Treasury of Chinese Poetry* (Hong Kong: The Chinese

University of Hong Kong, 1976), 10.

8. For further understanding of these factors, see Liu, "Some Chinese Concepts and Ways of Thinking and Feeling," in *The Art of Chinese Poetry*, 48–60.

9. See Fenollosa, *The Chinese Character as a Medium for Poetry*, ed. Ezra Pound (San Francisco: City Lights Books, 1936), 6, 8, 9.

10. See Liu, *The Art of Chinese Poetry; The Poetry of Li-shang-yin* (Chicago: University of Chicago Press, 1969). See also Wai-lim Yip, *Ezra Pound's Cathay* (Princeton: Princeton University Press, 1969); *Chinese Poetry*.

11. Paul J. Liu, *A Translation of Lao Tzu's Tao Te Ching and Wang Pi's Commentary* (Ann Arbor: Center for Chinese Studies, University of Michigan, 1977), 4.

II
Drama

Phaedra Britannica

 TONY HARRISON

> Prétends-tu m'éblouir des Fables de la Grèce?
> Quoiqu-'au-dessus de nous ils sont ce que nous somnes,
> Et comme nous enfin les Héros sont des Hommes.
>   Pradon, *Phèdre et Hippolyte* (1667)

I

RACINE TOOK TWO YEARS to write *Phèdre*, and I took two years to adapt it for the English stage. My methods, such as they are, a mixture of what Dryden called metaphrase and paraphrase, are no more original than Johnson's *Vanity of Human Wishes* or than Racine's, who made his play out of the Greek of Euripides and the Latin of Seneca, as well as earlier dramatic versions of the myth in his own tongue. In a pre-Romantic age I would feel little need for self-justification, nor feel I need be defensive about the poet's role as adapter. Nothing better could be said on that issue than what was written by Lion Feuchtwanger in his poem "Adaptations" (1924) composed after collaborating with Brecht on their version of *Edward II* after Marlowe:

> I, for instance, sometimes write
> Adaptations. Or some people prefer the phrase
> "Based on," and this is how it is: I use
> Old material to make a new play, then
> Put under the title
> The name of the dead writer who is extremely
> Famous and quite unknown, and before
> The name of the dead writer I put the little word "After."
> Then one group will write that I am

Very respectful and others that I am nothing of the sort and all
The dead writer's failures
Will be ascribed
To me and all my successes
To the dead writer who is extremely
Famous and quite unknown, and of whom
Nobody knows whether he himself
Was the writer or maybe the
Adapter.

Critics of *Phaedra Britannica* have provided a spectrum of opinion as wide and as contradictory as that in the Feuchtwanger poem, from the English critic (to whom Racine was, no doubt, "quite unknown") who accused me of taking a "crowbar" to the original, to the French critic Jean-Jacques Gautier writing in *Le Figaro* and finding that in my version *"la noblesse linéaire, la flamme, la grandeur de l'ouvrage original est préservée."*

II

When a play becomes a "vehicle" only, the greater part of it has died. If we go to see *Phèdre*, wrote Roland Barthes, it is on account of a particular great actress, a certain number of felicitous lines, some famous *tirades* set against a background of obscurity and boredom. We tolerate the rest. Barthes was writing after the production by Jean Vilar at the TNP in 1957 with Maria Casarès, and his reluctant conclusion was prominently displayed in the program of a production I saw in Paris in 1974 at the Théâtre Essaion: *"Je ne sais pas s'il est possible de jouer Racine aujourd'hui. Peut-être sur scène ce théâtre est-il aux trois-quart mort."* Similarly Jean-Louis Barrault in his *Mise en scène de Phèdre* (1946) writes that audiences went to see Sarah Bernhardt as Phèdre, but they did not go to see the *piece*. They did not even go to see the divine Sarah in the *entire* role, but the two scenes in which she excelled: the declaration of act 2 and the despair of act 4. *"Phèdre n'est pas un concerto pour femme,"* Barrault warns us, *"mais une symphonie pour orchestre d'acteurs."* The solution to the problem offered by Barrault could well apply to the revival of any classic play that has become simply a one-role play by coming adrift from its social origins: *"Phèdre femme droit de nouveau s'incorporer dans Phèdre tragédie."* A play is "about" everyone who sets foot on the stage, principals and mutes alike. The way to re-energize *Phèdre*, setting aside for the moment the well-nigh insuperable problems of doing that for an English audience, is to rediscover a *social* structure which makes the tensions and polarities of the play significant again. To make the roles, neglected for the sake of the "vehicle" role, meaningful again. To grasp the *play* entire. It is only when the characters around her are duly reinstated that the central figure can be seen in her true light. One can begin by going back to the title displayed on the original edition of Racine's text in 1677: *Phèdre et Hippolyte.* In order to correct the theatrical imbalance and sharpen the focus, one needs such, perhaps overloaded, assertions as Leo Spitzer's that Thésée is the most important person in the play. He is after all left alive with the awareness of the consequence of his actions, and the knowledge of the deaths of his wife and son. He has the last word.

III

There is a mode of literary criticism built upon the ruins of neo-classicism, and deriving from a period which was beginning to value intensity of experience at the expense of structure, a mode of criticism that extracts the principle "beauties" of a work, Arnoldian "touchstones," as though the essence of poetry resided in a few reverberant lines, and long works like Homer's were nothing more than a handful of titillating monosticha, rooted out of gray, unappealing tracts by Romantic truffle-hounds. It is an attitude represented at its extreme by Poe's opinion that "there is no such thing as a long poem." It made the assayer Matthew Arnold call Dryden and Pope "classics of our *prose.*" Racine has suffered similarly in France. Henri de Montherlant thought that there were only twenty-seven lines of "poetry" in the whole *oeuvres* of Racine, some twenty thousand lines. Jean Dutourd thought that Racine's Alexandrines were 99 percent rhetoric and 1 percent "poetry." One line which has consistently seemed to glitter from all this dross is one which Flaubert thought the most beautiful line in the whole of French Literature, and which Proust valued for its *beauté dénuée de sens.* It is a line which, typically, can only be understood, like most of Arnold's rhapsodical nuggets, by referring it back to the total context from which it was prised, by reconstructing the strata from which it was hastily lifted. One has to assume the responsibility of the archaeologist among so many opportunist treasure seekers. The line in question is the famous one spoken by Hippolyte describing Phèdre as *"La fille de Minos et de Pasiphaë."*

Admittedly it is a crucial line. A line full of mythical reverbera-
tions. For those who know the myth. And it is not enough to refer
the *reader*, as most French editions do, to the *tableau généalogique*
or the *index mythologique*. For one thing, we are preparing a piece
for the stage and not the study. Tableaus and indices are not theatrical, at least in a would-be Racinian recreation. The line is the key
to the inner struggle of Phèdre, to her essential torment, for those
who are at home in the obscure genealogies of Crete. As an
eighteenth-century commentator puts its, this line *"semble préparer
le spectateur à ce caractère mélangé de vices et de remords que le
poéte donne à Phèdre."* The key word in this is *mélangé*. Many
simply stress that the line signals the bad heredity of Phèdre, as if
it were simply a case of the mother, Pasiphaë, though R. C. Knight
tentatively suggests that "Minos *may* perhaps stand for moral conscience." Both elements of Phèdre's parentage are of equal importance. The problem about expanding the line, and absorbing into it
the facts given in study texts by genealogies impossible to project
theatrically, is that the line occurs in a context of nervous reticence.
It is an old story for Hippolyte and Théramène. Théramène cuts off
Hippolyte with an abrupt *"J'entends."* The line foreshadows the
causes of Phèdre's shame and her need to break through the barriers
of shame; it articulates her tension, without Hippolyte having to
transgress his own sense of propriety by being specific. It is an
"enough said" situation. The polarities represented by Minos and
Pasiphaë are those which maintain the tension of the whole play
and not simply the character of Phèdre. Minos and Pasiphaë, an
emblematical marriage, are the opposite poles of the human consciousness. Minos (whose function we cannot ignore and who is
given a disastrously misleading emphasis in Robert Lowell's epithet
"homicidal") is one of the three judge figures in Greek mythology.

He is the judge who *punishes* crime, as opposed to Aeacus, who
represents division of property, and Rhadamanthus, the rewarder of
virtue. Interiorized psychologically, as he is in Phèdre, he is that
part of our selves which is judgment, prescription, that part that
creates moral codes, imposes laws, fixes limits, the "frontiers" of
experience, defines the acceptable, and punishes transgression.
Pasiphaë is the transgressor of the codes created by Minos, that part
of our selves that hungers for every experience, burns to go beyond
the frontiers of current acceptability, specifically, in her case, to
gratify her sexuality with a bull, incur the guilt of forbidden bestiality. She is what Henri de Montherlant made of her in his play
Pasiphaë (1928), the woman who wants to transcend morality, accept

every part of her nature, however "animal" or "bestial" it has been branded by the lawmakers, to assert that nothing is unhealthy or forbidden. She rejects the codes of her husband Minos. The Minos/Pasiphaë duality is yet another statement of "civilization and its discontents." In that sense we are all children of Minos and Pasiphaë. The wedlock of Minos and Pasiphaë is a dynamic power struggle for the upper hand fraught with matrimonial tension, uneasy even in brief armistice. The struggle lives on in their daughter Phèdre, with the father Minos continually more assertive. I have isolated the function of Minos and made him simply "the Judge," who represents internally the moral conscience and is, in the exterior political world, a representative of "the rule of reason," like the ambiguously placed Governor himself, only utterly unimpeachable:

> a judge so unimpeachable and just
> to have a wife destroyed by bestial lust!

That may well seem a far cry from the cherished "*La fille de Minos et de Pasiphaë*," and it is not intended as its formal equivalent. I have had to redistribute the energies of that renowned line over my whole version, surrender the more obvious nugget for a concession to work the whole seam more painstakingly.

The problem, then, of Phèdre, as of us all, is that she contains within herself both Minos *and* Pasiphaë. That is the essence of the genealogy. She condemns the mother/female/accepter/"transgressor" in herself with the voice of the father/the male voice of punishment/repression/rigid social code. That is the psychological dynamic of the character. As with the outer political dynamic I have sought to create an equivalent, but redistributed, nexus of imagery for the internal tensions. The "bestiality" of Pasiphaë is seen as part of the threat of the alien, of that personified, often apostrophized INDIA upon which the exiled British projected all that was forbidden in their own culture. The temple sculpture and painting of India depicts in a spirit of acceptance what one particular picture, reproduced in the National Theatre program for *Phaedra Britannica*, called "the love of all creatures." It is a painting from Rajasthan of circa 1780 showing not only pairs of animals copulating but women in joyful congress with a variety of beasts. One could well apply to it the long passage on the power of Venus from Seneca's *Phaedra*:

> The dolphin of the raging sea doth love:
> the elements by Cupid's blaze do burn:
> Dame Nature all doth challenge as her own,
> And nothing is that can escape her laws:

That in the translation of John Studley, 1581, the first English version of Seneca's play. But the Indian picture goes just a little further, extends the frontiers of Venus into bestiality. This is quite beyond the limits of acceptability for the British in India, totally alien, though no doubt present in the dark recesses of the imagination. To Western eyes India seemed actually to celebrate a world where everything was sexually possible. The Western reaction was both fascinated (Pasiphaë) and repressive (Minos). It is the voice of Minos we hear speaking through Lieutenant General Sir George MacMunn:

> In the description of the astounding indecency which to Western eyes the temples of Conjeveram, of Jaganath and the Black Pagoda offer, mention has been made of the bestiality recorded: the mingling of humans and animals in intimate embrace. . . . The ancient religions did permit such terrible abominations and India has always apparently been more openly aquainted with such matters than the rest of the world.

When the guilt of Pasiphaë, which, it should be noted, is never specifically referred to in Racine, although it is, characteristically, in Seneca, is mentioned in my version, it is intended with reference to what is depicted in the temples listed by Sir George MacMunn:

> Mother! Driven by the dark gods' spite
> beyond the frontiers of appetite!
> A *judge's* wife! Obscene! Such bestialities
> Hindoos might sculpture on a temple frieze.

And the monster which kills Thomas Theophilus (Hippolyte) and seems to represent the suppressed passions of all the principal characters is described by Burleigh as being

> like one of those concoctions that one sees
> in dark recesses on a temple frieze.

But on the faces of the women in the painting from Rajasthan, women being joyfully pleasured by everything from a peacock to an elephant, we have the spirit of Pasiphaë seeking the total joy that seems to lie beyond all remorse and moral codes. One senses the Yeatsian cry:

> When such as I cast out remorse
> So great a sweetness flows into the breast
> We must laugh and we must sing,
> We are blest by everything
> Everything we look upon is blest.

The nearest my *Memsahib* ever gets to understanding such a mood is, ironically, in her envy of the young lovers she imagines untrammeled by the agonies that destroy her:

> To follow one's feelings through nature's course
> without recriminations and remorse,
> not to feel criminal, and meet as though
> the sun shone on one's love and watched it grow!
> Ah! Every day they must wake up and see
> vistas with no black clouds, and feel so free!

The tensions of the Minos/Pasiphaë polarity are maintained too in my images of the hunter, the Victorian type, projecting his inner repressed desires onto the fauna of India, amassing tiger pelts, covering his walls with animal heads, collecting obsessive proof that he is in control of his own animal nature, that he is the fit representative of "the rule of reason." The Governor himself is renowned as a great hunter, naturally, often scorning the rifle with its distant rationally controlled despatch for closer gladiatorial combat with a bayonet. The images of the hunt are maintained, in one degree or another, in all the versions of the story: Euripides, Seneca, Racine. At the beginning of the Euripides play Aphrodite (Venus) herself complains of Hippolytus not only that he denies her by ignoring women but also by driving wild animals off the face of the earth (ἐξαιρεῖ χθονὸς κυσίν ταχέιαις θῆρας). Venus, the principle of generation, replenishes the stocks exhausted by the hunter. The nurse in Seneca tells the destructively chaste young man as much, imagining the world as an unpopulated desert without the influence of the love goddess:

> *Excedat, agedum, rebus humanis Venus,*
> *Quae supplet ac restituit exhaustum genus;*
> *Orbis iacebit squallido turpis situ;*
> *Vacuum sine ullis classibus stabit mare;*
> *Alesque coelo deerit, & silvis fera;*
>
> (469–73)

The first speech of the Seneca play is one in praise of the excitement of hunting and a list of quarry. Ironically one of the beasts listed—"*latis feri cornibus uri*," probably some sort of buffalo—is described in an edition of 1902 as "extinct" owing to the untiring perseverance of the hunter! There is another element to the obsessive animal slaying. What is part of human nature, but not acknowledged, tends to be labeled "animal." Even in today's papers behavior which does not even transcend the limits of acceptability as much as Pasiphaë's is labeled by the Minos voice of judgment from the British bench as "animal" or "bestial." We are very nervous of our status on what used to be called "the scale of Creation." And this is the point of the animal abuse with which the *Memsahib* finally rejects her "lower" self in the shape of her *ayah*, or with which the Governor denounces Thomas Theophilus, when he tries to reimpose *within* his household the rigid limits he himself has clearly gone beyond outside his home.

The Governor's own position on this shifting scale of transgression and animality, with Minos at one end and Pasiphaë at the other, is decidedly ambiguous. The Governor both accepts and represses, he is both law and transgression. He is in many ways the classic male hypocrite. He avidly seeks experience outside the limits of his own code, or the code his society ostensibly subscribes to, but to do so he finds it necessary, as too many Victorians did, to adopt "native costume." Sir Richard Burton is only one of the best-known models for such behavior. In some ways the Governor carries the whole burden of the male Victorian dilemma. I wanted to state the conflict at a social and political level as well as at the psychological, as it is in Racine in slightly different form. Another redistribution. I took the clues for this from what the Victorian imagination found not only in its Indian experience but also in its assessment of the Theseus legend itself. All ages have used the long surviving classical heroes like Odysseus, Aeneas, Theseus, to realize their own natures and preoccupations. W. B. Standford's *The Ulysses Theme* has charted the fortunes of Odysseus from Homer to Joyce, and Anne C. Ward's *The Quest for Theseus* (London: Pall Mall Press, 1970) has done more or less the same for the hero of our present play. To the Victorians, who often cast themselves into the roles of classical heroes reborn, Theseus was a type of Victorian. John Ruskin in letter 22 dated 1872 of *Fors Clavigera* sees in Theseus

> . . . the great settler or law-giver of the Athenian state; but he is so eminently as the Peace-Maker, causing men to live in fellowship who before lived separate, and making roads passable that had been infested with robbers and wild beasts. He is that exterminator of every bestial and savage element.

With this as a guide one may specify merely from those combats with monsters, grotesques, giants, and brigands that Racine uses:

> Les monstres étouffés et les brigands punis
> Procuste, Cercyon, et Scirron et Sinnis,
> Et les os dispersés du géant d'Epidaure,
> Et la Crète fumant du sang du Minotaure.

The accounts of early "law-giving," the establishment of "the rule of law" in British India, read like a British version of the same kind of heroic, semi-mythical exploit. And not simply the obvious sources like Sleeman's account of the suppression of Thugee, legendary brigands and murderers worthy of any Theseus, but others mentioned always in mythologizing tones by, for example, James Douglas in his *Bombay and Western India* (1893): "England is the St. George that has slain the great dragon of infanticide which among the Jhadejas ravaged Kach and Kathiawar." "*Jauhar*, that Cyclopean monster of self-immolation," "the *Hashashin*" (from whom we derive our word "assassin"), "*Dacoits*," "*Aghori Cannibals*," "the anthropophagous *Mardicura*." Douglas is also typical when he dramatizes in a mythological, almost hagiographical, way the tiger slaughter of, for example, Sir James Outram, who in ten years was present at the death of 191 tigers, 15 leopards, 25 bears, and 12 buffaloes. He does not mention what Aphrodite thought of Sir James Outram, but he hails him as "another St. Paul, [he] had been a day and a night in the deep and fought with wild beasts." "The wild beasts and wilder men" of accounts like Douglas's of the establishing of "the rule of law" in British India represent the same stage of civilization of the Greece before Theseus, and the Victorians saw their own confrontation in his. So the Governor in *Phaedra Britannica* is, as John Ruskin wrote, "that exterminator of every bestial or savage element," but, at the same time, he is also, as someone called Sir Richard Burton, "an authority on all that relates to the bestial element in man." This authority is acquired, of course, in his capacity as the Governor, who represents "the rule of reason" and suppresses alien bestiality, while at the same time, as his other ("lower") self he explores his own animality in his forays "in native costume." It is with these two contrasting elements in his father that Thomas Theophilus has to struggle. In an article in *MacMillan's Magazine* for August 1889 Walter Pater adds an important qualification to a summary of the character of Theseus that, in other respects, is similar to Ruskin's. His Theseus "figures, passably, as a kind of mythic shorthand for civilization, making roads and the like, facilitating travel, suppressing various forms of violence, *but many innocent things as well.*"

As lawgiver, then, Theseus/Thésée/the Governor shares an element of repression with the father of Phaedra/Phèdre/the *Memsahib*. But only part. The other side of his nature, the seeker of new experiences, especially sexual, often "in disguise" precisely because he cannot relate the two halves of his nature, goes hand in hand with the hunter of beasts and the suppressor of bestial custom. That which he is most fascinated by he represses most ruthlessly. He is a kind of mythic shorthand, if you like, for civilization *and* its discontents.

The Khan who imprisons the Governor in my version of "a season spent in Hell" lies, on this scale of transgression, somewhere between the Governor and Pasiphaë. There is even a slight note of envy perhaps in these lines of the Governor's:

> My captor was a beast, obscene, perverse,
> given to practices I won't rehearse,
> to crude carnalities that overrode
> every natural law and human code.
> He'd draw the line at nothing, no taboo
> would stop him doing what he wanted to.

The Governor has gone beyond "the frontier" both geographically and psychologically. Some of the vocabulary of territory from our Anglo-Indian experience marks the boundaries very well. "The frontiers of appetite . . . of virtue . . . of blood." The Governor has gone beyond "the frontier," beyond the Indus, known everywhere as "the forbidden river." H. Bosworth Smith in his *Life of Lord Lawrence* speaks of the Khyber Pass as "the forbidden precincts" over whose gloomy portals might well have been inscribed the words of Dante: "All hope abandon, ye who enter here." So the hellish overtones, the Stygian symbolism, were created for me by those with some historical experience of the Anglo-Indian period I chose for my setting. Whatever the Governor has experienced, and he is, possibly through fear or shame, vaguely unspecific, he has finally seen the limits of the acceptable. His version of hell is being subjected to another's unlimited will, and suffering in the way that many victims of his casual sexual whims might well have suffered. His experience is a vision of the monstrous, the non-human other, beyond all human access and control, even for a "lawgiver," something more terrible than mere animal or beast, something that cannot finally be suppressed or mounted on a Residency wall, nor even physically embraced. This monster defeats both Minos and Pasiphaë. A monster to whom victims must be fed. ("Is there not a home among us that has not paid blood tribute to that relentless monster," writes an Anglo-Indian lady, meaning India). The Governor's vision is probably a glimpse of the monster that finally destroys his son. Whatever the experienced he has had of hell, it is one which makes him long for the circumscribed, apparently ordered world of his marriage and home. But the boundaries of that he finds are now

shaken, the barriers in need of reconstruction, the edges blurred
between inner and outer, hell and earth . . .

A season spent in hell, I've no desire
for whiffs of brimstone from the household fire.

IV

Neoclassical plays are about sex and politics. From as early as classical times there has been a healthily vulgar if slightly overdone
satiric scorn for Phaedra's problems. The taboo of incest between
stepmother and stepson seems irrelevant in societies with different
kinship restraints. It is easy for us to feel self-satisfied at what we
think of as our own permissiveness and to sneer at sexual problems
which were at the time agonizingly real. If literature is what Ezra
Pound said it was, "news that stays news," then dramatic agony
should stay agony, but this is difficult when the tensions involved
have come adrift from their social origins. To Ovid, the Roman poet
of sexual opportunism, not only was Phaedra's passion not incestuous, but Hippolytus has to be chivied by her beyond *his* consciousness of taboo:

> *Nec, quia privigno videar coitura noverca*
> *Terruerint animos namina vana tuos*
> *Ista vetus pietas, aevo moritura futuro,*
> *Rustica Saturno regno tenente fuit.*
> (Phaedra Hippolito, *Heroides* 3)

And this in the translation of poet/dramatist Thomas Otway, who
also did a version of Racine's *Berenice* into heroic couplets:

> How can'st thou reverence thy Father's Bed,
> From which himself so Abjectly is fled?
> The thought affrights not me, but me enflames:
> Mother and Son are notions, very Names
> Of Worn out Piety, in Fashion Then
> When old dull *Saturn* rul'd the Race of men.
> But braver Jove taught pleasure was no sin,
> And with his sister did himself begin.

These attitudes to a "Worn out Piety," repeated often enough
throughout the ages, are mild enough compared with a version of
the story published only five years after Racine's play in Alexander
Radcliffe's *Terrestrial Hymns & Carnal Ejaculations* (1682). This is

a Phaedra Britannica, isolated in "a Farm-House in Putney in Surrey," who has no feelings of restraint whatsoever, either Euripidean Greek or neoclassical French:

> When Young, I cou'd have cur'd these am'rous stings
> With Carrots, Radishes, or such like things;
> Now there's no pleasure in such Earthly cures,
> I must have things apply'd as warm as yours.
> Where lies the blame, art thou not strong, and young?
> Who would not gather fruit that is well hung?

In this case Pasiphaë has triumphed over Minos, and, reworking the passage already quoted from Ovid and Otway, Radcliffe has:

> Wee'd no such opportunity before:
> Your Father is at London with his Whore.
> Therefore I think 'tis but a just design,
> To cuckold him, and pay him in his coin.
> Besides he ne're was marry'd to your Mother.
> He first whor'd her, and then he took another.
> What kindness or respect ought we to have
> For such a Villain and perfidious Knave?
> This should not trouble, but provoke us rather
> With all the speed we can to lye together.
> I am no kin to you, nor you to me.
> They call it Incest but to terrifie.
> Lovers Embraces are Lascivious Tricks
> 'Mongst musty Puritans and Schismaticks.

This is that "Anglo-Saxon irreverence" that Michael Billington mentioned in his review of *Phaedra Britannica*. One sees it too in Stevie Smith's poem *Phèdre*. And very necessary it is, too, though it scarcely helps to recreate the Racinian mode in modern English. We read such pieces in early rehearsals, partly for the couplets, but also to draw the fire of cheerful vulgarity before we tackled the main text. It is an irreverence not confined to our attitude to inaccessible foreign classics, and I associate it in my mind with one of my culture heroes, the comedian "Prof." Leon Cortez, who offered his own cockneyfications of Shakespeare, reducing the high-flown poetry of kings to an earthy demotic. Nor is such irreverence purely Anglo-Saxon, even toward Racine. Far from it. In June 1974 I saw a production of *Phèdre* I have already referred to, directed by Regis Santon at the Théâtre Essaion, which played the Racinian text as vulgar farce, a compound of Buñuel, Racine, and Feydeau, with *Tristan and Isolde* as background music, and a vaguely Latin American setting,

something like Torre Nilsson's film *La Casa del Angel*. The production had simply given up the struggle to present the play on its own
terms, and enjoyable as it was as a lively piece of juvenile iconoclasm,
very necessary for the French classic theater, it gave no help whatsoever to one desperately seeking access to the play for equally, if
not more, irreverent English audiences. With this constant sense of
total subversion I had, even more carefully, to consider solutions to
the play which would place the problem in a society where the sense
of transgression was once more an agonizing burden. Sexual problems
do not occur in a vacuum, in a theatrical never-never land, but are
created by social codes. The period I chose eventually, after many
false starts and crablike researches, envisaged a particular society,
early Victorian Britain, with a rigid code made even more formally
defensive by being placed in the alien environs of sensual India.

The politics of the play are also obscured by genealogical complications, with which we no longer have any spontaneous rapport,
and distanced by our distaste for the absolute monarchy of the court
of Louis XIV. Even the translator cannot shirk his responsibility for
historical criticism.

Everywhere in the imagery of seventeenth-century poetry, prose,
and drama, in England and France, the psychological structure of
man is seen as an interiorization of the political. "The Government
of Man," writes the Cambridge Platonist, Benjamin Whichcote,
"should be the Monarchy of Reason; it is too often a Democracy of
Passions." Passions are elsewhere, in Dryden, "unreasonable things/
That strike at Sense, as Rebels do at Kings." When Dryden came to
paraphrase the famous Latin hymn *Veni Creator Spiritus*, the simple
lines:

> *infirma nostri corporis*
> *virtute firmans perpeti*

became a typical piece of the politically expressed psychology. I
mean:

> Our Frailities help, our Vice controul;
> Submit the Senses to the Soul;
> And when Rebellious they are grown
> Then, lay thy hand, and hold 'em down.

The alignment of political synonyms in such imagery is: Reason/
King/Rule Monarchy (to which series we can add *raj* = rule) on the
one hand, and what they restrain on the other: Passions/Mob/Dem-
ocracy ("the Natives"). As Martin Turnell points out: "There are

only two classes in Racine: masters and servants, the rulers and the ruled, royalty and the people." Elsewhere discussing the psychology of Corneille and Racine, he writes that "reason has to operate *tyrannically* and repress by force an uprush of the senses." Hence, "the rule of law"; the use of words like "seditious" and "mutinous" of the passions. Hence also the time of the piece, defined as taking place a few years before the Mutiny. As I used the prospect of *"les évènements"* of 1968 in Paris as a political, historical "measure" of the realities of my setting of *Le Misanthrope* and of Alceste's status as a critic of society, so in *Phaedra Britannica* I imagine the tensions of the play continuing into the Indian Mutiny of 1857 (the year also of the Obscene Publications Act). My text demands that the political realities of Racinian society are reinterpreted physically, realized literally in "black and white." I sought to re-energize critically the political content by aligning it with the British "Imperial dream," which like Goya's dream of reason "produces monsters."

V

Aphrodite speaks in Euripides. In Seneca Venus is merely addressed. But even in Euripides the gods are, as his translator Philip Vellacott puts it, "no more than dramatic fictions." The gods in Racine, as Martin Turnell points out, are "projections of basic human impulses which means that in *Phèdre* they belong to the realm of psychology rather than theology." "*Vénus, c'est Phèdre, c'est Hippolyte . . . Neptune est dans Thésée,*" writes Jean-Louis Barrault in his production notes. The British projected their own suppressed nature onto the continent they subdued, personifying a destructive INDIA, devastating to those who gave in to its powers, who were seduced by its nakedly obvious allure. Personification is general throughout the literature and memoirs of British India. Everything psychologically alien or suppressed becomes "India" or "the dark gods" or, not detached enough to be theologically accurate, an apostrophized Hindu deity like Siva or some other menacing god from a bewilderingly diverse pantheon. Here, for example, is an Englishwoman writing about the "Hot Weather":

> One has to experience the coming of the Hot Season to understand something of the worship of Siva—Creator and Destroyer—the Third Person of the Hindu Trinity. For its approach—swift, relentless and inevitable—is like that of a living and sensate force—like the visible work of that terrible yet withal beneficent God who destroys and

tramples all things beneath His feet in an ecstatic harmonious dance, that He may create them anew. For in a sense there is a necessity for the hot weather. The intensity of the sun's power cracks and cleaves the dry, obdurate earth, in order that the blessed rains of the Monsoon may irrigate and revivify the whole, jaded, exhausted face of the land.

And as Jean-Louis Barrault speaks of the tragedy of *Phèdre*, giving the arc and carthartic trajectory of the play the same kind of cumulative, meteorological image, as *"un de ces orages de fin août,"* it seems to make Siva, as present in the British imagination, particularly fitted to preside over the passion of *Phaedra Britannica*. The same woman goes on to describe her feelings of helplessness in the Indian heat (which another woman, Mrs. E. M. Croker, likens to some "cruel vindictive animal") in terms which, typically, create the sense of powerful alien forces:

> And finally there is the close, hot evening, and an airless night of tossing and turning, of trying to find one cool spot in one's bed, giving it up in despair, and lying in still resignation to look up at the uncaring stars above the gently flapping punkah, helpless beneath the destroying feet of Siva.

Such projections onto an alien divinity are very common in Anglo-Indian writing, and they tend to stand for those things that are felt to be outside the sphere of reason, order, and justice (or the current concepts of them) which it is the function of tragedy, according to George Steiner, to reveal as "terribly limited." It was to insist on the role of the gods as projections that I conflated the function of Venus and Neptune in Racine. The sea which in Racine is the symbol of the uncontrolled, the formless, becomes in my version "the jungle," almost a synonym for chaos. I have unified the psychological projections represented in Racine and ascribed them both to Siva, as he was imagined by the British, not necessarily as a complex component of the Hindu pantheon. Contemplating the attributes of Siva, though, one can see that the god can well bear the parallels, being at once the god of regeneration and sexuality, and of destruction. He contains opposing forces. He is both associated with ascetism (Hippolyte) and yet everywhere reverenced under the symbol of the phallus or *lingam*. He is Destroyer/Creator, birth and death, Apollo *and* Dionysus, to use the Nietzschean pair that forge the tragic dialectic. Even the minor parallels can be maintained, to authenticate the transfer, as Siva has a bull as a vehicle, and as a weapon the *trisula*, or trident. But the matchings at this level hardly matter, even if they aid the metamorphosis. What matters is the function of projection, the use of pagan gods in a culture that dramatizes itself as an age of reason, and its equivalent in the British apostrophization of the dark gods of India.

VI

I do not remember the exact point at which I decided on a nineteenth-century Indian setting, but in retrospect there seem to have been catalysts and clues about me from the start, though I did begin with versions ostensibly in Ancient Greece and in the period of Louis XIV. Of all the many elements I now can recognize the following as particularly prominent:

1. Maria Casarès, who played Phèdre in Jean Vilar's production at the TNP in 1957, said of her character: "*J'ai toujours imaginée étendue dans l'ombre d'une chambre close, dans un lieu où le soleil explose.*" India! The all-pervading presence of the sun, either seen as light or felt as heat in a darkened room, became also a physical counterpart for Phèdre's mythological kinship in the original.

2. There was an equivalent, felt intuitively at first and then researched, between the way critics write about the character of the confidante, Oenone, and the way in which Anglo-Indian memoirs and fiction write of the *ayah* figure. Jean-Louis Barrault calls Oenone the "*valeur noire*" of Phèdre, and in my version she is literally that (the Anglo-Indians used the inaccurate and deliberately insulting adjective "black" of Indians). Racine also speaks, too aristocratically and high-handedly for my liking, of the *bassesse* of Oenone, and the servile propensities which make *her* able to accuse Hippolyte, and not her mistress as was the case in the Euripides version. As I have made it a *Memsahib* and *ayah* relationship, it is a way of absorbing into my version, without doing violence to the sense, my social reservations about Racine, and it makes the *Memsahib*'s final outburst of racist rejection of her faithful servant a terrible one, and one that is linked to the outside world of alien domination of which the psychological is a mirror aspect.

3. I felt the need of making the Amazon mother of Hippolyte physically present in the son, a constant reminder of the past of Thésée. My Hippolyte, Thomas Theophilus, becomes a "half-caste" embodying the tensions between Britain and India within himself, as much as he embodies the two conflicting selves of his father. The occurrence of marriage between British men and Indian women was by no means uncommon in nineteenth-century India, and if we need

historical authentication, it is enough to cite only the better-known examples like James Achilles Kirkpatrick, resident at Hyderabad; Job Charnock, who rescued a Brahmin widow from *suttee* and lived with her happily until her natural death fourteen years later; Colonel Gardiner; and Sir Charles Metcalfe, who had three Eurasian sons by an Indian princess probably related to Ranjit Singh. The railways were to bring the *Memsahibs* to India and put a stop to that. I have assumed that transition in mores to be taking place, creating a new distance between ruler and ruled that was to harden to a more rigid apartheid after the Mutiny of 1857. The Victorian male could not permit his women the same intimate insights into India which he had allowed himself before his ladies made the crossing over the "black water."

4. Assailed as the British felt on all sides by an irrational India with its dark sensual gods and "primitive" customs, they created in their imagination defensive roles for themselves as the inheritors of rational civilization. They constructed residencies and public buildings in classical style, attempting to realize in external marble what they felt unable to realize internally in their far from securely stable minds. The books of the period are full of engravings showing proud classical facades in clearings in dense jungle, with creeper and mangrove festooning the edges of the scene. It is an eloquent juxtaposition. Mark Bence-Jones in his *Palaces of the Raj* (London, 1973) describes the Residency at Hyderabad, with its Durbar Hall lined with Ionic columns, and a staircase which "was adorned with sculpture: the Apollo Belvedere, Leda and the Swan" (not Pasiphaë and the Bull to complete the circle, but almost there!) and "Venus rising from the sea." "The mirrors in neo-classical frames reflected the Durbar Hall to infinity." It reads almost like the description of a traditional set for *Phèdre* at the *Comédie Française!*

It is more than a convenient point of contact. It represents the effort of one era, with its values threatened, to define itself in terms borrowed from another, which would seem best to support and prop up what was felt to be most shaky. The drama of Britain and India was constantly seen in these terms. Even as late as 1924 (the year of *A Passage to India*) Bennet Christian Huntingdon Calcraft Kennedy could write: "We are here to govern India as delegates of a Christian and civilized power. We are here as representatives of Christ and Caesar to maintain this land against Siva and Khalifa." And the cleaned-up classicism of the corresponding architecture, deriving as it does from Greece and Rome via Palladio and Wren, is still, as David Gerhard writing about Lutyen's New Delhi Residency has it, "a favourite political symbol in our century ranging from the megalomania of Albert Speer and Hitler to the New Deal of Roosevelt." This belief in our being the chosen heirs of Greece and Rome gives a special poignancy to those pictures of the classical facade of the Lucknow Residency after the Mutiny, shattered by rifle-fire and shell, and littered with skulls. This kind of Residency and the life lived within it seemed to fit almost exactly Martin Turnell's summary of the dramatic and political function of the palace in the plays of Racine. They are "not simply impersonal buildings which provide a setting for the tragedy. . . . They represent a particular *order*. . . .":

> We are aware from the first of an almost suffocating tension in the air combined with a desperate effort to maintain some sort of control which frequently breaks down. The tension is pervasive; it is also contagious. It is the atmosphere which produces fascinating and frightening revelations about human nature—about ourselves.
>
> The palaces vary in style . . . they have one thing in common. There is something of the prison about them. We have the impression that the community is somehow confined within their walls. The sense of confinement is partly psychological, but in some parts of the palaces we shall find one or two members of the community are literally prisoners. . . .
>
> The palaces are huge, dark, claustrophobic. They give the occupants the alarming impression that they are constantly being watched, that their lives are in danger in that disaster may overtake at any moment.
>
> There are winding corridors with innumerable rooms leading off them. But we the visitors, are only admitted to a single room. The whole of the drama is concentrated inside it . . . at the same time we are aware that the room, or more accurately the palace, is a *world within a world it is trying to dominate.*
>
> (Martin Turnell, *Jean Racine, Dramatist*)

VII

Couplets keep the cat on the hot tin roof. Each spirit has its own custom-built treadmill. After the metronome, the comic pacemaker of the *Misanthrope* couplet, I wanted a more organic model for my iambics. I wanted to return the iamb back to its sources in breath and blood. In the silences one should hear the heart beat. Jean-Louis Barrault, writing of the Alexandrine in *Phèdre*, says:

> *le coeur, qui egrène, jusqu'à la mort, les deux temps de son tam-tam obsédant: systole-diastole; systole-diastole. Brève-longue; brève-longue etc: le coeur bat l'iambe.*

It was this heartbeat, this bloodthrob, that marked the time of my metric. The heart as *"tam-tam obsédant"* leads us straight back too to British India, where another woman writes in her memoir, "The throbbing tom-toms became almost like our heartbeats":

I sensed the gods of India were there
behind the throbbing heat and stifling air.
Heart beat like a tom-tom, punkah flapped
backwards and forwards and my strength was sapped.
I felt you mocking, India, you brewed
strange potions out of lust and lassitude,
dark gods mocking, knowing they can claim
another woman with the Judge's name,
picking off the family one by one,
each destroyed by lust and Eastern sun.

Aischylos: For Actors, in the Round

 MICHAEL EWANS

THE TITLE REFLECTS two interconnected biases of my approach to Aischylos: that a translation of a play which was designed for performance should itself be made with the needs of actors very much in mind, and that the act of translation must include developing an understanding of the conventions, and manner of working in the theater shape, for which a drama was originally conceived. As a result you will not be required to read yet another rehearsal of the literal/literate debate; nor will I offer a sustained consideration of the relative merits of different modern meters, or the virtues and defects of (e.g.) rhyme, half rhyme, and blank verse in the translation of Greek tragedy. Any such approach would encourage you to go back to your studies and your books; and it will be a central contention of this essay that if you are translating a drama, you need as soon as possible to get out of your study and into a workshop or studio.

I came reluctantly to being a translator. Of the available modern versions of Aischylos some strike me as too solemn and high-flown— created under the spell of the traditional vision of Aischylos as grandly poetic and "difficult." (This applies even to the monumental, but fairly faithful translation by Richmond Lattimore, let alone such versions as that by Robert Fagles)[1]. Goethe, on first reading the *Oresteia* in 1816, described it as "a primevally gigantic form, of monstrous shape, which shocks and overwhelms us"[2]—and this is all too often the impression achieved, consciously or unconsciously, even by versions for our own times, when, in contrast to most of the nineteenth century, at least the possibility of performance is admitted.

Others are just too free from the actual sense of the Greek, and should be characterized as adaptations rather than presented as translations of Aischylos.[3] If Hugo von Hofmannsthal, a great poet, was humble enough to term his superb re-creation in Nietzschean and Freudian terms of Sophokles' *Elektra* (which became the text for Strauss's stunning opera)[4] simply a *"Bearbeitung,"* or arrangement of the original, a *Tragödie nach Sophokles*, Raphael and MacLeish or Tony Harrison[5] should do the same with their efforts. William Arrowsmith, in the editor's general preface to the Oxford University Press series, called for "re-creations of these plays—as though they had been written, freshly and greatly, by masters fully at home with the English of our own times."[6] But the products of that ethos during the last twenty years, both inside and outside the series, have (with a few honorable exceptions) gravely disappointed. All too often the English poetry is in no way fresh or masterly enough (especially when they are considered as potential playscripts for performance) to counterbalance their sometimes gross freedom from the sense of the original.

As a teacher of classics and drama, with large classes of Greekless readers, I have constantly encountered the problem of needing closer versions, and having to make do with translations which my classics students can read only with difficulty and my drama students cannot act. Nor do many translations give evidence that they were conceived in stage terms. The stage directions are often incomplete, confused (for the ancient theater shape or the modern one—if the latter, which modern one?), or simply inadequate to the task of giving readers a basic mental image of the action; and the introductions make almost no reference to the practicalities of performance, ancient or modern. So I could not evade the need to provide a new translation myself, when I decided in 1983 to perform a whole Greek play.

Aischylos was not just a playwright, in the modern sense, but a *poietes*, literally a "creator"—the word includes our separated roles of writer, director, composer, choreographer, and lead actor; he was responsible for the creation of the entire competitive performance event called the *Oresteia*, which he exhibited for one performance only (and with which he won) at the festival of Dionysos in Athens in 458 B.C. Aischylos wrote the text—which is all that is preserved to us, with the dialogue and lyrics in a mutilated form and no stage directions whatsoever—solely to go together with the music, movement, and dance which he created to interact with that text in the theater of Dionysos. And therefore the translation of Greek tragedy cannot be the act just of the scholar, poet, or both in a study with a script; on the one hand stand Aischylos, his fellow actors, and his audience, and on the other the translator, director, composer, choreographer, and modern actors with our audience, attempting to transfer as much as possible of the entire experience into contemporary performance in our theaters. Let us recognize that we have a duty to help potential readers to see the performance in their mind's eye, and potential actors and directors in their task of preparing to re-create the Greek experience in a modern production. It simply will not do to translate, as Don Taylor has translated Sophokles for the recent, highly acclaimed productions of the Oidipous plays on BBC television,[7] in ignorance both of the Greek language (shrugged off because the translator is a minor playwright himself, backed up by a classicist who supplied a crib as basis)[8] and of the Greek theater shape—for in his introduction Taylor makes it plain that he thinks Greek plays were performed in the Roman theater design, with a semicircular dance floor separated off from a high, raised stage for the actors![9]

Aischylos wrote his script with the shape of the Theater of Dionysos in mind. It was the only theater space he knew, and he wrote all his plays for performance in that shape; on completing each script accepted for production, he then took it to the theater with his fellow actors and developed a blocking, a pattern of movement, to accompany it and to be illuminated by it. That blocking was itself an integral, essential part of the experience which the Oresteia was for the Athenians.

Translation (in the full sense of the word) must therefore include a thorough understanding of the theater conventions of the original space, and one of the translator's absolute responsibilities is to provide, in stage directions and commentary, a reconstruction of how that space was employed—including (e.g.) such basic questions as what costumes and properties were used in Aischylos' production, who was in the performing area at any given time, when and where they came on and went off. But our work must go further even than that, and include conjectural reconstruction of the kinds of patterns of movement that might have accompanied Aischylos' script, if we are to provide the essential data which students need to study these plays properly, and which contemporary directors and actors need if they are to make informed decisions when working toward a professional production. This is of course conjectural, creative work— and so somewhat hazardous in the eyes of many classical scholars— but if based on production experience it is methodologically far more sound than fantasies about staging evolved in the scholar's study. (Oliver Taplin's book on entries and exits, *The Stagecraft of Aeschylus*,[10] with its combination of highly shrewd insights and impractical absurdities, all veiled in the mandarin language of polemic academic debate, should stand as a warning against the limitations which can be exposed when traditional scholarship attempts this kind of work.) The main aim of my own research productions of the three *Oresteia* plays in Newcastle, New South Wales, was to explore possible answers to the conjectural questions, as well as to test in performance the answers that have been given to some of the basic questions about staging.

But first let us go back, for a moment, to the translation in a narrower sense; the text in itself. Sitting in his or her study, what should the translator aim for?

There are to my mind many subordinate criteria for a good translation of a Greek tragedy; but only two are of primary importance. The first is that it should be *accurate*—that it should stray as little as possible from the meaning of what the Greek text actually says; and the second is that it should be *actable*—that it should be composed of words which actors can easily speak, and in the lyric sections easily sing.

Aischylos wrote the *Oresteia* for performance in a vast open-air theater. Its capacity has been variously estimated, but it must have been something on the order of seventeen thousand people. We know from Aristophanes that the audiences were easily bored with the work of inferior tragedians (*Acharnians* 1ff.), also that, thanks to the theater's good acoustics, they were capable of minute attention to the quality of an actor's delivery (cf. the Hegelochos joke at *Frogs* 302–4). Aischylos' verse responds to these fundamental features of his playing space and of his audience. Though rich and sometimes complex, it was primarily a flexible and dynamic theater language, with a constant and almost irresistible sweep; it is never opaque, and it is always direct in its communication with an audience.

I think it is fair to say that you would not guess at these self-evident qualities of the original Greek text by taking up any of the English translations of Aischylos in widespread use today. I do not want to demonstrate my point overwhelmingly by showing how a translator influenced by the traditional vision of Aischylos' archaic grandeur, and innocent of the practicalities of theater language, can transform a complex but comprehensible stanza of Greek lyric verse into an English stanza so convoluted it can hardly be understood on the printed page, let alone in performance. Instead I shall take a simple, short dialogue scene from *The Libation Bearers*, scene 5, in which Aigisthos arrives back at the royal palace and is lured into it to his death by one of the slave-women of the house. We will look at some of the problems which two of the major published translations would present to actors and director; then I will attempt to justify my own new version by analyzing how, when conceived for production in a replica of the original theater shape, translation can become a part of the act of dramatic interpretation.

AEGISTHUS. It is not without summons that I come, but called
        by messenger, with news that there are strangers here
        arrived, telling a story that brings no delight;   840
        the death of Orestes. For our house, already bitten
        and poisoned, to take this new load on itself
        would be a thing of dripping fear and blood. Yet how
        shall I pass upon these rumours? As the living truth?
        For messages made out of women's terror leap
        high in the upward air and empty die. Do *you*
        know anything of this by which to clear my mind?

CHORUS. We heard, yes. But go on inside and hear it from
        the strangers. Messengers are never quite so sure
        as a man's questions answered by the men
                themselves.   850

AEGISTHUS. I wish to question, carefully, this messenger
        and learn if he himself was by when the man died
        or if he heard but some blind rumour and so speaks.
        The mind has eyes, not to be easily deceived.

    (Exit AEGISTHUS.*)*

Richmond Lattimore's version has a consistent tone of voice, but is marred as a potential theater text by being at times too literal ("not without summons," 838), and by consistent archaism (note the reversed word order twice in this extract, at "here/arrived," 839–40, and "empty die," 846). Otherwise the weaknesses are few ("a thing of dripping fear and blood," 843, and the clumsy diction—and, again, archaism, n.b. the use of "but," 853—in the last speech); and the translation does have, like the original, a sustained rhythmic pulse expressing the smooth running of the sequence in which Aigisthos is lured to his death.

    Robert Fagles, by contrast, persistently avoids smoothness. Right from the outset he usurps the director's role with the jerky rhythms of the first three lines, followed by the unnecessary (and unwarranted) additive repetition of "galled and raw."

AEGISTHUS. Coming, coming. Yes, I have my summons.
        There's news, I gather, travellers here to tell it.

No joy in the telling, though—Orestes dead.
Saddle the house with a bloody thing like that
and it might just collapse. It's still raw
from the last murders, galled and raw.
But how to take the story, for living truth?
Or work of a woman's panic, gossip starting up
in the night to flicker out and die?

Turning to the LEADER

Do you know?
Tell me, clear my mind.

LEADER. We've heard a little.
But get it from the strangers, go inside.
Messengers have no power. Nothing like
a face-to-face encounter with the source.

AEGISTHUS. —Must see him, test the messenger. Where was he
when the boy died, standing on the spot?
Or is he dazed with rumour, mouthing hearsay?
No, he'll never trap me open-eyed!

Striding through the doors.

This version is also seriously marred by its failures of tone—the weak word "thing" even more exposed than in Lattimore, then "it might just collapse"; and in the last two speeches the version descends into clichés—"a face-to-face encounter with the source"; "standing on the spot." Add to this the quaint refusal to supply simple connectives ("get it from the strangers, go inside") and pronouns ("—Must see him, test the messenger"); the flamboyant, free rhetorical flourishes (". . . dazed with rumour, mouthing hearsay"), and the ambiguous, if not simply wrong reading of the last line, and one is forced to conclude that this version gives a false vision both of the texture of Aischylos and of what he actually wrote for his actors to speak.

The version which follows does not claim to compete on the same poetic level. It does not attempt to reflect for today's audience the fact that Aischylos wrote in a *Kunstsprache* which incorporated words and phrasing which would have been archaic if spoken in daily life. On the contrary, the tone and structure of my rhetoric are designed to match the ebb and flow of the original in a speakable and direct modern English—and sometimes to match them in some detail (notice, e.g., the enjambment at the start of 841). I was at pains to bring out, by positioning at the ends of the lines, the vital sexual change from Aigisthos' speech ("fearful, women's words") to the libation bearer's encouraging "from man to man" (845, 850); and I also confess my failure to bring *amauras kledonos* fully into the English in the penultimate line. Otherwise I will leave the performance script to speak for itself.

Scene 5

(*Enter* AIGISTHOS, *left*)

AIGISTHOS. I come not of my own accord, but summoned by a
                                 messenger.
I understand that certain strangers have arrived
and bring some news that gives me no
                   delight—   840
Orestes' death. This would be a bloodstained burden
for the house to bear, already wounded as it is,
poisoned by bitter murders long ago.
How can I think it is a living truth?
Are these perhaps just fearful, women's words
which leap high in the air, then die in vain?
What can you tell of this to clear my mind?

1 L.B. We've heard. But you must go inside.
and find out from the strangers. It's nowhere near as
                                good
to let a woman tell you as to hear yourself,
                 from man to man.   850

AIGISTHOS. I want to see this messenger and question him carefully,
to learn if he was there and saw Orestes die,
or just reports a rumour he has heard.
My mind has eyes; it cannot be deceived.

(*Doors open. Exit* AIGISTHOS, *into the skene. Doors close.*)

The modern actor needs help if he is to perform a Greek tragedy. In the words, clarity and complexity are *not* incompatible. Fluent, sometimes colloquial, but not abrasively contemporary English was my aim. And in the sentences, each speech must mirror the constructions of the original, but not at the expense of creating breathing difficulties. The English must reflect the flow, pace, and rhetorical structure of the original Greek; the translator should devise pause-moments (which later become move-points in rehearsal), which correspond to those of the original and so reflect its structure.

But above all, the translation needs to be created and modified in the light of a coherent vision of the purpose of the scene, and a visual concept of how it would work in the circle. Here is part of my new draft commentary on this scene, to show the considerations which emerged during production as important, and one way of representing them in Aischylos' space.

Aigisthos enters, "summoned by a messenger" (838); and we have already seen the way in which that message was reshaped by the libation bearers. Deception and treacherous persuasion are clearly working; Orestes and his allies beat the usurpers by turning their own devices against them, as Apollo ordained that they should. In this scene once again the libation bearers take action, and again in an extraordinary way; just as there is no parallel for the chorus intervening to change the message in scene 4, so too there is no parallel for their luring someone to his death, as here.

Aigisthos makes his approach while the libation bearers conclude a lyric appeal for Orestes to kill him without hesitation; and his step from the *parodos* into the playing area is the cue for the most violent of those transitions from expression of their inner emotions to feigned subservience, which is the most important aspect of the libation bearers' part in scenes 3 to 6. In our production the libation bearers moved at this moment from the erect position, with arms extended in salutation of Orestes' imminent triumph, in which they concluded the choreography of chorus 5, to the total submissiveness of an oriental salaam; they knelt prostrate, in an echo of Klytaimestra's outrageous homage to Agamemnon in the tapestry scene.

Short though it is, this scene allows the director to consolidate the atmosphere of political menace under the tyranny of the usurpers. In the speech an actor can establish not merely the hypocrisy of Aigisthos' condolences on the "death of Orestes" but also the sinister, decadent character into whom the self-justified *poseur* of *Agamemnon* scene 8 has been corrupted by power. And there is also the dynamic tension between the libation bearers, apparently weak and cowering before the tyrant but in fact strong, and Aigisthos who is the exact reverse. We tried to express all this by having the libation bearers kneel and prostrate themselves in a supposedly reverent, but in fact menacing ellipse in the *orchestra*; Aigisthos delivered his speech circling nervously around the centre of this ellipse, pausing only to ruminate (841–43) on the implications of the "death of Orestes." Circling again in and after 844, he paused at the words "die in vain," and then suddenly crossed to address 847 to one of the libation bearers.

Aischylos crystallizes the contrast between Aigisthos and his deceivers around a central issue of the trilogy, simply by taking advantage of the difference in sex between the tyrant and the libation bearers. Aigisthos pours scorn on Klytaimestra's message in 845f., and these lines remind the audience both of Orestes' confidential aside to Pylades at 665f. and—more directly, though over a larger span of time—of the Elders' sudden distrust of Klytaimestra's beacons at the end of *Agamemnon* chorus 2, 475f. Those parallel essays in male sexism, though subjected to almost immediate deflation, were at least addressed at the time to men alone; here however, with supreme irony, Aigisthos is made to voice his distrust of women's words to a woman, who then with consummate hypocrisy agrees with him and applies his teaching to herself. But the irony of the scene is not yet at its apex; going to his death even more blindly than Agamemnon, Aigisthos tells the woman who has duped him that "my mind has eyes; it cannot be deceived."

The movements and gestures here must establish the contrast between Aigisthos' false assumption that he has power and the true power of the slave woman who answers him and lures him to his death. For example, in our production Aigisthos suddenly grasped the libation bearer by the chin at 847, jerking her half erect to make her answer his question; but she rose fully to her feet on "we've heard" and delivered the rest of her speech standing uncowed, after moving slightly back away from him to assert her control over her own space. Aigisthos' transition from sadism to bemused acceptance of her words was conveyed simply by his acquiescence, as he moved steadily towards the doors during the next three lines. It was then almost irresistible to play the last line as a parting address, delivered from the doorway back to the libation bearer who had answered his question, before a purposeful, unsuspecting exit.

So the production itself (evolving into the commentary) became part of the act of translation. The attempt to respond to the feel of the original text, and to the real situations and issues at stake in it, had to go beyond the act of translation in the usual, narrower sense of that word and evolve into the gradual acquisition of a working knowledge of how the text works in its space. And as a result of using, in the round, a play text conceived in the style described earlier, we developed over the three productions a new concept of what Aischylos' dramatic style might have been; a concept which stresses the role of the chorus as an active, participating character— overturning at last (we hoped) the deep-rooted, but grossly misleading vision of the chorus as an "ideal spectator" mediating between solo actors and audience. As part of this process, I also abandoned the view that the chorus was represented in dialogue with the solo actors by one spokesperson. As many other modern productions have found, vigor and dramatic life are imparted to the staging of Aischylos as soon as this traditional belief is abandoned. If we regard the chorus as made up of twelve individuals who collectively form a group, their utterances during the scenes can be assigned to the individual actors in the chorus in such a way as to bring out a particular temperament or attitude to the action in each of them, which can be developed over the duration of the play.

This approach has been resisted because it disturbs the authoritarian assumption that the name-role solo actor is far more important and interesting than the anonymous group—just as the raised stage was imported into Aischylean tragedy to separate the solo actor from that group, and the chorus's responses to the action were misread as spectatorial reflections which denied their speakers their true role as participants in that action. But under the test of production the orthodox scholarly view collapses. The effect of dividing between a number of individual chorus members such moments as the edgy dialogue with Klytaimestra which opens scene 2 of *Agamemnon*, or the cross-examination of Orestes and Apollo by the Furies in the trial scene of *The Eumenides*, has to be seen to be believed. At once a balance and an impetus to dramatic flow are given to an action which is lame and halting if only one person speaks for the chorus.

Workshopping this translation with actors led also to what is certainly the most radical, and perhaps also therefore the most controversial, aspect of my recent work on Aischylos. Thinking about the successes and failures of the first production in the series, I concluded that there were two things which needed to be changed. First, the production concept had not responded as much as the translation itself implies to the flow of the original; by insisting overmuch on a sharp stylistic division between choral odes and scenes, we had not sufficiently undermined the traditional stereotyped view of a Greek tragedy as alternating between static dialogue scenes, in which the participants are almost motionless and the spoken word predominates, and sung choral odes in which choreography predominates. This clear demarcation worked to the play's disadvantage, and over the next two productions I attempted increasingly to explore the alternative picture of Greek drama as a mixed media event in which there are two different, complementary kinds of word/movement combinations: the choral odes, which are danced and sung, and the dialogue scenes, which are spoken and accompanied by unchoreographed (i.e., less strictly or symmetrically patterned) movement. As a consequence the musically accompanied lyric sections came more and more to blend seamlessly into the continuity of the play; and I believe that this is how Greek drama was and should be. This concept led to a considerable increase in the amount of movement in the *orchestra*.

Second, I resolved that the second and third plays should be performed in modern dress. I was influenced in this partly by the success of some Royal Shakespeare Company productions of the plays of Shakespeare—and even more by two opera productions of the late 1970s which I greatly admired. One was Patrice Chéreau's centenary *Ring* at Bayreuth, with costumes and sets drawn eclectically from the European culture of the last two hundred years to illuminate the sources of Wagner's work in the power politics of the industrial revolution;[11] the other was Jonathan Miller's *Rigoletto* for the English National Opera, in which the court of sixteenth-century Mantua is recreated in 1930s America as the "court" of a Chicago mafia boss. Both productions were notorious on first appearance; but both managed to outlast the inevitable conservative backlash against all modernization of a classic. They did so because they transcended mere trendiness and used costume and décor to evoke potent images, which could assist a modern audience toward understanding the characters in the opera, their dramatic interaction, and the real spiritual and political issues enshrined by the composers in that interaction, far better than the traditional "period" costumes which have lost their subtleties of meaning for a modern audience. If major professional actors—I think in particular of Donald MacIntyre as Wotan for Chéreau—could have their performances transformed by working in a modern dress production, would it not help student actors as well?

Modern dress turned out not only to be easier for the actors (the men did not have to play heroes while showing their knobby knees, and the women were no longer obliged to trail dresses of a length they would never wear in their own daily lives); it also proved to involve the audience more in the action. I wrote in the program note:

> *The Eumenides* is not a museum piece, but a work with much to say to us today about politics, society, and personal relationships. Accordingly we resolved to set the action in a period whose costumes and manners would illuminate, for a modern audience, the nature of the characters and the social tensions between them.
>
> We chose England, in the earlier years of Victoria's reign. Here Apollo's easy assumption of his own superiority—both as a male, and as a hereditary landowner—makes sense, with the Furies portrayed as downtrodden victims who have returned from the early, hideously exploitative phases of the Industrial Revolution to haunt the more prosperous, and supposedly more equitable, society of the 1870s. Athena's greater tolerance, and her serene confidence in the imperial grandeur of her city-state, are also appropriate responses for that time and place; and the confidence is undermined, for us, by our knowledge of how

much Britain's imperial pride was humbled over the ensuing decades. In just the same way Aischylos' own vision raised despairing and ironic thoughts in the minds of both Euripides and Aristophanes, as they watched revivals of the Orestes trilogy in the Athens of the late fifth century, while their city fell prone to civil strife and headed for total defeat in the protracted Peloponnesian War.

The production concept therefore became itself part of the act of translation. This is a task whose burden cannot simply fall on the shoulders of the "translator" in the restricted sense of the word; as these notes show, the director and costume designer can (and should) themselves play a central role. Translation (in the normal, strict sense of the word) now came into a profitable mutual interaction with interpretation. The Victorian setting allowed, for example, for a full emphasis in the script on the comic elements in Aischylos' presentation of Apollo, and especially of his arguments in the trial scene (elements which are all too often neglected in modern productions); and also gave us the chance to make some subordinate statements of key importance simply through costume (for example, both Klytaimestra and Orestes were costumed with deliberate anachronism—Klytaimestra as an Elizabethan queen and Orestes as a Byronic hero—to enforce the point that they bring the disputes of another age, and in some senses of another world, back to haunt Athena's fledgling aristocracy). But in general, and more importantly, the decision to reset the play swung us irrevocably onto the road of stressing in production those aspects of Aischylos' men, women, gods, and goddesses which remind us of the affinities between the Greek world and our own, rather than those which tend to emphasize the differences.

And so I found myself innocently involved in a controversy, which became even more marked with my final production, an *Agamemnon* set in an unnamed corner of Southeast Asia under British rule—Rangoon, perhaps, or Singapore?—in the late 1920s or early 1930s. One important element in the opening drama of the trilogy is the racial contrast between the Greeks and the Trojans (which Aischylos, by deliberate anachronism, reinforces by having Agamemnon and Klytaimestra confer on Priam's Troy some of the customs which the Athenians knew and despised in contemporary Persia). Despite his own innate assumption of superiority, Agamemnon falls as decisively as the city he has conquered. Setting this play from the heyday of Athenian imperialism in the framework of a modern empire, with equal delusions as to its own cultural superiority over the "barbarians," seemed to match key aspects of the original text—as well as allowing skin color to mark the all-important difference between Kassandra and all the Greek characters. And while there is far more to *Agamemnon* than the racial interplay, this is an essential substratum which must be revealed for any effective realization of the play in performance.

In Newcastle, ironically, the modern dress productions were resented by the local theater critics (and worried some drama staff who had responded warmly to the style of the classical-costume *The Libation Bearers*) but received the fullest imaginable support from the staff and students of the classics department. They were quite happy to forgo the doubtful pleasures of authenticity (e.g., male actors in masks, as seen in Peter Hall's London production of the Harrison script for the National Theatre), in return for a production which brought over to them, and also conveyed to members of the public not educated in the classics, some of the fundamental human reality, the vigorous life, and the psychological cut-and-thrust which can be sensed in the original text but rarely felt in contemporary performance.

And here I know I am on dangerous ground. Even to use the word "psychological" in reference to Greek tragedy is, of course, to commit anachronism; and to place emphasis on the fundamental human reality of these plays is at first sight openly to flout the equal or greater claims to fundamental status which may be lodged on behalf of the religious or philosophical truths for which Aischylos has been rightly acclaimed by all but the most philistine of his scholarly commentators. For refusing to use masks, even in a relatively small indoor theater where the distancing effect would far outweigh any possible gain, I have even been accused of opening the door to sub-Stanislaviskian depth character analysis as a tool in the interpretation of Greek tragedy.

That, of course, is out of the question. But everything can be overdone; and one thing that most definitely is overdone is the book which I and many others worshiped as undergraduates, John Jones's landmark study of 1960 entitled *On Aristotle and Greek Tragedy*.[12] For all his deep insight into the primacy of the *oikos* or household rather than the isolated individual, and his correct demolition of all attempts to Bradleianize Greek drama, Jones's book committed a fundamental outrage to common sense and theater practice by trying to remove virtually all human interaction between characters and audience from our picture of Aischylean tragedy. Years of learned argument (including a characteristically balanced contribution from Pat Easterling,[13] and an equally characteristically wild one from

Roger Dawe!)[14] were needed before some writers on Greek tragedy
(Brian Vickers[15] outstanding among them) dared to come out of the
trenches and claim once again that, yes, these plays were designed
to make an emotional impact on the audience as well as stimulating
their minds, and that they did this by involving their audience in
the situations of the characters and inviting them to feel a human
reaction to their fate.

In 1982 I myself added to this debate, in an article[16] designed to
reassert the obvious fact that *Agamemnon*, while most certainly a
play which raises important spiritual and metaphysical questions
about the nature of our world and our relationship with the powers
that control it, does this not through the means of abstract,
philosophical reasoning but through the progressive unfolding of a
story pattern[17] in a real social and political situation; the pattern of
the preparations by the Queen and the Elders of Argos for the return
of the King, and the ways in which Klytaimestra subverts the normal
processes of a Greek *nostos* or homecoming during the first half of
the play. If you fully appreciate the role of this story pattern in the
play's structure, then the passages which seem most difficult for the
modern reader and director—the chorus's long meditations on
human destiny—immediately gain dramatic life, as expressions of
the attempts of Elders, trapped in a real, sinister, and unfolding
situation, to probe the depths of the past and understand an increasingly ominous future.

When I turned, soon after writing that article, to producing a play
by Aischylos for myself, I developed the absolute belief that, whatever production style is adopted, a vision of the characters as real
people in a real situation is essential to involve the audience in the
story. Aischylos wrote not abstract parables based on legendary figures but plays about great individuals and cities whom the playwright
and the audience believed to have been real historical people and
places.

I apologize for stating so vigorously what ought to be a truism;
but I have been subjected too often, in the name of Greek tragedy,
to sterile and boring theater experiences by directors so obsessed
with "ritual" and with their own image of the archaic or primitive
that no part of the true meaning of the Aischylean, Sophoklean, or
Euripidean text crosses the divide between actors and audience. Why
should it be that directors (and some scholars) strive, in producing
the comedies of Aristophanes, for contemporary immediacy at any
cost—sometimes at the cost of any feeling at all for the original
play—while imposing on the tragedies an austere remoteness which

increases their already legendary difficulty and inaccessibility? I leave others to answer that question.

My central contention is that in the translation of a drama—any drama from any historical period—the act of verbal translation of the script cannot stand alone. It is, on the contrary, only one of a number of different, complementary parts of the act of translation; the English-language play script should be regarded simply as one of the tools available to the director for the interpretation, and re-creation on the modern stage in modern terms for a modern audience, of the meaning which the original theatrical experience, in the theater of Dionysos, had for the original audience. Playing space, costume, acting style, movement, and even music (which there is not space to discuss here) are all part of the act of translation, in this wider sense of the word. And the translation itself, in the narrower sense of the word, lives in constant mutual interaction with the conception of the original theatrical experience which is enshrined in these other media. In the Peter Hall production of the *Oresteia* at the National Theatre in London, for example, it is impossible for an outsider to tell which came first: the decision to use male actors with masks, the long raised stage (above a foreshortened *orchestra*) which was used for much of the work of the solo actors, the intense rhythmic quality of Tony Harrison's rhyming, neo-*Beowulf* text, the ritualized monotony of Harrison Birtwistle's music, or the stylized, hieratic manner of acting; all these elements worked together to create a picture of Aischylos as remote, massive, and primitive in his effects.

I hope it is obvious now that I attempted to bring out quite different values, both when I translated the three plays and when I realized those translations in performance for the first time. By the time I came to the most difficult one (*Agamemnon*, of course), I had, I believe, developed a degree of clarity and fluency, together with some ability to translate passages of quite difficult rhetoric, such as Klytaimestra's speeches when she emerges in triumph over the bodies of Agamemnon and Kassandra (printed below), in such a way that even a student actor could handle them without too many problems; I had also learned that, if you employ the circular shape with confidence, the psychological flow and interaction between characters, which for me are at the heart of these dramas, can be brought out effectively through the blocking. Costume and lighting may also be powerful; and music, though of course it should be of prime importance during the choral odes, may also be used to translate effects which might otherwise be lost. For example, in the last part of the final scene of *Agamemnon*, as the confrontation between Aigisthos and the Elders reaches such a height of bitterness that they almost come to blows, and Klytaimestra has to intervene to calm them, Aischylos marked the extra degree of tension by changing the meter of the dialogue from the regular iambic trimeter to the trochaic tetrameter. I could not find an effective way to echo this in my English verse in the script, so instead asked the composer of the electronic score for this production if he could find some simple musical way, contrasted with the complex accompaniment to some earlier choral lyrics, of marking off the final section.

Here, as an example from the edition in progress, is the opening of scene 7 in the version performed at Newcastle. It is preceded by an extract from the draft commentary.

> [After Agamemnon's death-cry] the focus turns inexorably from the deed itself to its consequences; and by the end Klytaimestra's position has been completely undermined. Though she begins scene 7 in absolute triumph over the bodies, she is soon obliged to retreat from her exultant stance. The Elders are armed, after Kassandra's death has proved her veracity, with all that she has said; and they add that knowledge to the wisdom they have gained from their own earlier meditations on the pattern implied by the sack of Troy. They find the power to counter much of Klytaimestra's self-justification and to make her see that her deed is merely one link in what now threatens to become an unending chain of vengeance and counter-vengeance. By the end of scene 8, though the usurping regime of Aigisthos is firmly in military control of Argos, the Elders can look forward with confidence to the prospect of requital in turn for Agamemnon's death. . . .
>
> But here, as earlier with Kassandra, the conflict does not bring deeper knowledge to only one of the participants. The Elders, when they recover from the immediate impact of her opening speech, denounce Klytaimestra's deed as monstrous and insane; she must have been high on drugs to dare such an act (1407f.). But this is not an adequate viewpoint, any more than her initial conviction that she is wholly justified. In two powerful speeches Klytaimestra puts before them the depth of the affront to her womanhood when Agamemnon slaughtered Iphigeneia, the humiliation of her husband's many infidelities outside the walls of Troy, and the crowning insult, the bringing back of Kassandra. Nor will she shirk conflict; with Aigisthos as her king and protector, she is prepared to meet all opposition on equal terms.
>
> This forces the Elders to reflect more deeply. Klytaimestra's command of language and of the situation is total, and she is clearly not insane. They must seek further if they are to find the true causes and make an adequate response to the death of the king. And so they turn back. . . .

(Doors open. Enter KLYTAIMESTRA *on the ekkuklema
over the bodies of* AGAMEMNON, *covered by a net,
and* KASSANDRA.*)*

KLYT. Much I have said before to suit the moment, and
I'm not ashamed to contradict it all;
how else could anyone contrive hostilities against an
enemy
who seemed to be a friend, and fence the hunting-nets
of pain up to a height beyond escape?
This conflict is the climax of an ancient feud—
it's been long in my mind, but still at last it came.
I stand just where I struck; the deed's been done.
And I will not deny that I made sure   1380
he had no chance to escape or ward off his fate.
I cast an endless mesh around him, like
a net for fish—a rich and evil robe.
I strike him twice, and with two cries
his limbs went slack, and when he's fallen
I give him a third, a votive offering
of thanks to Pluto, saviour of the dead.
And as he lies he breathes his life away,
and blowing out a rapid spurt of blood
he strikes me with black showers of murderous
dew, 1390
and I rejoice no less than does the growing corn
in Zeus' rain during the birth-pangs of the sheaf.

Elders of Argos, this is how things are;
be glad, if that's your will—and I will glory openly.
If it were right to pour libations now
upon this corpse, it would be just, it would be more
than just;
such was the bowl of cursed evils this man filled
inside our house, and drains it now on his return.

1 ELD. We marvel at your tongue, the boldness of your speech,
for you to make a boast like this over
your husband's corpse.   1400

KLYT. You try me like a woman of no sense,
but I speak out to you, who know it well,
with fearless heart; whether you wish to praise me or
to blame,
it's all the same. This is Agamemnon, my husband,

now a corpse, the work of this right hand,
a just executant. And that is all.

ELDERS A1. Woman, what evil drug
grown in the earth, or drink
sprung from the sea did you consume
to give the daring for this act of murder? You
reject and cut away the people's curses;
you will be   1410
cast out, a hateful burden on the citizens.

KLYT. So now you judge it right that I be exiled from this land
and have the hatred of the citizens and peoples' curses,
who never showed the slightest opposition to this man
when he, not caring much about it, just as if an animal
was dead
out of abundant flocks of fleecy sheep,
killed his own daughter, dearest fruit sprung from
my labour-pangs, to charm away the winds from
Thrace.
Should you not rather then have driven him out of this
land
to expiate that crime? But when you come to look   1420
into my deeds, you are a savage judge. I tell you this;
if you make threats, know I'm prepared
on equal terms: if someone conquers me by force,
then he may rule; but if the god ordains my victory,
you'll learn discretion, late although the lesson comes.

ELDERS A2. You aim too high,
your words are over-proud; your mind
is maddened by your murderous deed,
your eyes are flecked with blood.
Bereft of friends, you will one day pay for this
crime
with blow in turn for blow.   1430

KLYT. Now hear my solemn, righteous oath:
by the fulfilling Justice of my child, and by
Destruction and the Furies, goddesses to whom I
sacrificed this man,
my expectations do not tread the house of fear
so long as fire is kindled at my hearth
by Aigisthos, who now, as always, cares for me;
he is my mighty shield of confidence.

Here lies the man who has defiled my womanhood,
the one who charmed each Chryseis he saw outside the
                                                  walls of Troy,
and here's the captive, portent-reading   1440
concubine who gave him oracles—
his faithful mistress, who wore out the benches of the
                                                  ships
beside him. They have both received what they deserve:
he died as I have told, while she sang her last song,
her funeral lament, just like a swan, and lies
beside him as his lover; she has given me
a dainty side-dish for my feast of sexual ecstasy.

ELDERS B1. Oh, if only sudden death—not fraught
                with agony or lengthy pain—
                could come, and bring to us   1450
                eternal, everlasting sleep, now that
                our kind protector's been struck down. . . .

As every wise translator realizes, all translation is a necessary
loss; but we must *choose* what to lose. In this work I have turned
my back on what I profoundly believe to be a false ideal of grandeur
and ritual; the new translation of Aischylos is as lucid and accurate
as possible, contains no private poetry or inserted imagery of the
translator's own invention, and has successfully been played, uncut,
before an audience which lacks any tradition of live verse drama. It
will be published not alone but accompanied by a commentary which
is devoted to Aischylos' dramatic aims and what we can sensibly
conjecture as to how he himself realized them in his original, round
theater. I believe this format offers a new and profitable direction
in which the translation and interpretation of Greek tragedy might
well proceed.[18]

NOTES

1. Aeschylus, *The Oresteia*, tr. Richmond Lattimore (Chicago: University of Chicago Press, 1953); tr. Robert Fagles (London: Penguin, 1976).

2. Cited in W. Nestle's introduction to J. G. Droysen tr., *Aischylos: die Tragoedien und Fragmente*, 5th ed. (Stuttgart: Reclam Verlag, 1977), ix.

3. Cf. *The Serpent Son* (Aeschylus, *Oresteia*, tr. F. Raphael and K. McLeish (Cambridge: Cambridge University Press, 1979)).

4. See my article "Elektra; Sophokles, von Hofmannsthal, Strauss," in *Ramus* 13, no. 2 (1984): 131–54.

5. In *Theatre Works 1973–1985* (London: Penguin, 1985).

6. Cf. Euripides, *Iphigeneia in Tauris*, tr. Richmond Lattimore (New York: Oxford University Press, 1973), vii.

7. Sophocles, *Plays*, tr. D. Taylor (London: Methuen, 1986).

8. Ibid., 192f.

9. Ibid., xxiii.

10. Oliver Taplin, *The Stagecraft of Aeschylus* (Oxford: Oxford University Press, 1977).

11. Cf. my review article "The Bayreuth Centenary *Ring* by Patrice Chéreau and Pierre Boulez," in *Miscellanea Musicologica* 14, 167–73.

12. John Jones, *On Aristotle and Greek Tragedy* (London and New York: Chatto & Windus and Oxford University Press, 1960).

13. Pat Easterling, "The Presentation of Character in Aeschylus," *Greece and Rome* 20 (1974): 3–19.

14. Roger Dawe, "Inconsistency of Plot and Character in Aeschylus," *Proceedings of the Cambridge Philological Society* 189 (1963): 21–62.

15. Brian Vickers, *Towards Greek Tragedy* (London: Longmans, 1973).

16. Michael Ewans, "The Dramatic Structure of *Agamemnon*," *Ramus* 11, no. 1 (1982): 1–15.

17. I borrowed this term from Richmond Lattimore's short, underestimated monograph *Story Patterns in Greek Tragedy* (Ann Arbor: University of Michigan Press, 1964).

18. I append for interest the alterations to the text of scene 7 which we made during the rehearsals for our production of *Agamemnon*.

1375–6	*originally* torture	*finally* pain up
1384	*originally* struck, gave	*finally* strike, give
1412	*originally* think	*finally* judge
1447	*originally* a dainty side-dish for my feast of ecstasy; *then* a side-dish for my feast of sexual ecstasy; *and finally* a dainty side-dish for my feast of sexual ecstasy	

III

Anthropology

Language, Politics, and Translation: Colonial Discourse and Classic Nahuatl in New Spain

 J. JORGE KLOR DE ALVA

AMONG SO MANY OTHER THINGS, language en-
codes power relations. The translation of literature, always more
than a strictly linguistic or interpretive exercise, is no exception. It
is subject to power plays and responds to tactical moves that serve
the personal and collective interests of the original author, the translator, the audience, or (where relevant) the publisher or reviewer.
At another level, the process of translation into the language of the
dominant sector can constitute a way of speaking or writing about
the project that sustains the power relations of the society (e.g.,
Christianization, Anglo-American neo-colonialism, Nicaraguan so-
cialism). This latter phenomenon occurs when ideologies and ideas
that help to express and shape the socio-political hierarchy are for-
mulated and propagated in the course of translation. For this to take
place it is not necessary that personal intentions be the driving force.
Instead, the politics of a translation (or interpretation) are more likely
to be configured by the unspoken and usually unperceived assumptions making up the reigning ideas and exegetical rules that guide
the translator. Indeed, it is because these dominant ideas and rules
are conceived as obligatory (not subject to personal choice) that they
have the power to determine the truth, relevance, and propriety of
a literary decipherment. However, in a situation where one language
group is clearly dominant over another, as is generally the case in
a colonial context—like the one that existed in sixteenth-century
Mexico—the nature of language use and policy is so highly politi-
cized that the hegemonic assumptions prompting the socio-political
ends of those in control are generally quite transparent. A post-structuralist form of discursive analysis is particularly useful for studying

these conscious and veiled relations between the effects of colonial power and the translation of Classical Nahuatl.

Following, in part, Michel Foucault (1973), I use the concept of discourse—broadly defined as a bounded register of signs (statements or "serious speech acts" [Dreyfus and Rabinow 1983:48]), codes (rules for ordering the signs and assessing their truth value), and meanings (resulting significations)—in an interpretive manner to help uncover and analyze statements whose truth value is determined by passing a test made up of the rules of combination and argumentation accepted as appropriate to the discourse (e.g., biblical hermeneutics, dialectical reasoning, or the calculus of economic advantage). For the purposes of this essay, one of the central aims of this type of discursive analysis is to find the ideological devices that permit elements from one discursive formation (or register) to become part of another (e.g., the use of claims about salvation [religious discourse] to support arguments on behalf of Spanish claims to sovereignty [political discourse]). Thus, by "colonial discourse" I mean the ways of talking, writing, painting, and communicating that permit ideas to pass from one discourse (say, religion or philology) to another (like politics or economics) in order to authorize and make possible the ends of colonial control (e.g., Fabian 1986:78–84).

Classical Nahuatl as Colonial Discourse

The impositions of control (and acts of resistance) found in the process of translation take place primarily as linguistic moves. Through these a politics of aesthetics, building on the foundation of a pre-existent politics of linguistic assumptions and beliefs about language use, is encoded in the selection of texts, vocabulary, phrasing, style, and form (e.g., Fabian 1986; Rafael 1988). These choices, usually perceived by translators as merely the "natural" result of logical reasoning and aesthetic tastes, have a long history of service in the interest of dominant cultures in multilingual environments.

In the Castilian effort to bring all of the Iberian peninsula and the New World under the dominion of the Crown(s), one of the most important tactics was to appropriate the native languages and to impose their own. A lapidary statement from the fifteenth century summarizes the official Spanish design in pursuing its linguistic concerns at home and abroad: When Antonio de Nebrija, who in 1492 authored the first grammar of a modern European language, was asked by Queen Isabella, "What is it for?" the bishop of Avila answered for him, "Your Majesty, language is the perfect instrument of empire" (Hanke 1970:8). Though accurate, the bishop was not pretending to be novel or insightful; Nebrija in his introduction to the *Gramática de la lengua castellana* had already stated that "language has always been the partner [*compañera*] of empire" (Hanke 1970:127, n. 31).

Spanish language policy in New Spain (which includes most of the Nahuatl-speaking areas) was always subject to contradictions and dissensions: the officials of the Crown attempted, unsuccessfully for the most part, to force the inhabitants to speak Spanish; the missionaries, who manned the front lines of all language contact encounters, sought to protect the natives from secularizing influences and extreme forms of exploitation by isolating them linguistically from the Spaniards. Both sides employed the control of everyday language use to promote their distinct versions of the same goal: the peaceful colonization of Indian bodies and souls. Nevertheless, because the demographic ratios overwhelmingly favored the natives and a multiplicity of languages confronted the Europeans' limited number of colonial agents, the Spaniards were forced to establish linguistic order primarily by disregarding certain languages and promoting others. To make up for the lack of official recognition and use of some languages (generally those spoken by peoples with limited demographic and economic resources, in possession of marginal lands, or living a non-sedentary existence), Nahuatl was foisted on a number of native communities throughout Mexico. This was a logical maneuver because at the moment of contact the majority of central Mexican city-states were controlled by Nahuatl speakers, and the use of the language had already been widely diffused among non-Nahua groups because of the Aztecs' own nation-building efforts.

The transformation of Nahuatl into an official language of colonization (i.e., into a lingua franca) was also determined by the need to maximize the political usefulness of the native nobility. For instance, the training of a cadre of literate noblemen who could mediate between the Spanish officials and the local native rulers and laborers was an absolute necessity. And Spanish-style Nahuatl literacy, though always subject to being appropriated for pro-indianist concerns, contributed to the acculturation process, thereby helping to establish political control over the newly developed sector of native colonial leaders. Furthermore, the need to make the natives intelligible and predictable required that every effort be made to establish a common language throughout central Mexico. Not surprisingly, most of the native-language documents, books, and manuals from the colonial period are written in Nahuatl.

Beyond the practice of choosing and promoting Indian languages to serve the colony's communication and political needs, the pre-contact hierarchical ordering of Nahuatl was maintained and modified to address new ends. First, after alphabetization was introduced, the Nahuatl spoken by the *macehualtin* ("commoners"), the so-called *macehuallahtolli* or "rustic, common speech," became the vernacular or notarial Nahuatl that was employed by low-ranking notaries in the course of local political administration. Second, the *pillahtolli*, the elegant, affected speech of the *pipiltin* or "nobles," formed the basis for Classical Nahuatl, the literary or "vehicular" language of instruction, Christianization, and ritualized communication. Vernacular Nahuatl, with its straightforward prose that closely adhered to the everyday speech register, was used throughout the colonial period primarily for local record keeping and town (or city) council administrative tasks. Its evolution (except for the periodization of its various linguistic transformations) followed the path expected whenever languages are in contact over long periods of time: phonetic shifts, adoption of loanwords, morphological and syntactic innovations, and semantic modifications (Karttunen and Lockhart 1976; Karttunen 1985).

Given that formal language instruction took place in Classical Nahuatl, the fact that most non-literary colonial documents are written in the vernacular points to both the colonists' incomplete control over the development of the literacy they introduced, and the failure of the missionary schools either to inculcate fully their version of "correct" Nahuatl or to monopolize the instruction of native literacy. Furthermore, the speed and thoroughness with which the natives appropriated Spanish-style literacy in the vernacular to serve local needs, coupled with their general disregard of Classical Nahuatl, especially after the sixteenth century when the native nobility began its precipitous decline, underline the tenuous hold missionary Nahuatl had within the native communities. Lastly, the contrasting uses and ultimate fates of these two forms of Nahuatl help to make evident a telling paradox: Classical Nahuatl, the language modeled after the one used by those who controlled the ideological machinery of pre-contact central Mexico, and which claimed to represent the purest ritual speech of the indigenous secular and religious leaders, functioned within the colony as the most important vehicle for acculturation; while the vernacular of the local communities greatly enhanced their capacity to pursue their interests in the new socio-political order.

By Classical Nahuatl I mean the ritual and imaginative language used by the elites in the urban centers of central Mexico before and after contact. For two interrelated reasons this was the language that served the friar-grammarians as the exemplar when they adapted Nahuatl to alphabetic writing. First, the earliest efforts to bring the Nahuas under the control of the Europeans rested on the cooptation of the native nobility. The education under Spanish tutelage of the cooperative elite adults and children was one of the many tactics employed to ensure this cooptation, and having been the first to be instructed, it was their speech that came to be represented in alphabetic writing. Second, in order to employ language successfully as an "instrument of empire," the missionaries appropriated the authority already encoded in the discursive practices of the nobility. This they accomplished by translating the literature necessary for the Christianization process using the rhetorical moves and vocabulary of the newly alphabetized Classical Nahuatl. The ritual language, by which the native leaders had long helped to shape the ideology of the masses of commoners, became both the language of instruction about the ways of Europeans, and the language by which the ideological speech of the native leadership was domesticated to serve the ends of colonial discourse.

The adoption of Classical Nahuatl as the official language of the colonized also responded to a primary political requirement: the economical and efficient exploitation of native communities on behalf of colonial interests. To begin with, it simplified and thereby made possible language instruction for a large number of religious and secular colonial officials. In doing so, it both multiplied the number of points at which Spanish-dominated language contact could take place and increased the level of intrusion possible on these occasions, all without the need for physical force. In addition, although Classical Nahuatl was not the language of the pragmatic texts of the native notaries (usually the only literate Nahuas in the villages or small towns), it facilitated the Spanish-style organization of the Nahua communities by making language instruction at the local level more accessible and by contributing to the replacement of the native record-keeping apparatus with Spanish-style documentary forms (testamentary, judicial, tributary) that meshed better with the political and economic structure of the new colony. Also, the literacy made possible by the codification of Classical Nahuatl eased the flow of communication from the colonial authorities, which was critical for the efficient dissemination of regulations, the orderly collection of bureaucratic and tactical information (and tribute), and the adjudication of Spanish-Nahua disputes. Lastly, even if the everyday prose of the notaries served local indigenous needs better than the trope-ridden language of the elite, because it lacked the finesse of Classical Nahuatl the contrast between the two linguistic modes contributed to marking vernacular Nahuatl as a "degraded" or rustic speech, thus helping to legitimate the prejudices and discriminatory acts that generally accompany a people whose language is considered inferior. (To this day in Mexico the "rustic" native languages are considered "dialects" rather than "real" languages.)

For the missionaries who devised the official language of the colonized, the explicit primary goal of language instruction was proselytization. Since this endeavor was their raison d'être for coming to the New World, they lost no time in composing a variety of appropriate texts, written with the aid of the native scholars whom they had taught to read and write in Nahuatl (and sometimes in Latin). With their native assistants the priests produced vocabularies and grammars; bilingual catechisms, devotional works, and confessional manuals; and translations of sermons, psalms, parts of the Bible, hagiographies, religious dramas, and secular morality tales like Aesop's fables. These materials provided the local priests with their most important ideological tools for molding native social and cultural practices into the image of those of (exploitable) Spanish peasants. Furthermore, these scholarly teams also redacted ethnographies of pre-contact native customs and institutions, along with indigenous histories, myths, legends, didactic dialogues (huehuehtlahtolli), and poetic expressions. Such works were complemented by the pre- and post-contact histories, chronicles, poetry, and mythical tales inscribed by the few literate Nahuas writing independently of the missionaries (but within the European grammatical and lexicographic canons). Together, these two sets of native language texts constitute what modern scholars call Classical Nahuatl literature.

Classical Nahuatl was the centerpiece of New Spain's colonial discourse. Its use permitted the colonists to press into service the language of the native elites so as to secure their assistance in the colonial project. It thereby led to the illusion, at the level of the Indian town, that the social order dominated by the Spaniards differed little, or not at all, from the one that had preceded their arrival. This effect resulted in part from the maintenance of the contrast between the language of the elite and that of the majority. As the vernacular was appropriated by local native authorities, its use established an asymmetrical form of communication making possible socio-linguistic practices that reinforced the colonial hierarchy. For instance, regulatory statements emanated from Spanish-speaking or pro-Spanish authorities in Classical Nahuatl or Spanish, while petitions and assertions of compliance flowed to the centers of power in the vernacular. At the same time, the continuous subjection of public utility, as determined by ecclesiastical and secular colonial officials, limited the self-serving use by the Nahua elite of *unmonitored* Classical Nahuatl. Furthermore, the overwhelming control exercised by the Spaniards over formal Nahuatl, and the limited use of rustic Nahuatl outside the notarial setting (because of a lack of generalized literacy), functioned to limit the topics, vocabulary, and ritual settings permitted for the enunciation and performance of traditional (non-Christianized) native texts. As a consequence, most of the literature that came to be inscribed either had been purged of its anti-colonial and non-Christian elements or had encoded these in extremely opaque metaphors and rhetorical devices decipherable only by the initiated.

In short, Classical Nahuatl was clearly a device aimed at facilitating the movement of ideas from one set of discursive formations (Christianity, pre-contact ethics) to another (ethnic subordination, political order). And although the exclusions and intrusions that resulted from the regulatory practices of colonial discourse delimited the formation, circulation, and survival possibilities of *traditional* Nahuatl literature, its colonial versions, particularly as modified for the purposes of proselytization, and their translations, especially for priests who were supposed to use them to identify and root out idolatrous rites, played an important role in the colonial project. But none of this would have been possible without the translation of oral speech into alphabetized writing. With Nebrija's *Arte* and *Vocabulario* under one arm, and the *Doctrina cristiana* under the other, the missionary linguists set out to appropriate Nahuatl for use on behalf of the Spaniards. Few exercises of colonial power were to prove as effective and long-lasting as this initiative.

The Colonization of Oral Literature and Its Translation

The pre-contact central Mexican writing system was complex, composed of a combination of ideograms, pictograms, a few syllabic glyphs, color codes, and the symbolic use of pictorial space and image orientation. It was used by Nahua government officials for recording tasks that relied on the quantitative representation of objects, like censuses or tribute lists; maps; chronologically ordered histories and genealogies, including records of natural phenomena; and administrative memoranda, along with the transmission of military and bureaucratic information. Priests wrote (or had scribes write) calendric/divinatory almanacs, liturgical guides, prayers, descriptions of deeds of the gods, and other accounts concerning the supernatural. However, the interpretability of the more narratological, less quantitative or chronological accounts, was limited not only by knowledge of the meanings of the glyphs but, more importantly, by the reader's previous memorization of the accompanying oral text. Thus, when pre-contact Nahua writings were employed to transmit literary, imaginative texts, as opposed to straightforward accounts or general descriptions, they seem to have served primarily as systemic guides to assist the memory.

This form of literacy required that the narratives associated with the pictorial books, whose hieroglyphs served as mnemonic devices, be taught in the schools of the urban centers or handed down across the generations and social sectors via groups of ritual specialists and creative artists. The independence of writing from orality made possible by alphabetization had the effect of weakening the link between literacy and the authority of the native leaders (the keepers of the correct "reading" of the hieroglyphs). Needless to say, the missionaries quickly rushed into the space created by this rupture.

The invention (or improvisation) of written Classical Nahuatl took place through the registers of the Roman alphabet (adapted in part to Nahuatl phonology), and Spanish grammar, as originally set out by Nebrija. Through these European prototypes the missionary linguists codified the syntax, morphology, phonetics (orthography), and lexicon of oral Nahuatl. In doing so, colonial praxis was served not only in the many ways described above, but in other important forms. First, as just noted, it helped to replace the authority of the native priests and teachers by that of the missionaries. Second, the standardization of the language imposed a canon that contributed to the delegitimation (if not necessarily the abandonment) of regional dialects. The attempt to homogenize the population contributed to colonial control by promoting the breakdown of regional differences (linguistic, cultural, and social), whose presence, for instance, militated against the efficient allocation of labor and made proselytization and acculturation more difficult. Third, the implanting of linguistic uniformity slowed and in some place made impossible the creation of parochial indigenous writings that reflected local speech patterns, interests, and demands. Lastly, alphabetization had the effect of colonizing native oral literature.

As Dennis Tedlock (1983) and Dell Hymes (1977) have observed, literary texts transmitted orally—like any other oral literature—are most likely versed during their performance to simplify their recounting, to aid in memorization, and for aesthetic reasons. Although the Nahuas distinguished prose (*tlahtolli*) from poetry or song (*cuicatl*) (León-Portilla 1983), the inscription in alphabetic writing of their literature had a standardizing effect, transforming almost all the narratives and much of the poetry into unversed prose. The flattening out of the Nahua literary taxonomy in the process of inscription, although some missionaries made much of the richness of native genres, suggests the extent of control over indigenous aesthetics made possible by alphabetization.

Despite the missionaries' extensive use of chants and Christianized native songs in the colonization process, and quite apart from some very insightful arguments to the contrary (Haly 1986), most of the performative aspects of the traditional works have been lost, making their reconstruction necessarily speculative (e.g., Karttunen and Lockhart 1980). This loss, coupled with the lack of consensus around the type and degree of versification, meter, and stress, has forced modern scholars, until very recently, to translate into narrative prose the Nahuatl literature that is not already versified. Although frequently one cannot know if what is being translated was prose or poetry, much excellent work is being done on native taxonomies to help keep the genres straight (León-Portilla 1983).

Alphabetization, which greatly facilitated the deployment of the Spanish mechanisms of control, did not come about easily. The linguistic difficulties encountered by the missionaries and their native colleagues during the early stages of the inscribing process were legion, and their solutions, or lack of them, affect how Nahuatl is translated and understood today. One critical problem was how to represent Nahuatl phonology with the Roman alphabet, using primarily Spanish phonetic values. The pioneering work of Frances Karttunen and James Lockhart (1976:64–74) on orthography and diacritics has helped to clarify the way the missionaries met this difficulty. In brief, Nahuatl phonemes were left firmly framed within the still polemical phonemic structure of the sixteenth-century Spanish alphabet, notwithstanding the fact that during the early stages of language contact Spanish orthography was itself undergoing profound transformations. When the friars employed the Spanish alphabet to encode in script a set of alien phonemes (like unfamiliar consonants and a broad range of vowel contrasts) that were found, for instance, among the Mayas and Tagalogs, they employed several diacritical marks or invented non-Roman characters (Karttunen 1985:79–80; Rafael 1988:39–54). For reasons that are not clear, however, when dealing with Nahuatl they generally resorted to undifferentiated spellings of distinct sounds. Since it seems that only the native speakers discriminated among these subtle variations (and they had no need for diacritical markings), the less than adequate orthography served the colonial ends for which it was developed.

Nonetheless, the lack of distinction in Nahuatl between some consonants, like *p/b, t/d, c/g,* and the absence of *f, r, s,* and *j* means that some texts have words that to the unsuspecting translator cannot be identified easily as Spanish, Nahuatl, errors, or previously unencountered attestations. Even more problematical is the fact that while every Nahuatl consonant is spelled with either one or two letters (e.g., *tç,* or *tz,* the geminate *ll,* or *tl*), the glottal stop was generally left unmarked, except for an occasional representative *h.* Furthermore, the Spanish-based Nahuatl orthographies rarely distinguish the difference between long and short vowels. Until the publication of the grammars of Nahuatl by J. Richard Andrews (1975) and Michel Launey (1978), and the dictionary by Karttunen (1983), little attention was paid to the need for diacritics to distinguish vowel length and the glottal stop. Yet diacritics or, more precisely, knowledge of the distinctions they could represent if present, is sometimes critical to resolving the semantic problems that result when words that are similarly spelled but have totally different meanings are encountered, as the following examples suggest (where, ´ = short, ˆ = long, ` = glottal stop):

> âchtli (elder brother of younger sister), áchtli (seed)
> âhuic (toward the water), `ahuic (from here to there)
> `atlâcátl (inhuman, reasonless man), âtl `acátl (sailor, fisherman)
> mêtztli (moon, month), métztli (muscle, leg)
> t`atli (father), tâtli (you drink [from âtli])
> tlâtía nic (to hide), tlátía (to burn)
> tôca (plant, bury), tóca (to follow someone)

> Carochi 1983, 126v-128v

Beyond translation puzzles resulting from words spelled without diacritics, there are those caused by the tensions between an oral literature that follows the pronunciation dictated by the rules of Nahuatl morphology, and its inscription in Spanish-based orthography, with the latter in turn reflecting the tension of having been "caught in a tug of war between representing pronunciation and writing things in a predictive manner that [left] the fine points of pronunciation to the speaker" (Karttunen and Lockhart 1987:94). When phonetic representation predominates, as is frequently the case when the author was a native, the same word pronounced in different ways leads to significant confusion for the translator; however, a reliance on the canonical orthography might distance the inscribed word from its pronunciation so as to make its decipherment difficult.

This difficulty arises because Nahuatl is an agglutinative and polysynthetic language. As morphemes in the nature of affixes and roots combine to make up words, phrases, and even whole sentences, consonants and vowels are juxtaposed, causing one of the two to assimilate (to approximate fully or partially the sound of the other). In the absence of a consistent application of the rules of assimilation (or the erractic use of optional assimilations) by the author, the identity of the morphemes may become enigmatic, making their translation speculative (though the translator may not be aware of this). For instance, native speakers writing somewhat removed from the influence of Spanish overseers tended to disregard the latter's standard spellings (which were more or less consistent regardless of context). Instead, their reliance on a more phonetic orthography made their texts more sensitive to the assimilation, gemination, reduction, and intrusion of consonants. However, scholars today who rely primarily on the canonical forms of missionary grammarians and their native students have difficulties recognizing the equivalences between the two orthographies. Thus a Spaniard might write *oacico* (*ôahcico*) "he arrived," where a native writer may spell it *ohuacico*, introducing what might be construed as an additional morpheme (Andrews 1975:9–12; Karttunen and Lockhart 1987:94–100). Needless to say, this problem, common to the translation of all agglutinative and many polysynthetic languages, is the most ubiquitous of all for translators.

The sixteenth-century missionary-grammarians encoded unexpected and dissimilar Nahuatl grammatical details within the canons of the traditional Latin and Spanish grammars familiar to them. But they were aware that the European models did not fully represent Nahuatl. In his 1571 Nahuatl-Spanish dictionary Fray Alonso de Molina (1970: *Epistola nuncupatoria*), sensitive to the particular nuances of native grammar, stated, "the language and phrasing of these [natives], especially the Nahuas and Mexicans, is very different from the language and phrasing of Latin, Greek and Spanish." By "phrasing" Molina meant the morphology and syntax of Nahuatl (León-Portilla 1980:11–14). Fray Andres de Olmos was no less cognizant of the problem when he noted that

> In the art of the Latin language I believe the best manner and order that can be found is the one followed by Antonio de Nebrija in his [text], but because in [Nahuatl] the order he used would not fit, because many things are missing that in the grammar are very important, such as declensions, supines, and the types of verbs used to note the diversity among them . . . , I will not be subject to reprimand if I do not follow in everything the *Arte* of Antonio.
>
> Olmos 1885,9

The reference to Nebrija is to his Spanish grammar, the *Gramática [Arte] de la lengua castellana* (1926 [1492]). As noted above, this work and the *Vocabulario de Romance en Latin* (1973 [1516]) made possible the earliest Nahuatl grammars and vocabularies that, subject to necessary modifications, were modeled after them (Karttunen 1988). A careful reading of the pioneer Nahuatl grammars (e.g., by Molina, Olmos, or Carochi) makes it possible to articulate the linguistic idiosyncrasies of Nahuatl despite their forced labels and sometimes stilted structure. Without these prototypes it is difficult to imagine how the missionaries would have been able, in a matter of decades, to fix in script a language that, with the exception of the use of ideograms, pictograms, numerical symbols, and a limited number of phonograms, existed almost exclusively in oral form.

Otherness and Colonial Discourse

The otherness experienced when confronting a text recognized as Classical Nahuatl literature is not only the result of its being an inadequate representation of the oral original. The non-linear structure of Nahuatl poetics, where verses focus on a common theme rather than following each other in a logical narrative (Karttunen and Lockhart 1980:16–17), and the seemingly inescapable labyrinths of its figurative language differ strikingly from Western aesthetics. While the apparently straighforward and pragmatic vernacular Nahuatl documents like wills, notary records, letters, and petitions present even more complications than those identified by their interpreters, the elite texts that span from narrative historical accounts to esoteric poetry are far more opaque.

In the sixteenth century (as is sometimes the case today, e.g., Bierhorst 1985a:16–41), the desire to make the meaning of these texts transparent could conflict with the need to maintain or increase their surplus meaning. Space for interpretation was needed to locate in the natives' own words support for the Europeans' assumptions about the origin and nature of the inhabitants and cultures of the New World. A common topos of missionary hermeneutics that served this end was the observation that translation without the assistance of native interpreters was impossible. Assertions of this sort were used as arguments to advocate the maintenance of schools for Indians, to gain political and financial support on behalf of ethnographic research into native life, and, ironically, to permit the missionary-teachers to claim for themselves a monopoly on the authentic comprehension of indigenous ideas, motives, and needs. Therefore, the desire to dominate the lives of natives (paternalism) and personal and collective self-interest, as much as genuine ignorance of Nahuatl tropes, led sixteenth-century missionaries, like Fray Diego Durán, to summarize the problem of interpretability and its solution as follows:

> All of their chants are composed of such obscure metaphors that there is hardly a person who can understand them, unless they are very deliberately studied and discussed so as to understand their meaning. I have intentionally set myself to listen with much attention to what they sing. And between the words and terms of the metaphor it seems nonsense to me; but, afterward, having been discussed and conferred, they are admirable sentences, both in the divine things they compose today and in the worldly songs.
>
> Durán 1971, 299–300

Even more than in Europe, irony was the master trope of sixteenth-century colonial Mexico. As the dominant modality of figuration, ironic troping was the soul of colonial discourse; without it the identity of Christian morals with the colonial ethos would have been impossible. It characterized the rhetoric of priests like Durán when they sought to monopolize control over the interpretation of Nahua reality by admitting to the inadequacy of their own comprehension of their discourse. Irony also appears as a basic fact of colonial praxis in that the desire to make Indians confess themselves so that they might be understood, and thereby "saved," was ultimately an intelligence gesture whose object was submission and control. Furthermore, Durán, who like other early students of indigenous customs believed it was his duty to tell on Indians, claimed that he was moved to write about the Nahuas "by the zeal of informing and illuminating [the] ministers so that their task may not be in vain" (Durán 1971:386). But if the supplement that completes the signification of the Nahuatl chants (verses/songs/poems—presumably the core of Nahua religious beliefs) can be provided only by indigenous hermeneutics, then the real object of missionary research was persuasion or subterfuge, rather than exegesis.

Fray Bernardino de Sahagún, writing at the same time but from a more informed perspective (having spent many years studying the language and culture), was even more transparent when it came to explaining the political function of the space between the meanings of the words and the sense intended by the tropes:

> Our adversary the Devil . . . planted in this land a forest or mountainous thicket full of scrubby undergrowth in order to perform his business from it and to hide in it as the wild beasts do. . . . This forest or thicket are the chants that in this land he plotted to have sung in his service . . . without their being able to be understood except by those . . . who are native and fluent in the language.
>
> Sahagún 1975 II:172–73

Sahagún clearly recognized that between (let us say) lexical or linguistic competence (knowing what the words mean) and a comprehension of the semantic code (knowing what they signify) lies a strategic terrain. Given the tropological mode of figuring colonial experience that reigned in his day, by a transposition of intentions the field of contestation is characterized as where the Devil (read Indians), rather than the missionaries, creates surplus and/or no meanings to counter the initiatives of the opposition. Like Durán, Sahagún insists that in this battlefield only those Indians adept at deploying semantic ruses can overcome their damage. With this maneuver Sahagún conflates, in a colonial discourse context, the politics of interpretation and the problems of translation.

Fray Bernardino was so sensitive to Nahuatl's political dimensions and actual and potential linguisitic complexities that he refused to try his hand at translating the twenty religious hymns that followed the quotation cited above. Even when the topic to be translated was Christian doctrine, he argued that only those works "written with [the Indians] . . . can appear and may be free of all heresy . . . , [adding that] whatever is to be rendered in their language, if it is not examined by them . . . cannot be free of defect" (Sahagún 1950–82:10:83–84). From what we know today about the language (its syntax, morphology, and figurative lexicon), it is easy to appreciate the otherness experienced by the friars when confronting Nahuatl, but our concern here has been mainly with the intentional (religiously and socio-politically motivated) otherness of Nahuatl, for the uninititated *and* the native speakers.

With regard to the deliberate projection of otherness by the Indians, it was well known in the sixteenth and seventeenth centuries that Nahuas who engaged in traditional religious, curing, and divinatory practices shared an esoteric language, *nahuallahtolli*, that was ostensively used to communicate with supernatural beings. The opaqueness of this language, which is used to articulate a significant part of the Nahuatl literary corpus, had at least four practical functions. First, it constituted a magical discourse that, like the language of Roman Catholic sacramental speech, operated *ex opere operato* in order to effect specific results as a consequence of its mere utterance. Logically, this instrumental language was considered powerful and dangerous; its tropes were obstacles helping to confine its circulation so that witchcraft and unintended effects could be minimized. Second, the restrictions placed on the communication of this discourse contributed to maintaining the boundary between the professionals who used it and the uninitiated who were the recipients of its effects. Thus, like the jargons of lawyers or doctors, which by restricting the dissemination and/or intelligibility of the code keep the initiated in power and in possession of prestige or wealth, *nahuallahtolli* and cognate literary discourses were meant to keep the specialists employed and the social/ethnic boundaries firm, before and after the arrival of the Spaniards. Third, the tropological richness of Nahuatl poetics served as a discursive form of resistance to the advances of colonial and Christianizing forces. As was well known by local priests, it made possible a secret communication system whose proper use distinguished the conspirators who employed it from the collaborators who denounced it. Lastly, because Classical Nahuatl literature is composed primarily of the affected speech of the native elite, it was a mark of breeding that also contributed to the maintenance of a border between those who labored to pay tribute and those who collected it. In effect, there were many reasons for the Nahuas to conspire with the missionaries in promoting the latter's claim that only the indigenous could understand the thicket of tropes that hid the satanic motives.

The Translation of Nahuatl Literature Today

If Durán and Sahagún were correct, and only natives privy to the esoteric discourse could provide supplement needed for its rendition in another language, the modern translator is in a difficult position. Without informants to do the explaining (cf. Tedlock 1983:124–47), the challenges surrounding any move to unravel the metaphorical tangles found throughout Nahuatl literature are overwhelming. Consequently, the clearing of the semantic underbrush has been the single most important and challenging task for contemporary scholars who, following the practices of their sixteenth- and seventeenth-century counterparts (Gingerich 1983:112–14), are making use of and contributing to the development of lists of metaphors (Karttunen and Lockhart 1987:51–63), building concordances to assist in the identification of particular uses in differing contexts (Bierhorst 1985b), and creating indexes of morphemes to help uncover the nuances of the language (Campbell 1985). In addition, literary critics working on deciphering the creative works of the Nahuas have combined the interpretive tools of folklorists, structuralists, post-structuralists, and others with those of the ethnohistorians to come up with strikingly nuanced readings of heretofore formidable texts (Gingerich 1977, 1986, 1987; Bierhorst 1983; Carr and Gingerich 1983).

However, the tropological exuberance of Nahuatl is far from being the only obstacle to the decoding of its meaning. After all, solutions to the complications entailed by the use of metaphor, metonymy, and synecdoche are limited by our knowledge of how the sculptural, pictographic, and alphabetic texts, upon which our representations of Nahua culture are based, permit us to understand the ways in which the natives assigned signification to their idiomatic and figurative words and phrases. Some of the semantic matrices of the culture have been uncovered by art historians applying stylistic and iconographic tools to decipher the carved images and painted codices (e.g., Pasztory 1983). Their work and that of some of the more interpretive archaeologists make possible the testing of translations of inscribed works against cognate symbolic representations. However, our understanding of Nahua literature is still at an early stage of development and continues to be subject to the kinds of polemical interpretations that result from overly focused speculations and isolated research. Despite a lack of consensus on the possible meaning of key ideological issues or on the interpretation of various aspects of the culture and its myths, real progress has been made on the linguistic and literary fronts.

After the "golden age" of missionary ethnography, little attention was paid to the imaginative labors of the Nahuas (beyond that of a few colonial grammarians and collectors) until the study of Classical Nahuatl texts as literature resumed at the end of the last century. At that time scholars like Daniel G. Brinton (1969 [1887]) and Eduard Seler (1902–23) transcribed, translated, and published commentaries on the style, content, and meaning of a number of Nahuatl master-works. However, work on the subject stopped in the United States after Brinton's nineteenth-century studies and resumed only with the appearance in 1963 of Miguel León-Portilla's *Aztec Thought and Culture: A Study of the Ancient Nahuatl Mind*, followed in 1969 by his *Pre-Columbian Literatures of Mexico*. In contrast, beginning in 1934 León-Portilla's teacher, Angel Maria Garibay K., published in Mexico a series of volumes on the topic that established the literary production of the Nahuas as a legitimate scholarly field of inquiry (Garibay 1971). In turn, the Garibay–León-Portilla precedents inspired a host of translators (particularly into English and French), poetic innovators, and genuine critics working in Europe, the United States, and Mexico (Bierhorst 1985a:121–33; Gingerich 1987:87).

Since the 1970s the number of scholars who can translate Nahuatl texts has grown substantially, and the new students of the language and culture have brought with them significantly different perspectives and more diversified tool boxes than those common among the scholars who initiated the field. Not surprisingly, a quantum leap has taken place in our understanding of the language (including its transformations at contact and in the centuries that followed) and the material and ideational characteristics of Nahua culture (e.g., Klor de Alva, Nicholson, and Quiñones Keber 1988). This flourishing of Nahuatl scholarship and the widespread dissemination of its results make evident that a discussion of the translation of Classical Nahuatl and its attendant problems is no longer only an esoteric exercise for linguists or solely a matter of chauvinist, nation-building romanticism on the part of Mexicans or Chicanos.

BIBLIOGRAPHY

Andrews, J. Richard. *Introduction to Classical Nahuatl*. Austin: University of Texas Press, 1975.

Bierhorst, John. "American Indian Verbal Art and the Role of the Literary Critic." In *Smoothing the Ground: Essays on Native American Oral Literature*, Brian Swann, ed. Berkeley: University of California Press, 1983.

————. *Cantares Mexicanos: Songs of the Aztecs.* Stanford: Stanford University Press, 1985a.

————. *A Nahuatl-English Dictionary and Concordance to the "Cantares Mexicanos" with an Analytical Transcription and Grammatical Notes.* Stanford: Stanford University Press, 1985b.

Brinton, Daniel G. *Ancient Nahuatl Poetry.* New York: AMS Press, 1969. (Reprint of 1890 ed.; originally published 1887).

Campbell, R. Joe, ed. *A Morphological Dictionary of Classical Nahuatl: A Morpheme Index to the Vocabulario en lengua mexicana y castellana of Fray Alonso de Molina.* Madison, Wis.: Hispanic Seminary of Medieval Studies, 1985.

Carochi, Horacio. *Arte de la lengua mexicana.* Miguel León-Portilla, ed. *Facsimiles de Lingüística y Filologia Nahuas* 2. Mexico: Universidad Nacional Autónoma de Mexico, 1983.

Carr, Pat, and Willard Gingerich. "The Vagina Dentata Motif in Nahuatl and Pueblo Mythic Narratives: A Comparative Study." In *Smoothing the Ground: Essays on Native American Oral Literature*, Brian Swann, ed. Berkeley: University of California Press, 1983.

Dreyfus, Hubert L., and Paul Rabinow. *Michel Foucault: Beyond Structuralism and Hermeneutics.* 2d. ed. Chicago: University of Chicago Press, 1983.

Durán, Diego. *Book of the Gods and Rites and The Ancient Calendar.* Translated and edited by Fernando Horcasitas and Doris Heyden. Norman: University of Oklahoma Press, 1971.

Fabian, Johannes. *Language and Colonial Power: The Appropriation of Swahili in the Former Belgian Congo 1880–1938.* New York: Cambridge University Press, 1986.

Foucault, Michel. *The Order of Things: An Archeology of the Human Sciences.* New York: Vintage Books, 1973.

Garibay K., Angel María. *Historia de la literatura náhuatl.* 2 vols. Mexico: Editorial Porrúa, 1971.

Gingerich, Willard. "Tlaloc, His Song." *Latin American Indian Literatures* 1 (1977): 79–88.

————. "Critical Models for the Study of Indigenous Literature: The Case of Nahuatl." In *Smoothing the Ground: Essays on Native American Oral Literature*, Brian Swann, ed. Berkeley: University of California Press, 1983.

————. "Quetzalcoatl and the Agon of Time: A Literary Reading of the *Anales de Cuauhtitlan.*" *New Scholar* 10 (1986): 41–60.

————. "Heidegger and the Aztecs: The Poetics of Knowing in Pre-Hispanic Nahuatl Poetry." In *Recovering the Word: Essays on Native American Literature*, Brian Swann and Arnold Krupat, eds. Berkeley: University of California Press, 1987.

Haly, Richard. "Poetics of the Aztecs." *New Scholar* 10 (1986): 85–133.

Hanke, Lewis. *Aristotle and the American Indians: A Study in Race Prejudice in the Modern World.* Bloomington: Indiana University Press, 1970.

Hymes, Dell. "Discovering Oral Performance and Measured Verse in American Indian Narrative." *New Literary History* 8 (1977): 431–57.

Karttunen, Frances. *An Analytical Dictionary of Nahuatl.* Austin: University of Texas Press, 1983.

———. *Nahuatl and Maya in Contact with Spanish.* Texas Linguistic Forum 26. Austin: Department of Linguistics and Center for Cognitive Science, University of Texas, 1985.

———. "The Roots of Sixteenth-Century Mesoamerican Lexicography." In *Smoke and Mist: Mesoamerican Studies in Memory of Thelma D. Sullivan,* J. Kathryn Josserand and Karen Dakin, eds. Oxford: B.A.R., 1988.

Karttunen, Frances, and James Lockhart. *Nahautl in the Middle Years: Language Contact Phenomena in Texts of the Colonial Period.* Publications in Linguistics 85. Berkeley: University of California Press, 1976.

———. "La estructura de las poesía náhuatl vista por sus variantes." *Estudios de Cultura Nahuatl* 14 (1980): 15–64.

———, eds. *The Art of Nahuatl Speech: the Bancroft Dialogues.* Nahuatl Studies Series 2. Los Angeles: UCLA Latin American Center Publications, 1987.

Klor de Alva, J. Jorge, H. B. Nicholson, and Eloise Quiñones Keber, eds. *The Work of Bernardino de Sahagún: Pioneer Ethnographer of Sixteenth-Century Aztec Mexico.* Studies on Culture and Society 2. Albany and Austin: SUNY-Albany Institute for Mesoamerican Studies and University of Texas Press, 1988.

Launey, Michel. *Introduction à la langue et à la littérature aztèques 1: Grammaire.* Paris: L'Harmattan, 1978.

León-Portilla, Miguel. *Aztec Thought and Culture: A Study of the Ancient Nahuatl Mind.* Translated by Jack Emory Davis. Norman: University of Oklahoma Press, 1963.

———. *Pre-Columbian Literatures of Mexico.* Translated by Grace Lobanov and Miguel León-Portilla. Norman: University of Oklahoma Press, 1969.

———. "A propósito de algunas aportaciones lingüísticas." *Estudios de Cultura Nahuatl* 14 (1980): 11–14.

———. "Cuícatl y tlahtolli. Las formas de expresión en náhuatl." *Estudios de Cultura Nahuatl* 16 (1983): 13–108.

Molina, Alonso de. *Vocabulario en lengua castellana y mexicana y mexicana y castellana.* Facsimile edition of 1571 original, edited by Miguel León-Portilla. Mexico: Editorial Porrúa, 1970.

Nebrija, Antonio de. *Gramática de la lengua castellana.* Edited by I. González-Llubera. London: Oxford University Press, 1926. (Original published 1492.)

———. *Vocabulario de Romance en Latin.* Seville: Johannes Varela, 1516. (Republished with an introduction by Gerald J. MacDonald. Philadelphia: Temple University Press, 1973; and Madrid: Editorial Castalia, 1973.)

Olmos, Andrés de. *Arte para aprender la lengua mexicana.* Written in 1547, published by Rémi Siméon (Paris: Imprimerie Nationale, 1875). Mexico: Imprenta de Ignacio Escalante, 1885.

Pasztory, Esther. *Aztec Art.* New York: Abrams, 1983.

Rafael, Vincente L. *Contracting Colonialism: Translation and Christian Conversion in Tagalog Society under Early Spanish Rule.* Ithaca: Cornell University Press, 1988.

Sahagún, Bernardino de. *Florentine Codex: General History of the Things of New Spain.* 12 vols. Translated and edited by Arthur J. O. Anderson and Charles E. Dibble. Sante Fe and Salt Lake City: School of American Research and the University of Utah Press, 1950–1982.

———. *Historia general de las cosas de Nueva España.* Angel María Garibay K., ed. Mexico: Editorial Porrúa, 1975.

Seler, Eduard. *Gesammelte Abhandlungen zur Amerikanischen Sprach- und Altertumskunde.* 5 vols. Berlin: Verlag A. Asher and Verlag Behrend, 1902–23.

Tedlock, Dennis. *The Spoken Word and the Work of Interpretation.* Philadelphia: University of Pennsylvania Press, 1983.

The Translator;
or, Why the Crocodile
Was Not Disillusioned

a play in one act

 DENNIS TEDLOCK

Characters

PALEOGRAPHER
MANUSCRIPT
DICTIONARY
ETYMOLOGIST
EPIGRAPHER
TRANSLATOR
LITERALIST
NATIVE

Scene

Center is a desk with a swivel chair that faces downstage; stage right, barely in reach from the chair, is a bookcase the same height as the desk, facing stage left. Between bookends on the downstage edge of the desk top and in the bookcase are various volumes, many of folio size and some about to fall over or fall apart. Stage left is a window, the only source of light; otherwise, the stage left, stage right, and upstage walls are completely covered with overstuffed bookshelves. Suspended above the swivel chair is a giant cut-out cartoon balloon with a cloud outline, bearing these words:

POPOL VUH:
THE MAYAN BOOK
OF THE DAWN OF LIFE

Seated in the chair is TRANSLATOR, *reaching around for books in fits and starts, sometimes finding them at his feet. Most of them come from the case to his right; he lifts these over to the desk top with pain. Once a book is in front of him, he looks something up in it, turning pages back and forth and then scribbling on a pad of paper. Now and then he massages his right shoulder or picks his nails or looks out the window. Each book is placed on top of the one before, until the heap topples to the floor. As* TRANSLATOR *dives for the books, the light goes down quickly. When it comes back up the desk and bookcase are gone but* TRANSLATOR *is still seated in the chair.* PALEOGRAPHER, MANUSCRIPT, *and* ETYMOLOGIST *stand in a group to his left, with* DICTIONARY, EPIGRAPHER, *and* LITERALIST *to his right. He swivels around as they speak.*

PALEOGRAPHER. (*examining the folds of* MANUSCRIPT's *tattered cloak*) Here on the verso of folio nine the writing is clear enough. I read (*stiffly*), "Are chic uchacatajic, ucamic zipacna." But as you know, whoever wrote this book often left out glottalization, so that "cha" in "uchacatajic" could be "ch'a." And on top of that, the writer seldom made the distinction between the frontal sound of the consonant in "ca" and the back sound of "ka," something like the different *k*'s in Arabic. When you take both these problems into consideration, the "ca" in "chacatajic" could be "ca," "ka," "c'a," or "k'a." Put these together with "cha" and "ch'a" at the front of "uchacatajic," and you've got eight different ways of reading this one word. What does the dictionary say?

DICTIONARY. I don't have all those words, but I'll tell you what I do have. If it's "ucha*ca*tajic" you want, that means "his or her being-stood-up on four or more legs." If you want to read "ucha*ka*tajic," then you've got "his or her being disillusioned." If you want to read "ucha*k'a*tajic," then it becomes, "his or her being cooked," or perhaps "being ripened" or "fattened." Now let's try changing "cha" to "ch'a." Here I've got the possibility of u*ch'a*catajic, which would be "his or her being defeated." And then—

ETYMOLOGIST. I'd like to point out that "ch'a" means "arrowhead," so that the original meaning of "uch'acatajic" might have been "his or her being pierced," or "shot with an arrow."

EPIGRAPHER. And that reminds me that in the pre-Columbian books of the Mixtec—

ETYMOLOGIST. But the Mixtec are a thousand miles from the Maya Quiché and speak an unrelated language—

EPIGRAPHER. But this expression, "his being arrowed," might have originated in *reading* rather than in *speaking*. These Mixtec books could have been read in *any* language in this part of the New World, probably, because the writing is ideographic. Let me explain, please. In the Mixtec books, each town that is mentioned has an emblem glyph, built around the basic sign for a mountain—

TRANSLATOR. Well, it's true that in the Maya Quiché language, "juyub," the word for "mountain," is also used as a metonym for "town." That's because towns should be on the tops of mountains, or at least surrounded by canyons. We would seem to be getting a little beyond the reach of our Etymologist here, if being an Etymologist means worrying about the fact that the Quiché and the Mixtec words for "town" or "mountain" may *sound* completely different. But go on.

EPIGRAPHER. Now, as I was saying, each town has an emblem. When a town has been defeated, conquered, by one of the kings mentioned in one of these books, its emblem is shown with an arrow passing through it. So maybe the writer of the Popol Vuh was looking at an ideographic book when he wrote the word "uchacatajic"— or, as he should have written it, "uch'acatajic."

ETYMOLOGIST. Or maybe people spoke that way with or without actually having such a book in front of them—though I'll grant that the expression *could* have originated in the process of reading emblems, in this case, *impaled* emblems. But it could just as well be that the practice of painting arrows through emblems, in its turn, started with how people spoke aloud about war.

TRANSLATOR. And they could have spoken that way in more than one language. But they borrowed one another's *meanings*, not one another's *words*. That's where we get outside the territory of our Etymologist. And they could have done this with or without actual ideographs in actual books, which is how we get beyond the territory of our Epigrapher.

DICTIONARY. Isn't that enough now? Are you all done? I wasn't really finished with my bit when you went off to the land of the Mixtecs. There's one more possible reading of "uchacatajic." Do you want to hear it?

ALL. Yes, yes, go ahead.

DICTIONARY. Well, it's this: it could be "uch'*aka*tajic," which would mean, "his or her being hung up to dry."

ALL. (*with descending tone*) Oh.

DICTIONARY. So that's it for "uchacatajic." You shouldn't complain: there were eight different possible pronunciations, and I can attest to the actual occurrence of only five of them. Whoever "it" is in this word, it's either being stood up on four or more legs, disillusioned, cooked, defeated—or, if you like, pierced with an arrow—or else it's being hung up to dry.

PALEOGRAPHER. But are we really done? There's another *c* in this word, right at the end—"uchacatajic." Can't that be pronounced in four different ways too? Aren't we back up from five to twenty possibilities?

ALL. (*groans and moans*)

LITERALIST. Don't get excited. I can answer that before we even hear from our dictionary friend. The ending of "uchacatajic" consists of two very common suffixes: "-taj-," which explains why all the possible readings we've been getting were passive constructions, and "-ic," which makes a verb into a noun. So "-tajic" it is, just as it's written, and we've run out of alternative pronunciations. Not that I know which of the five to choose.

PALEOGRAPHER. We may be done with "uchacatajic," or whatever it is, but what about the next word, "ucamic"? It's got two *c*'s in it. Does that make sixteen possible combinations?

ALL. (*moans and groans*)

DICTIONARY. Don't worry. I've already thought about this, and there are only two that really work. There's "ucamic," just as it's written, which would be "his or her dying," and there's "uc'amic," which would be "his or her arriving." It's got to be one or the other. Are we ready to try for a literal reading of the whole line?

LITERALIST. Well, as for the first two words I don't even need to ask our dictionary. "Are chic"—and that *is* the way the words are pronounced—means, "this is now." And then come the two words we've been talking about, and then comes this word "zipacna." Zipacna, whatever or whoever it is, will be the one to whom those problem words belong. It's Zipacna who's being stood up on four or more legs, disillusioned, cooked, impaled, or hung up to dry, and it's Zipacna whose death or arrival is being talked about.

TRANSLATOR. Here we'll have to remind ourselves that in an earlier passage, the word "Zipacna" is identified as a *name*, or "bi" in Maya Quiché. It's the name of a character in a story.

LITERALIST. But can we translate this name, or shall we just leave it as a name?

DICTIONARY. I know of no such word as "zipacna." And there's something odd about the sound of the name.

ETYMOLOGIST. Well, I don't want to offend anyone, but "zipacna" sounds an awful lot like a Quiché corruption of "cipactli." And "cipactli" comes not from a Mayan language but from Nahua, the language of the Toltecs.

LITERALIST. And what does it mean?

ETYMOLOGIST. It means "crocodile."

LITERALIST. All right. So far, then, leaving our two problem words untranslated, we've got, "This is now uchacatajic, ucamic Crocodile." But I'm at a loss as to what's happening to Crocodile.

TRANSLATOR. And I'm not sure you should've called him "Crocodile" instead of calling him "Zipacna." After all, this is a *name*, not just a *noun*, and the text itself has previously called our attention to the fact. And nowhere does the text offer an etymology of this name, though it does etymologize other names from time to time.

ETYMOLOGIST. Those are merely *folk* etymologies.

TRANSLATOR. I would call them *interpretations*. Sometimes it's more interesting to hear what a Maya Quiché thinks the text means than to hear what *you* think it means.

But let's get back to the point. Instead of exploring Zipacna's name, the text lets him identify himself. He says, "I am the maker of mountains." But that's not a translation of the word "zipacna"; it simply explains who this character named Zipacna *is*. So, our friend the dictionary doesn't offer a translation of Zipacna and neither does the Popol Vuh itself. We've got one more possibility: let's ask someone who speaks Maya Quiché as a native language.

DICTIONARY. What would a native know that I don't know?

TRANSLATOR. Lots. Is there a native in the house?

(NATIVE *comes up on stage from the back row and approaches* TRANSLATOR, *who rises to greet him.*)

The sun's gone past the meridian, father, sir.

NATIVE. The sun's gone past the meridian, father, sir.

(NATIVE *stands to the left of* TRANSLATOR *and they shake hands.*)

TRANSLATOR. I am a sifter of ancient times. I want my words to come out as clear as day. Could you tell me something, sir?

NATIVE. What is it, sir? Tell me.

TRANSLATOR. What does "zipacna" mean?

NATIVE. Zipacna. Zipacna. That sounds like a name to me, but I don't know the name. Or at least we don't know the name in my town. Now, over at Rabinal, they have a story about someone named Zipac, but I don't think it's a story about a crocodile. Crocodiles are called "ayin."

TRANSLATOR. (*turning from* NATIVE *to the others*) So it was a name to whoever wrote the Popol Vuh and it's still a name today. It may mean "crocodile" in Nahua, but if we were to translate it that way, it wouldn't fall on the English-language ear the way it falls on the Quiché ear. It doesn't sound like "crocodile" to our Quiché friend, so it should't sound like "crocodile" in English.

LITERALIST. All right, all right. Zipacna it is. Now, how do we decide how to translate these other two words, "uchacatajic" and "ucamic"? I'm still at a loss.

TRANSLATOR. (*sitting down*) Well, did you ever hear of context? In the good old sense of intratextual context? I've been reading ahead, and skipping over any number of problems along the way, and I can tell you that this Zipacna character is destined to get crushed under the weight of an entire mountain. At the end it says something like, "He breathed a last sigh and was calm." And all of this happens because a couple of boys, twins, outsmart him. They don't stand Zipacna up on all fours—far from it—nor do they cook him or hang him up to dry. As for disillusionment, he never gets a chance to feel that. He has no idea he's been tricked until the moment the mountain crushes him. So, our victory in the struggle with "uchacatajic" must lie in the only other possibility, which is defeat. And as for that other word, "ucamic," he dies in defeat, he doesn't just arrive at it.

PALEOGRAPHER. But there's something that bothers me here. Isn't this a strange way to *begin* a story? By giving away the end in advance, announcing that Zipacna will be defeated and meet with death?

NATIVE. What's being given away? All the storyteller is saying is that he's going to tell the story through to the end, he's going to finish it. And don't stories end with death and defeat? Haven't you been listening to *us* when *we* tell stories, sir?

TRANSLATOR. Well I have, sir. But nobody else.

PALEOGRAPHER. All right, then. Our emended text will read as follows (*stiffly*): "Are chic uch'acatajic, ucamic zipacna."

LITERALIST. Which translates as, "This is now his or her being defeated, his or her dying, Zipacna."

TRANSLATOR. (*jumping up*) That's *not* a translation. Even as a crib it's a little hard to take. I can do better, even without forcing a choice between "his" or "her," which English sometimes needs but Quiché doesn't. Here's my solution (*to the audience*): "Now this is the defeat and death of Zipacna."

LITERALIST. I really must object to that word "and." There's no conjunction in the text. Where did you get it?

TRANSLATOR. From *English*. The text is perfectly good Quiché without it, and the translation is perfectly good English *with* it.

PALEOGRAPHER. "Now this is the defeat and death of Zipacna," you say. And is that final?

TRANSLATOR. (*sitting down again*) Well, some day I might wonder whether I should have translated Zipacna as Cayman.

ETYMOLOGIST. But that came into English from Spanish, which got it from Carib. It's barely even an English word.

TRANSLATOR. Precisely. And Cayman isn't quite like Crocodile in English, in the same way Zipacna isn't quite like Ayin in Quiché.

ETYMOLOGIST. But the trouble with that is, our text doesn't give an etymology, folk or otherwise, for Zipacna, and neither does our native. That means your Cayman solution would be appropriate only for readers who, on top of feeling strange about the sound of the *word* "cayman," aren't clear just what a cayman *is*.

TRANSLATOR. (*looking out the window while the light goes down*) Well, I was just wondering . . .

IV

History

Uilix Mac Leirtis: *The Classical Hero in Irish Metamorphosis*

 *FREDERICK AHL*

Introduction: Narcissus at the Well

"TRANSLATION" IS TOO MILD a word to capture
the violent process whereby a text written in one language and time
is taken apart and rebuilt in another. Perhaps "metamorphosis"
comes closer. For such radical changes in sense and sound occur
during the process of translation that the end product is generally
no longer intelligible to the author of the original or his cultural
community. The recreated work belongs to its new language and
culture—and, very largely, to its recreator.

We tend, however, to talk about translation as if the process were
reversed, as if the translator whisked his readers away from their
own environment to that of the original, as if we, rather than the
text, were being moved. The illusion is as misleading as it is pleasant,
especially when the original is centuries old and in a language no
longer spoken, such as Latin or ancient Greek. For almost all European cultures, however different from one another, have been conditioned to feel, despite distance in time and language, an intellectual
kinship with the classical world. It is the "cradle" of our cultures.
It is ourselves when we were infants.

Classical literature is the reflecting pool of European (and Euro-
pean-based) culture. Yet we, like Narcissus, are often more interested
in our mirrored image upon the waters than in the waters themselves.
Such narcissism may be creative and enriching, provided we do not
take our own reflections to be separate, ancient beings. Translators,
however, do much to encourage our illusions. Although the language
and cultural milieu of Euripides, when translated, becomes modern
English or French, translators often leave the illusion that their ver-

173

sions give us the next best thing to a seat in an ancient Greek theater. We even feel reassured about the authenticity of a version when something in it does not quite make sense: we are witnessing some facet of the original language or culture that is more primitive than or intriguingly different from our own. Here is proof that the image is not just our own reflection. So we may pursue our sense of the exotic to the extent of going to Greece and watching a Euripides play in modern Greek translation, and in a theater built in Euripides' own day—in an environment where translator and reader share the illusion of an archaeological "recreation" of an ancient drama.[1]

We have reached a point in our culture where the most widely accepted translations of Greek and Latin poetry *are*, to all intents and purposes, the original texts that we read and study. "The business of classics is in recession," Richard Stoneman observes, "but translation goes on."[2] Even classicists now need help with less familiar texts. And their preference is usually for what is taken to be a more literal "crib" than a poetic recreation of the original. For the assumption persists among scholars that the more wooden and "literal" the translation, the more accurate it is. Translators of classical literature have an acute (and justified) fear of being attacked by scholars for making mistakes. By mistakes, they do not necessarily mean actual slips or "howlers," but the selection of words and expressions which might seem somehow less than "objectively" accurate. Thus Richmond Lattimore, in the preface to his *Iliad*, remarks: "I must avoid mistranslation, which would be caused by rating the word of my own choice ahead of the word which translates the Greek."[3] Lattimore's comment suggests his "objectivity" and "accuracy." He is subordinating personal instincts to the demands of the original. We feel reassured. Hence translators who take more liberties than, say, Richmond Lattimore, have to inform the reader, as Douglass Parker does in the introduction to *Lysistrata*, that his version is "interpretative rather than literal. It cannot be used as a by-the-line crib."[4]

Such notions of objectivity lure us into accepting that a line can be drawn between the "substance" of a text (which we feel is translatable) and its language and form (which we feel are not wholly, if at all, translatable). We ignore Werner Winter's warning that "meaning and form . . . cannot be dissociated from one another" even at the level of the individual word.[5]

Many readers and translators start with an unspoken but troubling assumption that poetic form is separable from factual substance—as if poetry were the frame to the picture rather than part of the picture itself. If we are scholars, as many translators of Greek and Latin literature are, we incline to transpose what we read in ancient authors into a "factual," historical format before analyzing it. Our goal is the "objective" reality of the ancient world, and we are concerned to filter out the impurities which centuries of laxity have allowed to creep in. Modern Hellenists, for example, are keen to disentangle the Greeks from their Latin successors of the medieval and Renaissance world, to remove the corrupting taint of Latinity from Greek epic and Greek poetry. The traditional Ulysses is abandoned in favor of Odysseus; Socrates and Sophocles acquire a Greek *k* in place of the Latin *c*; Achilles fades into Achilleus, even Akhilleus—though we still call him Achilles to the eternal confusion of our students. The result (aside from pedagogical chaos) has been to distance the texts and the names from us, to enhance the illusion that we have been "beamed in" as observers into an exotic world.

The Oedipal Image

The translator's pose of objectivity may easily diminish our alertness to the various ways a translation may mirror not what the texts say, but what the scholarly consensus of the day thinks they ought to be saying. Too often, however, the modern translator interposes himself between us and some critical puzzle in the ancient text by removing a difficulty that would have been present even for an ancient reader. Let us take a simple illustration. When a messenger from Corinth arrives in Sophocles' *Oedipus the King*, announcing that he has news, Jocasta asks him two questions at the same moment:

JOCASTA. What sort of news? And who have you come from?

Her second question is a good one, and of a type not generally posed to messengers in Greek tragedy. It is usually assumed that the bearer of news is qualified to report what he reports. The messenger responds to her second question first (935–36):

MESSENGER. From Corinth. And the word you soon will learn
            could please—how not?—perhaps upset you too.

His answer is not entirely satisfactory, since Jocasta appears to be asking *who* has sent him, rather than *where* he is from.

Translators deal with the problems posed by the messenger's reply in some curious ways. Luci Berkowitz and Theodore Brunner, and Robert Fagles dispose of the dilemma before it reaches the reader's eyes. Here are their versions of 935–36. First Berkowitz and Brunner:

> JOCASTA. Where do you come from?
>
> MESSENGER. From Corinth . . .[6]

Now Fagles:

> JOCASTA. Who sent you?
>
> MESSENGER. Corinth . . .[7]

The first translation adapts Jocasta's question to the answer she receives. The second implies that the messenger has been sent by the city of Corinth. Although the messenger introduces himself as the bearer of good tidings, he goes on to suggest that his news is more ambiguous: it could be pleasing or upsetting. So the clarification Jocasta now seeks is about the messenger's ambiguous tone, not his unclear identity:

> JOCASTA. What is it? And what is its double force?

Here is the messenger's reply (939–40):

> MESSENGER. He'll be dictator. The Corinthians will give him
> power. So it is rumored there.
>
> JOCASTA. How so? Does not old Polybus still rule?
>
> MESSENGER. No more. For death now has him in the grave.
>
> JOCASTA. Are you then saying Polybus is dead?
>
> MESSENGER. If I don't speak the truth, *I* risk dying.

Jocasta is so distracted—in fact, delighted—by the news of Polybus' death that she fails to notice how odd the first part of the messenger's announcement is. He does not say Oedipus *has been* appointed tyrant (dictator) of Corinth, but that Oedipus *will be* appointed tyrant, if *rumor* is correct.[8] But several translators again confer official status on his mission and his message. Kenneth Cavander has the messenger say:

> MESSENGER. The people of Corinth—it was already announced
> there—will make Oedipus their king.[9]

Berkowitz and Brunner write:

> MESSENGER. Your husband now is ruler of the Isthmus![10]

These translators' changes in the text and force of the Greek are a reminder of the perils of reading *Oedipus* or any other ancient work without consulting the original. We may lose the critical awareness that we are dealing not with fact but with hearsay, and hearsay which is at least doubly removed, since the (rather evasive) messenger is reporting rumor. Dawe is quite right to comment that line 940 shows the messenger is "not an official representative, but one hoping to earn a reward on his own account by enterprisingly informing Oedipus of local gossip."[11]

But modern criticism is no more interested in the identity of the Corinthian messenger and what his credentials are than is Jocasta, or for that matter, Oedipus. We approach Sophocles with pretty fixed assumptions about what his play means. The messenger is the purveyor of information we take to be true. We are, if may one say it, as culturally programmed to accept that Oedipus committed the crimes he comes to believe he committed as is Oedipus himself.

Irish Epics

It is only as times and interpretations change that following generations can come to see how far the translations of their predecessors imposed, consciously or unconsciously, the values of their own cultures. It is, of course, easy enough for us to laugh at the foibles and idiosyncracies of translators past and present. Dryden's *Aeneid* or the first book of Pope's *Thebaid* bear the marks of seventeenth- and eighteenth-century England, just as contemporary versions of Sophocles' *Oedipus* bear the imprint of post-Freudian criticism. But occasionally we may learn more than we might anticipate from looking at translations of another era, especially when the translators concerned are quite obviously *not* working under the guise of objectivity—when they are quite clearly and unambiguously transposing and adapting the original into their own culture.

My object, then, is to give an overview of what are arguably the earliest translations of Greek and Latin epic into vernacular languages: the Irish (Gaelic) versions of medieval times. These translations offer not only a glimpse of how a scholarly culture on the westernmost fringes of medieval Europe decided to present Latin poetry to non-Latin speakers of the day, but also provide a more general insight into the ways in which societies or subsections of societies translate works from earlier or "parallel" cultures into their own languages. To read a little of the Irish *Aeneid*, or the already brief Irish *Odyssey*, is to glimpse some different possibilities of translation, possibilities which occupy a curious modern no-man's-land between what we accept as translation and what we would call outright re-moulding.

We will, I am sure, laugh at some of the foibles of Irish translators as we look at excerpts here and there. For they and their language bear the unmistakable mark of medieval Ireland's blend of Christianity and ancient Celtic paganism. And we are unused to dealing with translation as the Irish translators of the classics did. While we are concerned with creating the illusion of distance between ourselves and our originals, the Irish translator was doing quite the reverse. He was incorporating the figures of Greek and Roman history and myth into his own very Gaelic culture. J. H. Delargy observes: "From the Gaelic cauldron of rebirth they emerged Gaelic in tongue as well as in appearance, taking on Irish dress, names, and citizenship, at liberty to move freely in the company of the stock characters of Irish oral fiction."[12] Delargy was thinking, particularly, of the mysterious Irish version of the *Odyssey*. But his observations might equally well apply to some of the other works of mostly Latin epic that were translated into Gaelic somewhere between the tenth and the fourteenth centuries A.D.

Anyone who has read parts of the Venerable Bede's history of the church is well enough aware of the enormous power and influence of Irish scholarship in the seventh and eighth centuries A.D. Ireland's preeminence stirred no little jealously in Britain: the Anglo-Saxon scholar Aldhelm, writing around A.D. 680–690, expostulates angrily:

> Why, I ask, is Ireland, to which hordes of students flock by the fleet load, bolstered by this inexpressible privilege? It is as if here in the fertile sod of Britain teachers who are citizens of Argos and Rome cannot be found, men who can unknot for learners the dark secrets of a library, and unlock their offices to the enquirer. Admittedly the countryside of the Ireland that I mentioned is rich and springlike, so as to speak, a pastureland rich in flocks of scholars as the heavens glisten with the stellar shimmerings of twinkling stars.[13]

The suzerainty of Irish scholarship was, however, well on the wane by the time that the large corpus of Irish translations of important works of Latin epic appeared, probably in the twelfth century. Ireland had been wracked by Norse and Norman invasions, and her students, without a university, were traveling to England and the continent to study.[14] Latin learning in Ireland had faded. So the Irish translations of Latin epic, notably of Vergil, Lucan, and Statius, appeared in a culture under siege, with a declining knowledge of antiquity and Latin. The Irish versions may well have had to serve the same sort of purpose that English translations do today: to keep alive an interest in and memory of ancient authors and traditions in a culture which has lost its grounding in Latin and ancient Greek.

Given the dominantly negative modern view of most Latin epic poetry after Vergil, it may seem surprising that there exist Middle Irish versions of the *Thebaid* and Lucan's *Pharsalia* in addition to versions of the tale of Troy and the story of Alexander. But we should recall that it was not until the mid-eighteenth century that Statius fell from critical favor, and not until the mid-nineteenth that Lucan did. Before then these writers stood with Vergil and Ovid in the front ranks of Latin poetry.[15]

Not only must we register some surprise that anyone thought it worthwhile to translate ancient epics into Gaelic—was there really such a potential public for them in medieval Scotland and Ireland?—but also recall that they are the earliest translations of Graeco-Roman epic into *any* vernacular by almost two hundred years. They are also very different from the earliest English, French, and Spanish versions (in the sixteenth and seventeenth centuries) of these epics because they Irish them in a way no English version ever Englishes them. The Irish *Aeneid* and *Thebaid* are a far remove from their originals in many ways. Indeed, the classicist looking at them might be tempted to dismiss them as simply variants on the original, not translations. The versions range from fairly close approximation to the original Latin to what appear wild adaptations so apparently jumbled that we might (wrongly) dismiss them as being on a par with the mythical confusion of Trimalchio in Petronius' *Satyricon* (52): "I have bowls . . . showing Daedalus shutting Niobe up in the Trojan Horse."

Lucan

The Irish translation of part of Lucan's *Pharsalia* (*In Cocadh Catharda*) is the closest of all to the modern notion of translation. But even it departs substantially from the original, as the following excerpt from Julius Caesar's speech to his troops before the Battle of Pharsalia in 48 B.C. (*Pharsalia* 7.250–53) will suggest:

Tamer of the world, guiding genius (*fortuna*) of my achievements, Soldier: it's here, the opportunity for the fight you've so often hoped for. No need for prayers. Call fate with your sword. In your hands you control how great Caesar will be.[16]

Now the Irish version, translated by Standish O'Grady:

Good people, ye are they who to this day have put the world under me; my destiny and my fortune, my gods whom I adore, are ye. For all good things that I have had, to you I render thanks. And to you now is come that which of old time, and long and often, ye have craved and chosen [i.e., longed for]: even the Great Battle. That which henceforth ye need to do is not [any more] to solicit, but by dint of your hands and weapons to make good your fortune; for in your forearms' strength, in your shoulders' sockets and in your hearts' hardness my fortune lies or my misfortune; my increase or my diminution, in this the Great Battle's day.[17]

There is no question that the Irish translator had Lucan before him or was thoroughly acquainted with his Latin text. But he expands the Latin. He is at pains to make sure his reader catches the multivalence of *fortuna:* destiny, fortune, gods whom I adore. Yet his expansion of Lucan's last two lines significantly changes the emphasis from Caesar to his soldiers. Some of Caesar's megalomania is lost, his harsher overtones muted. A little later in the same speech the Irish Caesar adds a touch that has no parallel whatever in Lucan's text. He says of Pompey's triumphs in apparent contrast to his own (*In Cocadh Catharda* 76): "Often as he may have come to Rome after subduing of one or of another race from among all these, it was not as though he came after conquest of Gaul, of them of Lochlann, and of Britain's island. . . ."[18] Either the Irish translator has misunderstood the extent of the Roman Caesar's conquests (which I rather doubt), or he is adding, for the sake of his Irish audience, a triumph which Caesar never earned but which would have made him stand high in their twelfth-century eyes: the conquest of Lochlann—Scandinavia, land of the Norse predators so well known to Irish history.

The Gaelic Lucan is the "closest" to its original, is remarkably self-contained. Lucan presents more of what one needs to know to understand his epic than does Vergil, who is notoriously "allusive". John Conington observed of Vergil's scenes on the gates of Apollo's temple in *Aeneid* 6 that they are unintelligible to the reader who does not already know the story that they tell.[19] Lucan, however, is less inclined than most Roman writers to rely on his reader's knowledge of myth and history, and thus presents fewer difficulties for readers of later ages. Indeed, my encounters with Irish versions of

Latin epic suggest that Lucan (and even Statius) are much more comprehensibly and elegantly presentable in translation to an audience which lacks detailed knowledge of Rome and things Roman than is Vergil, even an audience of the present day.

Vergil

The Irish translator of the *Aeneid* flattens Vergil's epic into a kind of annalistic chronicle. So he freely rearranges the order of the *Aeneid*'s books: he does not present *Aeneid* 1 until after *Aeneid* 2 and 3. As a result, the complex perspectives of Vergil's epic are lost, as they are lost in the modern classroom where the *Aeneid* is taught, and for the same reasons. The modern reader and his medieval Irish counterpart both need "background" to understand what is going on, and the Irish *Aeneid* is a kind of teaching text which takes account of the *Aeneid*'s inaccessibility to those unlearned in Roman history and Graeco-Roman myth. The teacher-translator offers a simplified translation blended with commentary for a reader shaped by the traditions of medieval Ireland rather than imperial Rome. He delivers only what he feels he can make intelligible. And the form he chooses is that of the traditional Irish prose *sceal*, a prose saga, if you will.

The Irish *Aeneid* gaelicizes the characters much more thoroughly than does the Irish *Pharsalia*. To illustrate my point, here is *Aeneid* 1.589–93, where Vergil describes Aeneas as Dido first sees him: "In head and shoulders he was like a god. For his divine mother herself had given him alluring, unscissored hair and the bright glow of youth and had breathed a happy sparkle into his eyes—the way hands add allure to ivory or when silver or marble from Paros is circled with blond gold."[20] Vergil's Aeneas, after Venus' treatment, is quite appropriately likened to a gilded cult statue. We may recall, in fact, the famous statue made by the Cypriot sculptor Pygmalion, and often assumed to be a figure of Venus—appropriately enough in this context where Dido, sister of another Pygmalion, will fall in love, but more tragically. Vergil's close positioning of the epithet *genetrix*, divine mother, (the title under which Julius Caesar and Augustus in particular worshiped Venus) to the word "*caesa*ries" (unscissored hair), describing Aeneas' locks imparts a curious sense that Aeneas' "descendants" are at one with him in this moment. The Irish translator aims for a different effect, as we see in George Calder's English version:

Pleasantly, comely, and well-born was the hero that came there—fair, yellow, golden hair upon him; a beautifully ruddy face he had; eyes deepset, lustrous in his head like an image of a god, the expression which Venus, his mother, with love's splendour threw into his face, so that whoever looked upon him should love him.[21]

The echoes of Caesar are lost. But surely the hint of Pygmalionic magic is not. Aeneas is saved from being an ivory, marble, or metal statue by the addition of a blush of life, much as Ovid shows us the blush of shame vitalizing Pygmalion's ivory statue in *Metamorphoses* 10.283–93 when her creator kisses her.[22] Ovid turns the statue into a woman, the Irish translator turns Aeneas into an Irishman with a ruddy face. He is, after all, Aenias MacAnaichis. So he acquires an appearance to suit his name.

Greek and Roman writers rarely detail the actual physical appearance of their characters. The only persons described in any detail in the *Iliad*, for example, are the ugly Thersites and the small Tydeus. Such omission was clearly more than a Celtic bard or scribe could tolerate, as we see not only in Aeneas' case but in that of Aeneas' young ally, Pallas, in *Aeneid* 8.587–91:

> In the middle of the column was Pallas himself, you could see him in his cloak and his ornamented armor. Like Lucifer drenched in the water of Ocean, the evening star that Venus loves before other fiery lights of stars, he suddenly raises his face, all sacred, in the sky and lightly looses the grip of darkness.[23]

The ominous stellar beauty of Vergil's doomed Pallas gives way to images of nature in springtime in the Irish. The images of Ocean suggest coral and pearls:

> Comely was the youth that was in their midst. Golden was the hair upon him, slightly curling; a clear blue eye in his head; like the prime of the wood in May or like the purple foxglove was each of his two cheeks. You would think that it was a shower of pearls that rained into his head. You would think his lips were a loop of coral. As white as the snow of one night were his neck and the rest of his skin. There were fine robes long, almost white, to the extremities of his hands and his feet. A purple fringed mantle about him. A pin of precious stone set in gold upon his breast. A necklace of gold about his neck.[24]

The details of his dress and arms continue. But we have the idea. Pallas' beauty is that of a Celt, and his golden necklace, his *muntorc*, the standard mark of the Celtic warrior from the earliest archaeological records and traditions, to the dying Gaul statue at Pergamum, and the dawn of Celtic literature in the Old Welsh Lament of

Llywarch Hen for Gwen, the favorite of his twenty-four sons, who wore a gold torque and died fighting the Saxons.[25]

The halls of Dido's palace also have a rather Gaelic feel in the Irish *Aeneid*. Vergil's "massive silver on the tables and the brave deeds of ancestors embossed in gold—*ingens argentum mensis, caelataque in auro/fortia facta partrum*" (*Aeneid* 1.640) are elaborated into a strikingly Celtic panorama: "Many were the drinking-horns with embossings, and goblets, and beautiful ancestral cups of gold and silver in the hands of free-born boys of noble birth a-serving in it."[26] Of course the Greeks and Romans had drinking-horns. But they were not the characteristic vessels of the Graeco-Roman royal dining hall as they were of the northern European. Further, the Greek and Roman tradition of having slave boys wait upon high kings would have seemed degrading to an Irish audience. So the translator imports free-born boys to serve the drinks.

Vergil's geography also takes on an Irish touch. The tawny, yellow Tiber does not conform at all to the Irish notion of a beautiful river. So herewith Aeneas' arrival in Italy, first in Vergil (*Aeneid* 7.29–36):

> And here Aeneas saw a huge grove as he looked out from the sea-surface. From here the Tiber, in delightful steaming, bursts out into the sea with whirling eddies, blond with sand. Around and above in their variety, birds of the shore and marshy estuary incessantly beguiled the sky with song and flew out of the grove.

Now the Irish *Aeneid*:

> At that time Aeneas beheld a beautiful sacred grove on the sea bank whence issues the river Tiber and flocks of birds of every species of bird floating on the *clear* waters of estuary; and it was enough of joy to listen to the many strains which those birds used to sing.[27]

More like the entrance to Purgatory in Dante, according to Calder (p. 350).

The translator accommodates other features of the *Aeneid* to what may be Irish sensibilities. Aeneas' capture of the sons of Sulmo and Ufens in *Aeneid* 10.217–20 to use as human sacrifices at the funeral of Pallas is so muted and changed that Calder offers his own glosses in his translation of the Irish:

> *Sulmone creatos*
> *quattuor hic iuvenes, totidem quos educat Ufens,*
> *viventis rapit, inferias quos immolet umbris*
> *captivoque rogi perfundat sanguine flammas.*
> (*Aeneid* 10.217–20)

Then, four youths, sons of Sulmo, and as many reared by Ufens,
he takes alive, to offer as victims to the dead and to sprinkle
the funeral flame with captive blood.

(tr. H. Rushton Fairclough)

Dohoit les na ceithri cathmilid, iiiii meic. . . .

There fell by him ⟨sc. Aeneas⟩ the four battle soldiers [of Sulmo], four
sons [of Ufens] . . . .

(tr. George Calder, pp. 160–61)

The Irish translator is uncomfortable with Aeneas' human sacrifices.
He not only has Aeneas kill the young men instead of reserving
them for sacrifice, but he also suppresses the names of their fathers,
Sulmo and Ufens (even though he follows up with an extensive and
supplemented list of the names of Aeneas' other victims immediately
afterwards). Calder compensates by supplying the omitted names,
thus diminishing our sensitivity to what the Irish translator has done.

As the translator makes the *Aeneid* Irish and accomodates it to
Irish sensitivities, he dovetails it into the scheme of bibilical Christianity by means of curious supplements to the text. Latinus' genealogy in *Aeneid* 7.47–49, for example, runs as follows:

We have been told that he was the child of Faunus and a Laurentian
nymph, Marica. Picus was Faunus' father, and he says you, Saturn,
were his parent and the original source of his bloodline.[28]

The Irish translator (himself translated by George Calder) renders:

They reached Latinus son of Picus, son of Neptune, son of Saturn,
son of Pal (Apollo?), son of Picus, son of Pel, son of Tres, son of Tros,
son of Mizraim, son of Ham, son of Noah.[29]

At the other extreme, the Irish translator gives an altogether
different twist to Jupiter's famous comment to Venus in *Aeneid*
1.279: "I have given empire without end: *imperium sine fine dedi*"
which finds its expression in the Irish *Aeneid* at the very end of the
epic: "And from the seed of Aeneas, Ascanius and Lavinia, have
sprung Roman lords, and king-folk, and rulers of the world from
thenceforward till the judgment-day shall come. So that these are
the wanderings of Aeneas Meic Anaichis, as above."[30]

The modern commentator might sense a historical irony in the
notion of Rome's empire without end, as, a century after Vergil,
Lucan did. Lucan saw in Caesar's power the suppression of Roman
freedom: "We have," he said, "been cast down upon until the end
of time: *in totum mundi prosternimur aevum*" (Pharsalia 7.640).
But the Gaelic translator goes beyond even the most optimistic in-

terpretation of Vergil's Jupiter. He sees Rome as the capital city of Christianity, the *civitas dei* on earth.[31] Thus the foundation of that city, and the life of its migrant creator, have different, more personal, and *spiritual* significance for him than for either Vergil or the modern scholar. Perhaps appropriately, the Irish scribe concludes in a sentence identifying himself in a blend of Latin, Hebrew, and Gaelic:

> *Finit, Amen, Finit Solamh o Droma nomine scripsit.*
> Finished, Amen, Finished! He wrote it, Solomon O'Droma by name.

Not only does the Irish translator adapt the text to what I would assume to be the tastes of his contemporary reader, but, to ensure the reader is not alienated from the text, he either leaves out, or resolves in a straightforward manner, the incongruities and puzzles of the *Aeneid*, much as some of our modern translators of Sophocles do. He is obviously aware, for instance, that Aeneas' departure from the underworld through the Gate of Ivory presents a problem and demands an explanation, since Vergil specifically tells us that through the Ivory Gate "the spirits of the dead send dreams that deceive: *falsa ad caelum mittunt insomnia manes*" (*Aeneid* 6.896). Vergil is clearly leaving the puzzle to the reader to resolve, and does not even tell us where the Sibyl goes (6.897–99): "With these, then, Anchises follows Aeneas—and with him the Sibyl—with these words. And he sends them out through the Ivory Gate. He cuts a path back to the ships and joins his friends again."[32] So the Irish translator appends an explanation:

> They came away from out of Hades by the ivory door, and the Sibyl departed to her cave, and Aeneas to his ships; and of that history which he had seen, nothing remained to Aeneas but a vision in his mind like a man who has been dreaming, or who is at the point of death.[33]
>
> (tr. George Calder, p. 93)

This is not the only way the translator rearranges or develops what Vergil says. He routinely supplements Vergil when he feels such supplement is necessary, as does the translator of Statius' *Thebaid*, not only to explain his original, but to *correct* Vergil when he thinks Vergil is wrong, or has omitted something.

The Treacherous Aeneas

Like other medieval readers and critics of Vergil, such as the twelfth-century Bernardus Silvestris, who wrote a fascinating allegorical commentary on the first six books of the *Aeneid*, the Irish *Aeneid* translator obviously drew on the mysterious traditions best known to medieval writers from the second century A.D. writer Dares Phrygius.[34] Dares suggests that Aeneas, along with his fellow Trojan Antenor, betrayed Troy.

Startling as the suggestion of a treacherous Aeneas may sound to modern ears, conditioned by the solemn interpretations of Vergil's epic from the nineteenth century onwards, the traitor Aeneas was an ancient motif.[35] Dionysius of Halicarnassus, a contemporary of Vergil's, reports in his *Roman Antiquities* 1.48 that Menecrates of Xanthus (a writer of the fourth century B.C.) said that Aeneas himself overthrew Priam and became one of the Greeks. And the early Roman epicist Naevius seems aware that there is some doubt about "the terms under which Aeneas left Troy—*Aenea quo pacto/Troiam urbem liquerit.*"[36] The tradition of Aeneas the betrayer is hardly even mentioned in modern editions and translations of the *Aeneid* despite the presence of some curious traces of it in the text. But they are clearly presented by Vergil's Irish translator, who opens the *Aeneid* not, as Vergil does, with the vengeance of Juno on the Trojans and the great storm at sea, but in the Greek camp outside Troy, where Agamemnon faces a dispute among the Greeks and asks "what counsel they would give him respecting those that had betrayed the city." He continues: "The counsel which they voiced and decided on was to lay Troy waste and drive the traitors out of it without killing them. . . . Agamemnon enjoined Aeneas and Antenor to leave Troy waste."

At the same time, the Irish translator shows more evenhandedness than Dares Phrygius who, like the other much used early A.D. commentator on the Trojan War, Dictys of Crete, makes no mention of Aeneas' foundation of the Roman race—a theme which Vergil so mightily emphasizes. The Irish *Aeneid* easily integrates the Vergilian with the conflicting Dares and Dictys traditions. He also rearranges the early narrative so that it follows what Bernardus Silvestris would have called "the natural order of narration"—an order which Vergil, like Terence, often disregards in favor of what Bernardus calls "artistic" (*artificialis*) order.[37]

Statius

Statius made as profound an impression as Lucan upon, say, Dante, Chaucer, and Pope, not to mention the Gaelic-speaking lords of medieval Ireland; and there is no reason to doubt that he enjoyed considerable popularity in his own day.[38] Today the open-minded may give Statius' *Thebaid*, perhaps, a cursory glance in translation. Unfortunately, the only English translation of the *Thebaid* readily accessible to the modern reader is J. H. Mozley's, in the Loeb Classical Library; and Mozley observes in his preface: "To be the author of a great epic poem is to count as one of the few great poets of the world, it need hardly be said that Statius can make no claim to that honor."[39] The Latinless reader of Statius, or the classicist in a hurry, is at Mozley's mercy. He learns from the preface that the original is second-rate even before he gets to the translation—which does nothing to dispel that illusion.

It has been common to talk of the "excesses" of Latin epic from Lucan onwards, the emphasis on self-destruction and horror, as if these were not topics appropriate to literature and as if they were the products of a morbid fantasy rather than images of real life. H. E. Butler, for instance, argued in his influential *Post-Augustan Poetry* that Statius ought to have known better than to write on the subject of the war of the Seven against Thebes: "The Theban legend is unsuitable for epic treatment for more reasons than one. In the first place the story is unpleasant from beginning to end."[40] One could wreak havoc with Greek tragedy too if one applied this kind of tone in discussing, say, Sophocles' Theban plays. Of Statius' battles Butler remarks (p. 221): "Homer knew what fighting was from personal experience, or at least from being in touch with warriors who had killed their man. Vergil had come no closer to these things than 'in the pages of a book.' Statius is yet one remove further from the truth than Vergil." Whether Homer saw (much less fought in) battles, or anything else for that matter, we will never know. Some doubt his existence. But Vergil and Statius, of course, *had* known civil war in their times. And killing was never farther away than the arena.

The fallacies in Butler's reasoning have not prevented scholars from accepting his conclusions even if, when pressed, they would reject the steps by which he reached them. What is really being said by modern critics is simply this: What Statius is saying does not interest me and is not in accord with what Latin literature should be like. Even Statius' admirers often reason that the poet could not possibly be suggesting any parallel between the mythical civil wars between the two sons of Oedipus, Eteocles and Polynices, and the civil wars of Rome in his own day. It is, then, hardly surprising that the poet's detractors find him irrelevant.

The scribe who copied the Gaelic translation of the *Thebaid* in 1487 presumably did not share such feelings about the epic's lack of relevance to his own day, as these excerpts from his prefatory note will suggest. The English translation is that of George Calder in *Togail na Tebe* (Cambridge: Cambridge University Press, 1922), p. xxiii:

> This book was written in A.D. 1487, and, in the same year died O'Reilly, to wit, Turlough, son of John; and in the same year were slain the sons of O'Rourke, to wit, Tiernan and Brian Roe, to wit, Tiernan was slain by the sons of MacDermot and by Muinteir-Eolais in treachery, and Brian by a son of O'Rourke, to wit, by Owen, son of Felim, son of Donough, son of Tiernan; and in the same year was slain Tiernan Duv, son of Donough Blind-eye Tiernan by O'Donnell, to wit by Hugh Roe O'Donnell and by the sons of O'Rourke; and in the same year the fortress of Lough Oughter was taken possession of by the race of Donnell Ban O'Reilly, and by myself, Dermot. It was finished on the island of Inishannon upon Thursday during the feast of St. Catherine. . . . *And at the same period there were two bishops in the bishopric of Kilmore, to wit, Cormac, son of the bishop Magauran, and Thomas son of Andrew Mac-Brady, each of them alleging that he himself is bishop there.* . . . And in the same year was slain Ua Mael-Shechlain, to wit, Laighnech Ua Mael-Shechlain, by Conn, son of Art ua Mael-Shechlain. And may the blessing of God rest on the soul of him that wrote this book. And there was war between Magauran and O'Reilly, to wit John O'Reilly, in that same year; and another war between the descendants of Teige O'Rourke, etc.

The concluding *etcetera* is the most telling touch. The wars of the mere two sons of Oedipus and two mere cities would not, I think, have seemed overblown and exaggerated to the scribe (or the author) of the Gaelic *Thebaid*. And our century has witnessed horrors unimagined by the most extravagant flight of ancient or medieval fancy. But the Latinist persists in feeling that such horrors are not the proper subject of poetry.

The Irish Ulysses

So far I have discussed only Latin epics in Irish versions, for the fairly obvious reason that Greek epic was not widely known in medieval Ireland. But the most detailed section of this paper now examines the very brief, but fascinating, Irish tale based upon the *Odyssey*. It is a baffling work which *must* owe something of its origin, however little, to Homer, even though R. T. Meyer is right when he observes that it "contains only a few waifs and strays of the Homeric account."[41]

The chief episode of interest for us here is Penelope's recognition and acknowledgment of Ulysses after he enters her bedroom through a long tunnel. I cite the translation by Kenneth Jackson, adding, for completeness, the final interchanges of Penelope and Ulysses:

> "Good people," said the queen, "who are you at all?" "I am Ulysses son of Laertes," said he. "You are not the Ulysses whom I knew," said she. "I am indeed," he said, "and I will describe my credentials"; and then he told of their secrets and their talks together and their hidden thoughts. "What has happened to your looks, or your men," said she, "if you are Ulysses?" "They are lost," he said. "What was the last of your keepsakes that you left with me?" she said. "A golden brooch," said he, "with a silver head; and I took your brooch with me when I went into the ship, and it was then you turned your back from me," said Ulysses. "That is true," she said, "and if you were Ulysses you would ask after your dog." "I had not thought it would be alive at all," he said. "I made it a broth of long life," said she, "because I saw that Ulysses loved it greatly. And what sort of a dog at all is that dog?" she said. "It has white sides and a light crimson back and a jet-black belly and a green tail," said Ulysses. "That is the description of the dog," she said, "and no one in the place dares give it its food except myself and you and the steward." "Bring the dog in," said he. And four men went to fetch it, and brought it in with them. And when it heard the sound of Ulysses' voice, it gave a tug at its chain so that it laid the four men all over the house behind it, and jumped at Ulysses' breast and licked his face. When Ulysses' people saw that, they leaped towards him. Whoever could not get at his skin to kiss him covered his clothes with kisses.[42]
>
> "You are Ulysses," she said. "I am," he said.[43]

The key to Ulysses' recognition in the Irish version, then, is the acknowledgment of Ulysses by his dog in front of Penelope and the entire household. And it is a prelude to the joyful embraces of all present. We are given no hint that there is serious trouble on the home front. No suitors have been killed, the majority of the household staff has not been wiped out, as in Homer, before Penelope's acceptance of her returned husband. The only trace of Homeric suitors is the presence of an unknown man in Penelope's bedroom, whom Ulysses resists killing, and who turns out to be his son. The faithful dog, of course, does have a Homeric counterpart: Argus, who recognizes his returning master in *Odyssey* 17.290–327, long before Penelope accepts Odysseus as her husband. And the ragged, aged Argus is a far remove from the sprightly animal we see in the Irish text. Homer assures us that no one took care of Argus during Odysseus' absence:

> He lies cast away while his lord is away, upon a heap of manure from mules and oxen which was poured in good quantity in front of the gateway so Odysseus' servants could take it to manure his great estate. Here lies the dog Argus, teeming with dog-ticks. And when he sensed that Odysseus was near, he wagged his tail and pricked up both his ears. He no longer had the strength to come closer to his lord who saw him from a distance and, undetected by Eumaeus, shed a tear. . . . (297–305)

Argus, an outcast from his master's estate, has acknowledged his master as openly as he can; but his master cannot acknowledge his dog other than with a secret tear. Odysseus' recognition of Argus is as covert and personal as such moments can be in literature—between the hero, the poet, and ourselves. And the scene ends on a note of great pathos. For when Odysseus and Eumaeus leave him and head for the palace, the faithful dog dies: "His lot of dark death took Argus the moment he saw Odysseus—in this twentieth year" (326–27).

Argus and the Irish Wolfhounds

An Irish audience would have had some difficulties with Homer's Argus. In Irish tradition, dogs have a much more significant role than they have in classical epic and tragedy. The greatest of all Irish heroes, Setanta, is better known as CuChulainn, "the Dog of Culann (the smith)," because he killed the *archu*, the "slaughter hound" or guard dog that watched over Culann's house, and was thus obliged to serve as its replacement.[44] And hounds mark the end of CuChulainn's life too. He is forced by three old hags to violate the taboo (Irish *geis*) of eating "his namesake, the dog," as he heads off toward the battle where he will die.[45] When, weakened by his violation of *geis* and wounded in the fight, CuChulainn goes, with his enemies' permission, to wash himself in a loch: "an otter—the Irish word means 'water-dog'—comes to drink the blood. CuChulainn casts a stone at it and kills it. Now he knows that he must die, for it has been prophesied that his last heroic deed, like his first, will be the killing of a dog."[46] Nor is CuChulainn's association with the dog unique in the *Tain* tradition. One of CuChulainn's victims, Conbel, who is called both an *archu*, "slaughter-hound," and *cu*, "hound," is replaced by a dog when he dies, as Alfred W. De Quoy notes in his brilliant study of Irish wolfhounds in Irish culture; and the sound made by the warrior Conor's sword is compared "to the howls of a 'dog of war,' i.e., '*archu*.'"[47]

Hound and hero enjoyed, then, a curious closeness in Ireland. Indeed, ownership of hounds was a mark of high social class. De Quoy points out that of the seven grades of society recognized by the *Senchus Mor*, the "Great Old Law Book," only a king and the two highest grades of chief were permitted to keep hounds, and a law recorded in the sixteenth century reaffirms the point:

QUERY. Who is entitled to keep a greyhound?

ANSWER. A chief.

QUERY. Who is entitled to keep a lapdog?

ANSWER. A young Hospitaller; a Doctor; a Harper and a Chief's wife.[48]

Quarrels over the ownership of hounds could lead to violence: the *Book of Lecan* tells of Cosnamhach Mor, killed in 1162 in a dispute over a greyhound puppy.[49] And the loss of a fine hound elicits several touching laments, none better known than that for the departure of Bran, a wolfhound who ran away after being struck by his master Finn. There can be little doubt that the author of the Irish *Odyssey*, as he describes Ulysses' dog with its "white sides and a light crimson back and a jet-black belly and a green tail," has the following description of Bran in mind (despite its textual difficulties):

> Two white sides had Bran
> and a fresh crimson shining tail.
> His crimson haunch was well apportioned,
> stretching from his tail to the end of his back.
>
> He had four blue feet
> for going by night and day,
> green paws that . . . not battle
> and gleaming pale-red claws.[50]

The Homeric Argus has become like Bran, the Irish epic hound, in all its glorious color.

Argus *and the* Archu

The Irish *Odyssey* is a much more complete assimilation of a classical original than the Irish *Aeneid*. It is more like a dim memory of the *Odyssey* tradition preserved in a folkloric resin. The Irish archetype has almost completely absorbed the alien text into itself. Yet since all literary translation involves a massive assimilation of the original to the foster tradition, what has happened to the *Odyssey* in Irish differs in degree rather than in kind from what has happened to the *Aeneid*. It has been subjected to more stages of processing before reaching its surviving Gaelic form.

Yet the Irish *Odyssey* may, curiously enough, offer new perspectives on the Homeric original. The world of Bran and CuChulainn suggests a European hunter and herder society more primitive than that of the Greek *Odyssey*, even though the Homeric text predates the Irish by about two thousand years. Homer's *Odyssey* suggests a world where the hunting, herding hero with his fierce hounds has largely been absorbed into a more sophisticated warrior hero. The students of Cheiron (who, according to the *On Hunter* (1.1–5) attributed to Xenophon, was given charge of "wild beasts and hounds"— *agrai* and *kynes*—by Apollo and Artemis) include Achilles, Odysseus, Amphiaraus, Theseus, and Aeneas—prominent heroes in Graeco-Roman epic. But only Odysseus is shown as having a special dog or dogs. Outside the surviving epic tradition we have, of course, the club-wielding Hercules who, like CuChulainn, is famous for his participation in cattle raids, his capture of Cerberus, the guard dog of the underworld, and for his prowess in mastering confrontation with animals both wild and domestic. In fact, his monstrous, destructive rages are reminiscent of the battle fury of an Irish warrior. Similarly, Theseus' skill at dealing with wild bulls, and above all with the Minotaur, or the famous tale of the heroes who hunt the Calydonian boar, recall the world of the Irish *sceal*.

In Homer, heroic hunting and herding skills are subordinated to prowess with weapons and words. And there is not much to suggest that dogs are held in high honor. The word "dog" is more suggestive of contempt and distaste, the animals themselves reviled as seekers of carrion on battlefields and never hailed as participants in the struggle for cities. But there are glimpses of an older order. In *Iliad* 23.161–77 Achilles slaughters numerous humans and animals on the pyre of his beloved Patroclus, but kills only two of his friend's nine lapdogs ("table-dogs," Homer calls them). In the *Odyssey* we are not allowed to forget that it is the killing of the forbidden Cattle of the Sun, not the Trojan War, which robs Odysseus of his companions and leaves him to return alone. And Odysseus' connection with hunting and hounds first establishes his identity in Ithaca. The old Argus knows who Odysseus is before any human does. The old Eurycleia recognizes him by an old hunting-wound (*Odyssey* 17.361–502). The age and decrepitude of the Homeric Argus owe something not only to the realistic passing of time, but to the dog's symbolic importance as part of an older order of heroic narrative.

In that older order, which still survived in medieval Ireland, the relationship between hero and hound can amount, as we have seen, even to literary interchangeability. Thus an attack on the hero's hound can be tantamount to an attack on the hero himself. By the same token, a rejection of the hound may amount to the rejection of the hero. In the context of the Homeric epic, the fact that Argus is lying upon a heap of mule and cow dung may seem little more than a symbol of his total rejection by Odysseus' household. No one, including Penelope, has taken care of him. But one detail may hint at a larger significance. In one of the *Ancient Laws and Institutes of Ireland*, cited by De Quoy, we find the following provision in the event that a dog urinates or defecates on someone else's property:

> The excrement must be removed as well as the soil under it until there is no evidence of any liquid. Sod is put down and *covered with cow dung* for one month. The ground is then tamped down with the heel and fine clay of the same quality as that in the adjacent soil is added. Compensation must be paid to the landowner: butter, dough, and curds, each in the same bulk as that of the excrement. Moreover, if the offense occurred in the presence of the dog's owner, the latter is liable for trespass.[51]

The sense of the law is that if the dog is present on land long enough to relieve himself, he is establishing some kind of territorial claim on behalf of his master—a claim which demands legal recompense. The cow dung marks the attempt to separate, ritually, dog and master from their claim to the property. Thus one could envisage a scenario in which Odysseus' Argus is not simply lying in filth and on filth, but defying ritual attempts to alienate him—and through him, his absent master—from the estate in Ithaca. He dies as Odysseus crosses back into his own territory and can reclaim it for himself. The watchful hound is now replaced by his master. His role in the epic, and, in a larger sense, heroic Greek society, is over, and he dies.

The Irish *Odyssey* does not collaborate to the full and make the symmetry complete by playing on the hound's name, by making Argus an *archu*.[52] Ulysses' dog is not named; and he is called, as CuChulainn is most of the time, a *cu* rather than an *archu*. Nonetheless, the "slaughter hound," the Irish *cu* or *archu*, is as alive in Irish tradition as he is obsolete in Greek. Hence Argus, as he is transposed from the *Odyssey* to the *Merugud Uilix Mac Leirtis*, is revitalized, indeed metamorphosed, by the culture into which he is translated. He is not rejected by the household and Penelope, he does not have to die as his master returns.

Conclusion

Could it be, then, that there are moments when the Irish versions of classical works may open up windows on classical texts, as well as offer important insights into the development of Irish literature— not to mention entertainment in their own right? For whenever the early literature of a rapidly developing culture is translated into the idiom of an ancient culture of similar origin that has not "progressed" at nearly so rapid a speed, the forward flow of time is reversed, the new may seem to reach back beyond the old. We recognize in the Celtic Gloucester Head of the first century A.D. a Greek head of Mycenaean times, or in an iron age Irish building a structure echoing the tombs of Nestor's Pylos. As Vergil's Pallas is gaelicized by the Irish translator, his "up-dating" equips him with the warrior's torque necklace, examples of which are found in Ireland dating back to over a millennium and a half before Vergil's birth. How appropriate that the same reversal of time, through the metamorphosis of translation, can bring back to colorful life Odysseus' hound, who was obsolete and dying as the *Odyssey* was composed.

NOTES

1. See Peter Arnott's perceptive comments in "Greek Drama and the Modern Stage," in *The Craft and Context of Translation*, ed. William Arrowsmith and Roger Shattuck (New York: Anchor Books, 1964), 116–17.

2. Richard Stoneman, *Daphne into Laurel: Translations of Classical Poetry from Chaucer to the Present*, (London: Duckworth, 1982), 30.

3. *The Iliad of Homer*, tr. Richmond Lattimore (Chicago: University of Chicago Press, 1951), 55.

4. *Four Plays by Aristophanes*, ed. William Arrowsmith (New York: New American Library, 1984), 344.

5. "The Impossibilities of Translation," in Arrowsmith and Shattuck, eds., 96.

6. *Sophocles: Oedipus Tyrannus*, tr. Luci Berkowitz and Theodore F. Brunner (New York: W. W. Norton, 1970), 21.

7. *Sophocles: The Three Theban Plays*, tr. Robert Fagles, with introductions and notes by Bernard Knox (New York: Viking Press, 1982), 212.

8. Forms of the verb *audao* generally express the idea of not necessarily well-informed talk in the *Oedipus*. In line 731 Jocasta, commenting on the report that Laios was killed at a place where three roads meet, says: "This is what was said (*eudato*) and still is said." Similarly, in line 527 the chorus, talking to Creon about accusations that he "set up" Teiresias to accuse

Oedipus, comments: *eudato men tade, oida d'ou gnomei tini*: "That's what was said—though whether it was correct, I do not know."

9. *Sophocles: Oedipus the King*, tr. Kenneth Cavander with an introduction by Tom Driver (San Francisco: Chandler Publishing Company, 1961), 29.

10. Ibid.

11. *Sophocles Oedipus Rex*, ed. R. D. Dawe (Cambridge: Cambridge University Press, 1982), ad loc.

12. "The Gaelic Story-teller," *Proceedings of the British Academy* 31 (Sir John Rhys Memorial Lecture, 1945), 36.

13. The Latin text can be found in R. Ehwald, *Monumenta Germaniae Historica: Auctores Antiquissimi* 15 (Berlin: Weidmann, 1919), 492; for additional comments on this passage see M. Herren, *The Hisperica Famina* (Toronto: Pontifical Institute of Medieval Studies, 1974), 36.

14. W. B. Standford, *Ireland and the Classical Tradition* (Dublin: Allen Figgis & Co., 1976), 12–14.

15. The Irish versions of Roman epic are wholly or partially accessible to the reader with limited or no Irish in "literal" English versions, and there has been a small amount of scholarly discussion, most notably by R. T. Meyer, "The Sources of the Middle-Irish *Alexander*," *Modern Philology* 47 (1949): 1–7; "The Middle-Irish *Odyssey*: Folktale, Fiction, or Saga?" ibid. 50 (1952): 73–78; *Merugud Uilix Maic Leirtis* (Medieval and Modern Irish Series, vol. 17) (Dublin: Institute for Advanced Studies, 1958); "The Middle-Irish Version of the *Pharsalia* of Lucan," *Papers of the Michigan Academy of Science, Arts, and Letters* 44 (1959): 355–63; "The Middle-Irish Version of the *Thebaid* of Statius," ibid. 47 (1962): 687–99; "The Middle-Irish *Odyssey* and Celtic Folktale," ibid. 46 (1961): 533–61; "The Middle-Irish Version of the *Aeneid*," *Tennessee Studies in Literature* 9 (1966): 97–108; "The Middle-Irish Version of the Story of Troy," *Etudes Celtiques* 17 (1980): 205–18.

16. *O domitor mundi, rerum fortuna mearum,*
    miles, adest totiens optatae copia pugnae.
    nil opus est votis, iam fatum accersite ferro.
    in manibus vestris quantus sit Caesar habetis.

17. *adhedmuinter issib rotairbir indoman fumsa cosaniu. issib motoice ocus mo conach ocus mo dee adartha. is frib beirim buidi cachmaitiusa fuarus riam. doriact anois cucuib inni cafuilti iarraid ocus togha cofada ocus cominicc anallana i in cath mor. ocus ni herigti ales diarraid festa acht inconac do cosnam allos farlam ocus farnarm uairisanertaib barriged ocus ambonaib barnguland ocus icruas barcraided ita moconachsa no mo doc nac no mo medugad no mo laigdiugad isin losa in morcata (75).*

18. *cid minic tisad donroim arclod ciniuda dibsin nihinand occus tissad arclod nagallia ocus locta Loclainne ocus innsi Bretan.*

19. John Conington, *P. Vergili Maronis Opera* (3 vols.) 4th ed., rev. Henry Nettleship (London: Whittaker & Co., 1884), 2: 430 (note on *Aeneid* 6.28).

20. *os umerosque deo similis; namque ipsa decoram*
caesariem nato genetrix lumenque iuventae
purpureum et laetos oculis adflarat honores:
quale manus addunt ebori decus, aut ubi flavo
argentum Pariusque lapis circumdatur auro.

The Vergilian passage itself echoes *Odyssey* 23.156–62, where Odysseus' beauty is enhanced for the eyes of the hesitant Penelope.

21. *Mong findbuidi fororda fair, gnuis caem corcurda aigi, ruisc cochlacha*
caindelta ina chind cosmail re delb ndea, in delb rola a mathair i Uenir, o li
serce ina ghnuis, co rocarad gach aen he in nech rosillfed fair.

Imtheachta Aeniasa: The Irish Aeneid (London: D. Nutt for the Irish Texts Society, 1907), 22 & 23. For *caesaries* and Caesar see Frederick Ahl, *Metaformations: Soundplay and Wordplay in Ovid and Other Classical Poets* (Ithaca: Cornell University Press, 1985), 74–81.

22. The Irish translator seems well aware of the importance of the blush as a motif in Latin epic. See Ahl, 245–70.

23.   *ipse agmine Pallas*
in medio, chlamyde et pictis conspectus in armis:
qualis ubi Oceani perfusus Lucifer unda,
quem Venus ante alios astrorum diligit ignis,
extulit os sacrum caelo tenebrasque resolvit.

24. *Ba cruthach an maccaem robai etarru. Mong fhocos orbhuidhi fair, rosc*
gorm glainidi ina chind. Ba cosmail ri forcleithi cailli cetemuin no fri sian slebi
cechtar a dha gruadh. Anddar lat ba fras do nemandaib rolad ina ceand.
Anddar lat ba dual partlaingi a beoil. Ba gilithir ri sneachta n-aen aidchi a
braigi ocus a cneas ar cheana, at e seme fata fogeal co hindaib a lamh ocus a
cos. Brat corcra corrthorach uime. Liagdelg oir ara bruinde. Muntorc oir ima
braighit (Imtheachta-Aeniasa, 120–22).

25. See Ifor Williams, *The Beginnings of Welsh Poetry*, ed. Rachael Bromwich (Cardiff: University of Wales Press, 1980), 139, 158.

26. *Batar imda cuirnd ci n-imdenum, ocus bledheda, ocus buancopain ailli*
orda ocus airgit i l-lamaib mac saerclanda soicheneoil oc fri dail inti (24).

27. *atque hic Aeneas ingentem ex aequore lucum*
prospicit. hunc inter fluvio Tiberinus amoeno
verticibus rapidis et multa flavus harena
in mare prorumpit. variae circumque supraque
adsuetae ripis volucres et fluminis alveo
aethera mulcebant cantu lucoque volabant.

Adconnairc Aenias uadh in tan sin fidnemedh alaind for bru in mara bail asa
tic sruth Tibir, ocus elta do enaib gach ceniuil ein oc snamh for duim in inbir,
ocus ba lor d'aebnius cloisteacht frisna hil-ceolaibh doghnitis na heoin sin (93).

28. *hunc Fauno et nympha genitum Laurente Marica*
accipimus; Fauno Picus pater, isque parentem
te, Saturne, refert, tu sanguinis ultimus auctor.

29. *Laitin mac Puin meic Picc meic Neptuin meic Saduirn meic Pal loir meic*
Pic meic Pel meic Tres meic Trois meic Mesraim meic Caimh meic Noe (92–94).

30. *ocus is do shil Aeniasa ocus Asgain ocus Lavina rogenetar flaithi ocus*
rigraidh Roman ocus oirigh in domuin o sin riam co ti in brath (200).

31. The scribe seems to have worked around 1400; the translation itself is of uncertain date.

32. *his ibi tum natum Anchises unaque Sibyllam*
    prosequitur dictis portaque emittit eburna,
    ille viam secat ad navis sociosque revisit.

33. *Tancatar uad a h-iffern arin dorus n-eburnete ocus dochuaidh Sibill dia huaim, ocus docuaid Aenias dochum a long, ocus ni roibi d'Aenias don sceol sin adconnairc acht taibsi ina menmain amal bis duine iar n-aislinge no i remeg.*

34. For Bernardus Silvestris, see *The Commentary on the First Six Books of the Aeneid of Vergil Commonly Attributed to Bernardus Silvestris*, ed. J. W. Jones and E. F. Jones (Lincoln: University of Nebraska Press, 1977), and *A Commentary on the First Six Books of Virgil's Aeneid by Bernardus Silvestris*, tr. with introduction & notes by E. G. Schreiber and T. E. Maresca (Lincoln: University of Nebraska Press, 1979). Dares Phrygius was translated into Irish in the Middle Ages and known by the title *Togail Troi (Destruction of Troy)*. The text (of the sections corresponding to Dares Phrygius chs. 2–11 and 14–19) is found (with following English translation) in Whitley Stokes and Wilhelm Windisch, *Irische Texte mit Übersetzungen und Wörterbuch* (Leipzig: S. Hirzel, 1884), 1–141. The Irish translator felt free to supplement the original Dares, as Stokes observes (1). For a full discussion see R. T. Meyer, "The Middle-Irish Version of the Story of Troy," 206–18.

35. See G. K. Galinski, *Aeneas, Sicily and Rome* (Princeton: Princeton University Press, 1969), esp. 46–53 for a convenient summary of the various traditions.

36. Naevius' *Punica* fr. 23—*Aeneas quo pacto/Troiam urbem liquerit.*

37. See Jones and Jones, 1–2.

38. This section is a modified version of my discussion in "Statius' *Thebaid*: A Reconsideration," *Aufstieg und Niedergang der römischen Welt* 32.5 (1986): 2803–2912 (esp. 2804–2811 and the sources cited there).

39. J. H. Mozley, *Statius* (Cambridge: Harvard University Press, 1928), xiv.

40. H. E. Butler, *Post-Augustan Poetry* (Oxford: Oxford University Press, 1909), 208.

41. *Merugud Uilix Maic Leirtis*, xiv; cf. Meyer's "The Middle-Irish Odyssey," and Robin Flower, *The Irish Tradition* (Oxford: Oxford University Press, 1946), 137.

42. K. H. Jackson, *A Celtic Miscellany* (Harmondsworth: Penguin Books, 1971), 57–58.

43. *"A daine maithi," ar in rigan, "carsa cia sib-si etir?" "Uilix mac Leirtis misi," ar se. "Ni tu int Uilix rob aichnid duine-ne," ar si. "Is me co deimin," ar se, "ocus indesad mo chomartha duit." ocus docuaidh ina ruinib ocus ina comraitib ocus ina derridib. "Caidi do delb ocus do muinter," ar si, "masa tu Uilix?" "Docuadar amugu," ar se. "Craed fo derid dud chomartaib ro fagais agum-sa?" "Delg oir," ar se, "ocus cend airgid fair; ocus rucusa do delg-su leam ag dula dam isin luing ocus is and sin ro impois-siu uainn." "Is fir tra sin," ar si, "ocus damad tu Uilix, do fiarfochtha do chu." "Nir sailius a marthain etir,"*

ar se. "Doronadh brochan aisi di agum-sa," ar si, "uair do rathaigius a grad co
mor ag Uilix. Ocus cia halt con hi etir in cu sin?" ar si. "Da taeb gle-gela aice,"
ar Uilix, "ocus druim gel-chorcra ocus tarr cir-dub ocus earball uainegda." "Is
si tuaruscbail in chon," ar si, "ocus didiu ni lamund duine isin baili a cuid do
thabairt di acht misi ocus tuso ocus in rechtaire." "Tabar in cu asdeach," ar se.
ocus ro ergidar ceathrar ara cend ocus tucsat leo asteach hi. ocus amal
adcuala-si fogur gotha Uilix tug builli ara slabrad co tuc in cethrar ina laigi ar
fad in taigi ina degain gur ling i n-ucht Uilix ocus guro ligh a gnúis ocus a aigid.
O'dconncadar muinter Uilix sin ro lingsiud cuigi. In duine dib nach roiched a
chneas re phogad do pogad a edach ocus nir gluais a ben ris-sin. "Is tu Uilix,"
ar si. "Is me," ol se. (Meyer, Merugud Uilix Maic Leirtis, 8–9).

44. See *The Tain*, tr. Thomas Kinsella (Dublin: Dolman Press, 1969),
83–84.

45. Alwyn Rees and Brinley Rees, *Celtic Heritage* (London: Thames and
Hudson, 1961), 327.

46. Ibid., 332. The Irish text is in R. Thurneysen, *Die Irische Helden-
und Königsage* (Halle: Niemeyer, 1921), 563. The Irish for "otter" is
dobhar cu.

47. *The Irish Wolfhound in Irish Literature and Law* (McLean, Virginia,
1971), 78; see also T. F. O'Rahilly, *Early Irish History and Mythology* (Dublin: Dublin Institute for Advanced Studies, 1976), 78–80 and the sources
cited there. The element "cu" (= Greek *kyon*), "dog," is part of many Irish
names—not only those of ancient heroes, but those of families whose sur-
names are quite familiar in the present day, from Coleman to Macnamara:
see Kuno Meyer, *Contributions to Irish Lexicography* (Halle: Niemeyer,
1906), 539–40. For the meaning of *archu* as "slaughter hound" or guard dog,
but not "mastiff," see Alfred W. De Quoy, 35 and 77–79. For dogs in the
Irish Arthurian cycle, see *Two Irish Arthurian Romances* (*Eachtra an
Mhadra Mhaoil.* Sir Galahad and crop-eared dog), ed. and trans. R. A. Stewart
Macalister, vol. 10 (London: Irish Texts Society, 1908).

48. De Quoy, *The Irish Wolfhound in Irish Literature and Law* (McLean,
Virginia, 1971), 62–63 and the sources cited. Homer makes the same general
distinction between hunting hounds and "table dogs."

49. De Quoy, 54.

50. See Meyer's note on the Irish *Odyssey* (*Merugud*, 24). The translation
is that of Gerard Murphy, "Bran's Departure from the Fian," in *Duanaire
Finn* (London 1933), 198–203, and cited by Du Quoy, 39.

51. De Quoy, 63–64.

52. On the name "Argus" and its significance in Greek, see Ahl, 158–59;
on the city of Argos in Greece and its use of a dog's head as a symbol on
coins, see N. Davies, *Greek Coins and Cities* (London: B. A. Seaby, 1967), 39.

Sappho: Translation as Elegy

 ROSANNA WARREN

For Ruth Jaeger

> *Our dreams pursue our dead.*
> Swinburne,
> *"Ave atque Vale"*

Ille mi par . . .
He's like a god, that man; he seems
(if this can be) to shine beyond
the gods, who nestling near you sees
   you and hears you

laughing low in your throat. It tears me
apart. For when I glimpse you,
Lesbia, look—I'm helpless:
   tongue a frozen

lump, and palest fire
pouring through all my limbs; my ears
deafened in ringing; each eye
   shuttered in night. . . .

You're wasting your time, Catullus,
laying waste to your life. You love it.
Whole kingdoms and blissful cities
   have wasted away, like you.

I seem to have given a misleading title, for the poem I present
is not by Sappho, but by Catullus. And I revise further by pointing
out that it is not "by" Catullus either, but "by" me. There may

seem to be no little immodesty and downright foolishness in putting forward my own translation of Catullus' famous translation of Sappho's famous poem *Phainetai moi.*

My translation of Catullus' "*Ille mi par . . .*" occurs, with another Catullus poem in the Sapphic meter, in a volume of my own poems. But these possessive phrases become obtrusive, as indeed they ought in matters of authorship. The purpose in focusing on a translation of a translation is not to claim that the world *needs* yet another version of this perennially retranslated poem; nor is it to demonstrate that I have outpaced all my predecessors and found a perfect English equivalent for Catullus. Rather, I should like to offer it, impersonally, as a small instance of lyric lineage, a type or model for poetry's perpetual re-engendering of itself. It is to argue that poetry is, finally, a family matter, involving the strains of birth, love, power, death, and inheritance; and that, given such strains (in every sense), one is never "by oneself" however isolated the act of writing may appear. The so-called original poems in my book are, in their own way, translations of several lyric traditions into personal experience and idiom, and are possible only because of strenuous acts of reading, one form of which we know, conventionally, as translation. I am concerned here with the way in which the individual poet inherits poetry, or, in Eliot's formulation, is catalyzed by it; and I take translation as a specific and especially focused instance of the reception and transformation of literary tradition.

I was drawn to Catullus 51 ("*Ille mi par . . .*") not only because it has haunted me since adolescence, not only because I am more at home in Latin than in Greek, but precisely because I was touched by the pathos of its being a translation and not "the real thing." In Catullus' forging of a new poetry from his still rather primitive native traditions and Greek models, I recognized the situation of any poet in the strain of self-creation through confrontation with the foreign and the past, the choosing of a parentage. And that situation may be seen as an analogy for the self-creation of a whole literature which develops by exposure to the "other," as English literature, also fairly barbaric in its early stages, has done in burst after burst, and as American literature, given its colonial inception, could not avoid doing.

The word "inheritance" implies death, grief, contest, and riches. In presenting the literary genre of elegy as a model for translation, I shall be relying on Peter Sacks's *The English Elegy* (The Johns Hopkins University Press, 1985). This book traces the work of mourning from its anthropological origins on into complex literary codification. In elegy, with its association with the ritual death and rebirth of a fertility god, I see a figure for the work of translation, which involves the death, dismemberment, and (one hopes!) rebirth of a text, with relative consolation for the mourners, or readers.

Sacks's work is essential in restoring our sense of the primitive vigor, I could almost say sacred power, at the source of our inherited rituals of mourning, of elegiac writing, and, I will argue, of all writing. In recalling the rites of sacrifice and cannibalism associated with early cults of Dionysus, and the survival of such rites symbolically in ancient Greek and later funerary practice, Sacks reveals the terror and *virtú* latent in such an apparently artificial form as English pastoral elegy. He shows how individual loss may be integrated within larger rhythmic structures dramatized by the poem, and he provides a vision of literature as a communion perpetually renewed in the light of death. In considering Sappho and some of her progeny, I am trying to recover that visceral sense of the rite of poetry: that sense in which, as Auden said of Yeats, "the words of the dead / Are modified in the guts of the living," and in which Pound, also translating a translation, envisioned Odysseus summoning the dead in canto I of the *Cantos*: ". . . A sheep to Tiresias only, black and a bellsheep. / Dark blood flowed in the fosse, / Souls out of Erebus. . . ."

The term "elegy" requires more than a little elucidation. The word is a rather mysterious one, with veiled origins, and auspicious dual associations with death and with love. The original Greek elegiac couplets were not necessarily associated with funerals, but were used for a wide variety of exhortation and reflection.[1] But Hellenistic grammarians derived *elegos*, in an imaginative etymology, from *"e e legein"* (to cry 'woe, woe').[2] In Euripides it is used as a song of mourning associated with the *aulos*, a flute whose tone was considered woeful as opposed to the *barbitos*, the lyre associated with lyric. In *Heroides* 15, Ovid has Sappho say, in elegiac couplets, *"Flendus amor meus est—elegiae flebile carmen; / non facit ad lacrimas barbitos ulla meas"* (ll. 7–8: My love is lamentable—a weeping song of elegy; no lyre suits my tears). "Elegy," in that passage, is doubly anachronistic: in Ovid's time the term was used for witty amatory complaint, and in Sappho's sixth century B.C. the elegiac meter had no necessarily doleful connotation. However, there is a strong possibility that the *elegos* was at an earlier period specifically associated with ritual grief.[3] Sacks describes the evolution of elegy through Latin love poetry into the English pastoral elegy, which reclaims some of the primitive features such as structures of repetition, myth of a vegetation god, bursts of anger and cursing, procession of mourners, detachment from the deceased, and consolation through symbolic substitution.[4] For my purposes, which are to define a private ritual figure for translation, the perhaps fictive origin of elegy as the art associated with funerals, and thus with the death and resurrection of vegetation gods and the rechanneling of eros into song, serves beautifully. We are considering the death and resurrection of texts in a myth of literary metamorphosis whose deities are those grieving poet-lovers whose nymphs turn into the tools—or emblems—of the trade: Pan's Syrinx into the panpipes, Apollo's Daphne into the laurel. Its other deities are those vegetation figures Dionysus, Adonis, Hyacinth, who survive sacrifice to reemerge as myths of eternal song.[5] It becomes apparent then that two senses of elegy, love and loss, can only rarely be disentangled.

We shall find our way back to Sappho through *Lycidas*. The death of Edward King provided Milton with an occasion to negotiate with grief—in this case a rather ceremonial grief—and, more pointedly, with the inherited genre of pastoral elegy and his own ambition and fear of death. His apparent heartlessness, or at least jauntiness, in the twitch of the mantle blue and the turn from pastoral to epic has often been noted. A poet's elegy for another poet is somehow a translation of that poet or at least of a tradition, and involves some kind of transfer of powers, perhaps aggressively asserted by the survivor. In any case, the underlying question is not that of personal survival, but of the survival of poetry. If all real poetry is, as I believe, writing in the light of death, elegy is the genre which performs most consciously in that light.

In *Lycidas* Milton's grief, anger, and fear crystallize appropriately around the figure of Orpheus, in classical mythology the mystic singer whose death by dismemberment could be read either as the failure of art or as its resurrection and purification.[6] Orpheus' *sparagmos* and drowning in the Hebrus not only suit the fate of Edward King, but fit within Milton's cosmic pattern of drownings and ascensions of stars and the sun. Such a pattern is hinted at early in the poem when the shepherds sing undisturbed by the passage of time ("Oft till the star that rose at evening bright / Toward Heaven's descent had sloped his westering wheel"); the pattern is fulfilled at the end, in a Christian design: "So sinks the day-star in the ocean bed / And yet anon repairs his drooping head." The final couplet astonishingly detaches the surviving poet, the uncouth swain, from the natural cycle to which the dead poet has been assimilated; yet the solar association haunts the conclusion in the ambiguous pronoun "he": "And now the sun had stretched out all the hills, / And now was dropped into the western bay; / At last he rose, and twitched his mantle blue: / Tomorrow to fresh woods and pastures new."[7]

In a crucial turn *Lycidas* associates Orpheus with Sappho:

What could the Muse herself that Orpheus bore,
The Muse herself, for her inchanting son
Whom universal Nature did lament,
When by the rout that made the hideous roar,
His gory visage down the stream was sent,
Down the swift Hebrus to the Lesbian Shore?

(ll. 59–63)

The classical Orpheus envisaged in his humiliation emphasizes the death of Lycidas, in this phase, as horror. This Orpheus serves as anti-type to, and will give way before, "the dear might of him that walked the waves"; cut off from Christian revelation, he is an inadequate figure for resurrection. Even at this nadir, however, when the "hideous roar" of the Thracian women seems to overwhelm the "inchanting" powers of music, Milton hints at the resurrection of those powers by imagining the current of the Hebrus flowing south over a hundred miles along the coast of Asia Minor to wash Orpheus' head to the shores of Sappho's island. That "supreme head of song," as Swinburne called her, and the possibilities of poetry she represents, are immediately challenged in *Lycidas* by the speaker's questions and the visions of the blind Fury. In Milton's poem Sappho remains a faint allusion. It is significant, however, that she should be glimpsed here in the context of the drowned poet who will be raised, like the "day-star," into the morning sky, and into a familiar mythology of resurrected divinities. Sappho, too, is said to have drowned, disappointed in love, by leaping from the Leucadian Rock; as Gregory Nagy has shown,[8] she rises, in her legend if not in *Lycidas*, into a similar myth of solar resurrection as Sappho/Aphrodite pursuing Phaon/Phaethon.

But why Sappho? I have been considering her as a legend, not as a poet. Indeed, it is partly as legend that she presides over the family matters I want to trace, in translation, through Catullus, Baudelaire, and Swinburne. Nagy's argument linking her to Aphrodite/Istar/Eos and a solar myth of recurrent death and rebirth—an argument so intricate as to deserve Sappho's own epithet for Aphrodite, *doloplokos*, weaver of wiles—derives to some degree from Sappho's invocations to the goddess, but for the most part from a fragment of Menander's *Leukadia* preserved by Strabo, from Ovid's *Heroides* 15, and from a bristling array of mythological sources. Through Menan-

der and Ovid and earlier comic traditions, Sappho entered the Western imagination as a priestess of song and of illicit love who died
by flinging herself off the white cliff at Cape Leukas for the love of
the handsome ferryman Phaon. Satirically viewed in various plays
of Middle Comedy, the story is one of the insufficiency of poetry,
and perhaps also of the just come-uppance meted out to a woman
who has spurned too long the love of men. Even the burlesque plays
and Ovid's arch diagnosis, however, veil a glorious Sappho linked
to ancient cults at Cape Leukas. Through "Longinus," that is,
through the treatise *"De Sublimitate"* to which we owe the pres-
ervation of *Phainetai moi*, Sappho has imposed herself as the
exemplary sublime poet, with a halo of primacy for the lyric akin
to that of Homer for epic. She was known in the Palatine Anthology
as the Tenth Muse, and comes down to us as a kind of mother
goddess of poetry, of whom Swinburne said, "Judging even from the
mutilated fragments fallen within our reach from the broken altar
of her sacrifice of song, I for one have always agreed with all Grecian
tradition in thinking Sappho to be beyond all question and comparison the very greatest poet that ever lived."[9]

But again, why Sappho? Why such a legend? Why should she
seem to have engendered the Western lyric, not once, but over and
over again, as we see in the twentieth century's rapture over the
Oxyrhynchan fragments and their shaping touch on Aldington,
Pound, HD, Guy Davenport . . . ? We must turn to these fragments,
to the poems. If the legendary Sappho rising from the sea as the
evening star gives us an emblem of the translation and survival of
song, the actual survival of her texts in quoted snippets and in the
papyri of grave wrappings is all the more eloquent. In the idea of
elegy, with its dual allusions to love and death, we can sense something of the power of these mutilated poems stripped from mummies
but still casting erotic spells.[10]

The enchantment resides, however, not in an idea, but in her
"visible song," as Swinburne so rightly understood; supremely, in
the Sapphic stanza, which burned its shape into Catullus' brain five
centuries after Sappho's death, and which has shaped our desire ever
since. If we consider Sappho as a myth, it must be as a myth not of
love, but of form.

> Phainetai moi keinos isos theoisin
> emmen oner ottis enantios toi
> izanei kai plasion adu phonei-
> sas upakouei

kai gelaisas imeroen, to m'ei man
kardian en stethesin eptoasen;
os gar es t'ido, broke', os me phonas
ouden et' ikei

all' akan men glossa eage, lepton
d'autika kroi pur upadedromaken,
oppatessi d'oud' en oreimm', epirrom-
beisi d'akouai,

kad de m'idros psukros ekei, tromos de
paisan agrei, klorotera de poias
emmi, tethnakein d'oligo pideueis
phainomai . . .

It is a haunting shape. In Sappho's hands it plays release against restraint with unrivaled cunning: the poem runs from stanza to stanza like water pouring from basin to basin down a trout stream, twisting and flashing, unfurled and checked. As Charles Segal has observed, its very motion is the erotic persuasion, *peitho*, of which Sappho so often writes. Within each hendecasyllabic line the opening trochaic feet give way to the impulse which throbs forward in the choriamb, to be teasingly checked by the concluding bacchiac: ‑‿‑×|‑‿‿‑|‿‑‑. The halt teases because more often than not the sentence's propulsion launches us into the next line, sometimes through enjambment within a word: *phonei-* / *sas* (ll. 3–4), *epirrom-* / *beisi* (ll. 11–12). After three such hendecasyllables the adonic seems to dam up the current with its wedgelike, truncated shape and final pair of long syllables; but Sappho admits no such resolution, and spills her poem over barrier after barrier. Within this flow, the eddies of assonance and consonance complete the work of hypnotic enchantment. In its expansions and contractions this is a stanza fatally gauged to register the pulse of desire.

Can a living stream be translated? One of Sappho's finest interpreters, Swinburne, has testified:

To translate the two odes and the remaining fragments of Sappho is the one impossible task; and as witness of this I will call up one of the greatest among poets. Catullus "translated"—or as his countrymen would now say "traduced"—the ode of Anactoria—"*Eis Eromenan*"; a more beautiful translation there never was and will be; but compared with the Greek, it is colorless and bloodless, puffed out by additions and enfeebled by alterations. . . . Where Catullus failed, I could not hope to succeed.[11]

Swinburne is here mourning the death of the original. To pursue the elegiac analogy, he has brought himself to that stage of grief which recognizes irreplaceable loss. But just as the work of mourning proceeds by rehearsal of the trauma and ritual self-mutilation to detachment from the deceased and acceptance of a symbolic substitute, so the work of translation repeats the destruction of the original, dismembers and ingests it as in the Thracian sacrifice of Orpheus or the rites of Dionysus, and finally offers its transubstantiated version as consolation for, and recognition of, loss. In the passage just quoted Swinburne was defending his free translation of Sappho in his poem "Anactoria":

> "That is not Sappho," a friend once said to me. I could only reply, "It is as near as I can come; and no man can come close to her. . . . I have striven to cast my spirit into the mould of hers, to express and represent not the poem but the poet. . . . Here and there, I need not say, I have rendered into English the very words of Sappho. I have tried also to work into words of my own some expression of the effect: to bear witness how, more than any other's, her verses strike and sting the memory in lonely places, or at sea, among all loftier sights and grounds—how they seem akin to fire and air, being themselves "all air and fire"; other element there is none in them."[12]

We shall presently consider the fruits of such devotion; before that, we need to turn to her first translator, Catullus.

Sappho and Catullus

51

Ille mi par esse deo videtur,
ille, si fas est, superare divos,
qui sedens adversus identidem te
   spectat et audit

dulce ridentem, misero quod omnis
eripit sensus mihi: nam simul te,
Lesbia, aspexi, nihil est super mi . . .

lingua sed torpet, tenuis sub artus
flamma demanat, sonitu suopte
tintinant aures, gemina teguntur
   lumina nocte.

otium, Catulle, tibi molestum est:
otio exsultas nimiumque gestis:
otium et reges prius et beatas
   perdidit urbes.

Though Catullus seems to have written only two poems in the Sapphic meter, the extent of his debt to the poet of Lesbos may be judged from the name he gave to the woman he loved: Lesbia. The two Catullan Sapphic poems record stages in that affair. The translation of *Phainetai moi* can be seen either as celebrating an early, happy phase, substituting erotic rapture for Sappho's distress,[13] or, as had been plausibly argued, as commenting ironically on the destructiveness of his love for Lesbia through allusion to supposed marriage elements in Sappho's poem.[14] "*Furi et Aureli*," Catullus' other Sapphic poem (Catullus 11), is a savage and lyrical farewell to the unworthy lover. However Lesbia is seen by Catullus in these poems, it is through a Sapphic lens which emphasizes, by contrast, Lesbia's Roman corruption.

This is not the occasion to pore, syllable by syllable, over the transposition from Greek to Latin; a few details will have to suggest the enterprise. Most tellingly, however, we can observe right from the start that Catullus has "lost it" (to use current parlance) with the very first word. *Phainetai*, from *phaino* (to appear), shares a root with *phaos* (light), and with the verb *phao* (to give light, to shine). The "appearance" Sappho indicates is no mere seeming or being seen, but something more on the order of our "epiphany," an English cognate of *phaino*. It is used of the apparitions of deities. The man in Sappho's poem, *keinos*, that one, whoever he is who sits next to the beloved girl, blazes in the first stanza with a radiance reflected from Aphrodite, through the girl. It is an epiphany of Love, working upon the man and, beyond him, upon Sappho observing. We are confronted here not simply with a relative poverty in Latin and English verbs of seeming, but with an entirely different conception of the manifestation of the divine.

Another detail: Sappho's *imeroen* (l. 5). A long-drawn-out, caressing neuter adjective used adverbially ("and listens to you laughing *enticingly*"), it contains the words *eros*, and is charged with desire, with the dread and sacred power of love, to a degree that annihilates most dippy English substitutes and far outstrips Catullus' merely sensory *dulce* (sweetly). As if *imeroen* had not sufficient voltage, Sappho renews the charge in a phonetic echo, completing the line *kai gelaisas imeroen, to m'ei man*, whose sensuous alliteration and assonance can be savored even by the Greekless reader. A few final points: Catullus inserts a legalistic clause into line 2: *si fas est, superare divos* (if it is permitted, [he seems] to surpass the gods). It testifies to a peculiarly Roman attitude about men and gods, but it also slows up the poem, and a good deal is lost in line 6 in the replacement of Sappho's heart shuddering in her breast by the abstract *sensus* (general powers of apprehension).

What has Catullus salvaged? First and foremost, the stanza form, through which he knowingly pours his own poem. It was Catullus' muscular twining of sentences through lines and stanzas that mesmerized me years ago when I did not know the Greek. He has taken over, likewise, something of Sappho's vowel and consonant play, though his seems more programmatic and symmetrical: *"flamma demanat, sonitu suopte"* (l. 9). Where Sappho was entirely flexible, Catullus moves toward practices which will be codified in Horatian Sapphics, often making the fourth syllable of the hendecasyllable long, and ending a word after the fifth syllable. He does not have Sappho's radiance, but he grasps the simplicity with which she lists the medical symptoms of love, symptoms taken over from Homeric descriptions of shock and fear, the drama of war imported to the love chamber, epic into lyric. Where Sappho emphasized intimacy in stanza 1, Catullus insists on the recurrent nature of the scene with the rare adverb *identidem* (again and again) which appears in his other Sapphic poem, *"Furi et Aureli,"* in an obscene context. He misses the ring structure in her poem that linked the apparition (*phainetai*) of the rival man in line 1 through the sundering of her own body to a reunification of self in the strongly enjambed verb "to be" (*emmi*, l. 15) and felt apparition of self "I seem" (*phainomai*, l. 16). Where her poem went at this juncture is a wild surmise. Catullus seems to have omitted her remarkable fourth stanza, and his poem may or may not have ended with the famous *otium* stanza. If the *otium* lines did close his poem, as I sense they did, they set Catullus' passion in the typically Roman context of politics and empire at odds with private erotic life, and glance out again in the direction of epic.

That epic glance is given more scope in the *"Furi et Aureli"* poem. There Catullus addresses his two enemies as his "companions," and charges them, in a torrent of bombast mimicking imperial rhetoric, with a simple message of farewell to his "girl." After that calculated understatement, *"non bona dicta"* (not good words), explodes a stanza of obscene abuse which gives way to one of the most delicate of all Latin lyrics, the stanza recalling Sappho's cut flower:[15]

> But she'd better not look, like last time, for my
> love reviving. It's her fault it's fallen,
> a flower at the rim of the meadow, touched
>   by the plow passing.

Not surprisingly, the anatomy of love, and perhaps jealousy, in *Phainetai moi* has never lost its grip on the Western imagination. But the history of Sappho in English is by and large a sorry one. It is the story of the awkward adaptation of classical quantitative prosody to the English accentual-syllabic system.[16] The faint presence of stress in Latin meter only complicates the problem further. John Hall, translating *Phainetai moi* in 1652, sensibly opts for a loose stress equivalent to Sappho's quantities, and gives tetrameters with a dimeter for the adonic. The poor man can muster almost no other poetic resources beyond his common sense, however: his instinct for the rhyming couplet wars with the shape of the stanza, his meter thuds, his vocabulary is trite; to top it all off he has misunderstood (wilfully perhaps) the gender relations in the poem, rendering stanza 2:

How did his pleasing glances dart
Sweet languors to my ravish'd heart
At the first sight though so prevailed
  That my voice fail'd.[17]

E. M. Cox's 1925 version exemplifies the mess that results when a quantitative system is clamped arbitrarily onto English. One line will suffice. The conflict between natural word stress and fictive quantity results in verse which, if pronounced according to its own system, sounds downright idiotic: "Peér ŏf the góds | the hăppĭest | măn Í seém."[18] J. A. Symonds in 1887 was more successful in aligning English stress with the requirements of length; his version is hardly felicitous syntactically ("Nothing see mine eyes, and a noise of roaring / Waves in my ear sounds"), but his first line at least shows how an accommodation might plausibly be reached: "Peér ŏf góds hé | seémĕth tŏ mé, | the blíssfúl. . . ."[19] For an approach which ignores the Sapphic stanza but tries to approximate its simplicity and concision, we can turn to Mary Barnard's 1958 version:

He is more than a hero

He is a god in my eyes—
the man who is allowed
to sit beside you—he . . .[20]

Hers has the virtue of cleanliness, but it lacks the rhythm of expansion and contraction which sustains life in Sappho's form.

The twentieth century has in fact been rich in appropriations of Sappho's poem. In "Three Letters to Anaktoria" from *Imitations* (1958), Robert Lowell supplies in hyperbole, exaggerated assonance and alliteration, extraneous similes, and sheer gusto what he lacks in subtlety: the man sits next to the girl "like a cardplayer"; "refining fire," filched from Dante's Arnaut Daniel, perhaps by way of Eliot, purifies the speaker's flesh in a discordantly Christian way; and Sappho's pale grass becomes blindingly verdant: "I am greener than the greenest green grass." Basil Bunting, working freely from Catullus in 1965, turns the poem back to Sappho by imitating her ring structure: "O, it is godlike to sit selfpossessed / When her chin rises and she turns to smile," he begins, and concludes the last stanza: ". . . I dissolve / When her chin rises and she turns to smile. / O, it is godlike!"[21]

Examples could proliferate endlessly. I indulge myself in one final instance. John Hollander's canny "After an Old Text"[22] uses the fact of its being a translation and revision of Sappho as a figure for the speaker's nostalgia for, hence re-vision of, an old lover, with the pronoun "you" conflating Sappho and his own lost love. The final stanza runs:

This revision of you sucks out the sound of
Words from my mouth, my tongue collapses, my legs
Flag, my ears roar, my eyes are blinded with flame; my
    Head is in hell then.

I would like to close, not by nagging at the innumerable translations of *Phainetai moi* in English, but by penciling briefly a larger sketch of translation as an elegiac genealogy. I spoke of poetry as a family matter; a record of translations is a family tree. I want now to trace, through a series of elegies, a perpetuated acknowledgment of Sappho as lyric mother, and therefore of her progeny as siblings. At issue is the enduring life of poetry. The poems to bear in mind are Catullus' elegy for his real brother ("*Multas per gentes,*" poem 101), Baudelaire's Sapphic poems, Swinburne's "Sapphics," and his elegy for Baudelaire "*Ave Atque Vale.*" Through these elegies, I suggest, we can sense Sappho, the lyric impulse, rising again and again like Hesperus from the waters of language, and perpetually lost; and we will sense translation in action as the blood pulse of our continuing, shared literary life, keeping time with the larger cycles of nature. I freely confess it: this is a myth. A working myth for a poet and translator.

Baudelaire and Swinburne

Baudelaire studied Greek as well as Latin in the *lyçée*, and was surely familiar with Sappho's *Phainetai moi.* But the Sappho reincarnated in Baudelaire is not a metrical essence, as she was in part for Swinburne. Rather, Baudelaire is haunted by the myth of Sapphic sexuality. In a number of poems, two of which were excluded from *Les Fleurs du Mal* by the censor in 1857, he celebrates an eros which has nothing to do with the Greek Sappho's frank and splendid pleasure. Baudelaire's lesbian love is consecrated, not as joy, but as deviance. Set in the ghoulish context of Christian damnation on the one hand, and of "natural," socially useful, reproductive mating on the other, his lesbians are artists and outcasts in their pure search for beauty and sensation. "*O vierges, o démons, o monstres, o martyres, / De la réalité grands esprits contempteurs, / Chercheuses d'infini . . .*" ("O virgins, O demons, O monsters, O martyrs, great spirits contemptuous of reality, seekers of infinity . . ." from "*Femmes Damnées*"). Theirs is the true spirituality in, and against, a materialistic world, and, not surprisingly, they are associated with Baudelaire's cherished images of infinity: the abyss and the gulf, and their corollary, death: "*—Descendez, descendez, lamentables victimes, / Descendez le chemin de l'enfer éternel! / Plongez au plus profond du gouffre, où tous les crimes . . .*" ("Descend, descend, sad victims, descend the path of eternal hell! Dive to the depths of the gulf, where all crimes . . ." from "*Femmes Damnées: Delphine et Hippolyte*"). This *gouffre* has its analogies in Baudelaire's sense of Sappho's poetry: the nearest he comes to describing her verse is his evocation, in "Lesbos," of the lesbian embraces where the imaginary cascade behaves rather like a Sapphic stanza:

> Lesbos, where the kisses, like cascades
> teeming and turbulent yet secret, deep,
> plunge undaunted into unplumbed gulfs
> and gather there, gurgling and sobbing till
> they overflow in ever-new cascades![23]

At issue for Baudelaire is not the survival of Sappho's poetry. His Sapphic poems suggest something of the hell created in French nineteenth-century society for homosexual lovers, but his true absorption is with his own deflected eroticism as a figure for art. For him, art is and must be profoundly anti-natural; it joins in holy alliance with a sterile eros and with death, with infinity and the soul, in opposition to the squalid claims of nature and literal fact.

Though he claims to be Sappho's sentinel keeping vigil on the Leucadian cliff, Baudelaire takes us far afield from Sappho's hyacinths and the "dew on the riverside gleaming."[24] With Swinburne the inheritance is much more complex because it is expressed "genetically"—that is, in meter and stanza form. Sappho's strain is crossed, however, with the strong influences of Baudelaire and, at his worst, the Marquis de Sade. Before considering the fraternal relationship between Swinburne and Baudelaire, I want to address the matter of Sappho's more direct incarnation in Swinburne's poetry.

First, the meter. Swinburne's Greek was excellent and, more than excellent, it was passionate, so that he writes the Sapphic stanza naturally, translating long and short syllables to stress with an ease scarcely ever matched in English. I will now make a risky claim: that Sappho lives in English, not in any word-by-word reproduction of her texts, but in Swinburne's poems "Sapphics" and "Hendecasyllabics." I would claim in addition that Sappho's rigor and subtlety saved Swinburne from his own worst propensities toward prosodic exaggeration, and that his finest poems, to which we do not sufficiently confess our gratitude,[25] are those disciplined by Greek. In "Sapphics" Swinburne has allowed himself to be possessed by Sappho's "visible song," and his poem, in places, surges and pauses as delicately as hers down its streambed, its vowels and consonants as cunningly in play:

> . . . and I too,
> Full of the vision,
>
> Sáw thĕ whíte ím|plácăblĕ Á|phrŏdíté,
> Saw the hair unbound and the feet unsandalled
> Shine as fire of sunset on western waters;
>   Saw the reluctant
>
> Feet, the straining plumes of the doves that drew her . . .
>
>   (ll. 7–13)

I scan one line to show with what grace the stress corresponds to the Greek's requirements for length. In "Anactoria" the rhyming pentameter couplets make for a cruder versification. Here, however, actual translation of Sappho rises out of hyperbolic Sadean rhetoric, and so filially imbued is Swinburne with her spirit that those fragments from the "Hymn to Aphrodite" seem intrinsic to his own poem:

> Saw Love, as burning flame from crown to feet,
> Imperishable, upon her storied seat;
> Clear eyelids lifted toward the north and south,
> A mind of many colors, and a mouth
> Of many tunes and kisses; and she bowed,
> With all her subtle face laughing aloud,

Bowed down upon me, saying "Who doth thee wrong,
Sappho?"

(ll. 67–74)

Swinburne is straining to render the first lines of the ode
"poikilothron athanat' Aphrodite / pai Dios doloploke"; literally,
"Richly (dappled, intricate, with various colors) enthroned immortal
Aphrodite, child of Zeus, weaver of wiles." Swinburne has at least
made incantatory what in Barnard seems blunt and curt, though
clean ("Dapple-throned Aphrodite / eternal daughter of God, / Snare-
knitter!"), and in Davenport rococco ("God's stunning daughter
deathless Aphródita / A whittled perplexity your bright abstruse
chair . . .").

Swinburne has taken from *Phainetai moi* the conceit of love as
a pathology, "Yea, all thy beauty sickens me with love" (l. 56); he
has grossly exaggerated it with Sadean extrapolation that shies not
from cannibalism: "Ah that my mouth for Muses' milk were fed / On
the sweet blood thy sweet small wounds had bled!" (ll. 107–8). For
a modern reader such a passage can only be comic; nor is there much
to be said in defense of the workaday verse. I pause for a moment,
however, on the theme of cannibalism. For all its hysteria, the passage points back to primitive rites of communion associated with
funerals, and may recall my elegiac emblem of translation for which
Sacks provided the model. The erotic communion Swinburne so-
licits, an invitation to rather than a defense against death, is itself
merely a figure for the poet's real communion with the spirit of
Sappho, and, as such, is an elegiac act. At the end of "Anactoria"
the poetic eros does fend off death, for it allows Sappho, resurrected
through Swinburne, to assert the immortality of song:

I Sappho will be one with all these things,
With all high things forever; and my face
Seen once, my songs heard in a strange place,
Cleave to men's lives . . .

(ll. 276–79)

Communion with a ghost from antiquity is one thing; acceptance
of the death of an immediate poetic forebear is quite another
and more shocking matter. The loss felt is more urgent, as is the
threat to one's own life and voice. The death of Baudelaire was,
for Swinburne, such a shock, and one that elicited from
him one of the majestic pastoral elegies in English, *"Ave Atque
Vale."* The title conjures up Catullus' farewell in elegiac couplets to his brother, and proclaims a fraternity between Sappho's

lyric offspring: Catullus, Baudelaire, and himself.

Sappho, the mother, is immediately invoked in stanza 2:

> Thine ears knew all the wandering watery sighs
> Where the sea sobs round Lesbian promontories,
> The barren kiss of piteous wave to wave
> That knows not where is that Leucadian grave
> Which hides too deep the supreme head of song.

Peter Sacks has charted this poem with exemplary intelligence and learning. For my purposes, it will suffice to emphasize the way in which an elegy involves translation. In rejecting the traditional garland "rose or rue or laurel," in favor of "Half-faded, fiery blossoms, pale with heat," Swinburne is translating "Lycidas" into *Les Fleurs du Mal*. The poem proceeds to "translate" Baudelaire's own "translation" of Sappho: "Fierce loves and lovely leaf-buds poisonous . . ." (l. 25). Facing the death and, worse still, the silence of his brother poet, Swinburne is led to question whether poetry itself survives: "Thou art far too far for wings of words to follow / Far too far off for thought or any prayer" (ll. 89–90); note the lack of caesuras streamlining the distance. In this crisis, the poem attempts to assert poetic communion as the symbolic consolation proffered in traditional elegy: ". . . and not death estranges / My spirit from communion with thy song" (ll. 103–4); the whole lyric tradition appears as one long, shared lament: "Or through mine ears a mourning musical / Of many mourners rolled" (ll. 109–10). But this death and the impotence of Apollo and Aphrodite, poetry and love, seem to blight consolation: ". . . not all our songs, O friend, / Will make death clear or make life durable" (ll. 171–72). After much synaesthesia, the elegy seems to end in silence; the dead poet is not to rise as day-star or genius of any shore, and the figure of Sappho has blended into that of a more tragic mother: "And chill the solemn earth, a fatal mother, / With sadder than the Niobean womb . . ." (ll. 191–92).

The dead poet seems beyond the reach of poetry. This crisis corresponds to the moment in Moschus' lament for Bion in which "Bion is dead, and with him dead is music, and gone with him likewise the Dorian poesy."[26] The work of mourning, that is, would be completely blocked, were it not for the *translation* of Catullus that opens the final stanza, and in its very nature as translation belies the silence of death which it asserts. As long as Catullus speaks through Swinburne, he is neither dead nor silent, and neither, in some sense, is Baudelaire: "For thee, O now a silent soul, my brother, / Take at my hands this garland, and farewell" (ll. 188–89). Besides being one of the noblest versions of the Catullus we are likely to get, Swinburne's closing echo ensures that Hesperus will once again rise from Okeanos, that Sappho lives on, transmuted, in her children, and that poetry will continue to voice us to ourselves.

NOTES

1. D. A. Campbell, *Greek Lyric Poetry: A Selection* (MacMillan/St. Martin's Press, 1967), xxv.

2. Georg Luck, *The Latin Love Elegy* (Methuen, 1969), 26.

3. Peter Sacks, *The English Elegy* (The Johns Hopkins University Press, 1985), 3.

4. Ibid., 2.

5. Sacks, 26ff.

6. In the fourth Georgic, Virgil sets the defeat of Orpheus against the life-giving success of the peasant Aristaeus. Thanks to the narration of Proteus, Aristaeus is able to appease the vexed spirit of Orpheus and bring life out of death, reviving his beehive:

> When from the bellies, over the rotten flesh
> Of the corpses, bees buzz out from caved-in flanks,
> Swarm in heavy clouds to treetops, group,
> And hang in clusters down from the pliant boughs.

(Virgil, *The Georgics*, tr. S. P. Bovie (University of Chicago Press, 1956, 4: 555–58).

7. For an elegant and clear-sighted reading of the passage, with particular attention to the anaphora "And now" and the ambiguous "he," see Sacks, 116.

8. Gregory Nagy, "Phaethon, Sappho's Phaon," *Harvard Studies in Classical Philology* 77 (1973): 173–75.

9. H. T. Wharton, *Sappho* (John Lave, 1898, 4th ed.; repr. Libera, Amsterdam, 1974), 168.

10. Charles Segal, "Eros and Incantation," *Arethusa* 7 (1974): 139–160.

11. Wharton, 34.

12. Ibid., 36.

13. C. J. Fordyce, *Catullus, A Commentary* (Oxford University Press, 1961), 218ff.

14. T. P. Wiseman, *Catullus and His World: A Reappraisal* (Cambridge University Press, 1985), 152–54. I am not convinced that we need accept Wilamowitz's theory of a marriage ceremony as occasion for Sappho's poem in order to sense that poem bitterly invoked by Catullus. The elemental drama of *Phainetai moi*, a happy couple excluding the former lover, suffices in my mind to charge Catullus' address to Lesbia with retrospective anguish. Yes, the symptoms he enumerates appear to be those of passion, not jealousy,

since "*ille*" (ll. 1, 2: that man, any man is not as definite and particular as Sappho's "*keinos . . . aner*" (that man). In both poems, I think, attention focuses more on the painful mystery of love itself rather than on an interloper; and Catullus could be seen as recalling his own innocent, early passion only to underscore his disillusion by reference to Sappho's distress as well as to the destruction of whole kingdoms in the *otium* stanza. For further discussion, see Denys Page, *Sappho and Alcaeus* (Oxford University Press, 1955), 20, 21, and Anne Pippin Burnett, *Three Archaic Poets* (Harvard University Press, 1983), 229–43.

15. Wiseman, 146.

16. For a learned and lucid account of such efforts, see John Hollander's *Vision and Resonance* (Yale University Press, 1975; 1985), 59–70. It is an indispensable book.

17. E. M. Cox, *The Poems of Sappho* (Charles Scribners Sons, 1925), 34.

18. Ibid., 70.

19. Ibid., 72.

20. Mary Barnard, *Sappho* (University of California Press, 1958), 39.

21. Basil Bunting, *Collected Poems* (Oxford University Press, 1978), 119.

22. John Hollander, *Spectral Emanations* (Atheneum, 1978), 57. John Hollander, a rare *doctus poeta*, has written Sapphics with splendid ease throughout his career. The form has been for him a rich inheritance, allowing him serious spoofs of the modern relationship to Antiquity ("Making It" and "Epilogue: the loss of smyrna" in *Town and Country Matters* (Yale University Press, 1958), as well as a severely graceful meditation on love and representation, "The Lady of the Castle," over which Sappho, the poet of Aphrodite, presides through the evocatory power of her stanza (*Spectral Emanations*, 54, 55). Sappho's form affords Hollander more than thematic resonance; he uses Sapphic enjambment, so often avoided by her translators, to the hilt: "My desire, my memory was so intelli-/gently caressing" ("A Thing So Small," *Harp Lake* (Knopf, 1988), 80.

23. Charles Baudelaire, "Lesbos," stanza 2, tr. Richard Howard, *Les Fleurs du Mal* (Godine, 1982), 123.

24. Guy Davenport, *Archilochus, Sappho, Alkman* (University of California Press, 1980), 93, a translation of fragment 42. Guy Davenport has brought the Poundian imperative of clarity to bear in his long and honorable engagement with archaic Greek poetry.

25. A notable exception is Jerome McGann, whose sprightly *Swinburne: An Experiment in Criticism* (University of Chicago Press, 1972) begins to repair the wrong.

26. J. M. Edmonds, *The Greek Bucolic Poets* (Harvard University Press, 1938; 1950; 1960), 445.

Montale:
Translated, or Translator?

Extract from the Journal of Comparative
Poetry 23 (1987): 41–43

"SOME MONTHS AGO we received an anonymous
translation in a kind of ancient Greek of Montale's *'Meriggiare pallido e assorto.'* It was written in what appeared to be free verse,
although since it made use of many of the cola or metrical units of
classical choral lyric, it was not so much 'freer' than the strophes
of tragedy, or perhaps rather of Pindar, were they not paired with
matching antistrophes. The piece was accompanied by a note (again
anonymous) advancing the remarkable suggestion that this might
be an original composition from a hitherto unknown period of Greek
literature which saw a poetic revolution akin to that of our own
century, one that allowed poets to broach new themes, drawing
freely on the old poetic diction with whatever admixture of contemporary, prosaic elements, and departing from the rules of classical
metric (or simply ignoring them) whenever they wished. Clearly this
suggestion raised so many questions that it seemed best to treat the
whole thing as a joke, and we decided against publication.

"More recently we were sent another Greek composition of the
same sort, again apparently a translation of a poem of Montale's
(*'Gli orecchini'*). It was composed in a meter recognizably derived
from the classical iambic trimeter, treated as freely as we find English
blank verse treated in Jacobean drama or in Eliot's 'Gerontion.' Whatever the relation between the two texts, we were struck by their
consonance. The Greek, detached from its ancient moorings and
hence free to sound new reaches of experience, yet retaining something of the formal gravity of the tragic line, seemed to provide a
closer equivalent to the weight and complexity of Montale's diction
than modern English can. To put it this way is to assume that the

Ὠχρὸς καὶ ἀφεστώς τις μεσημβριάζει
κήπου παρ' ἡλιοβλήτοις αἱμασίαις,
ἐν δὲ βάτοις τε καὶ πρέμνοις ἀΐων
κοσσύφων κλαγγάς, ψιθύρους ὀφέων.

κατὰ χθόνα σχιζομένην ἐρυθροὺς καθορᾷ
μύρμηκας καὶ ὑπὲρ βοτάνας στοιχηδὸν ἰόντας
ἀτάκτως, τὰ δὲ συμπλοκῇ τεταγμένοι
σμικραῖς ἑλίσσονται 'π' ἀμάλλοις.

διὰ τῶν πετάλων δὲ τηλόθεν σκοπεῖ
πόντου τὰς λεπίδας ἐλελιζομένας,
τεττίγων λιγυρὰν κρεκόντων
ἠχὴν ψιλῶν ἐκ κορυφῶν.

πορευομένῳ δ' αὐτῷ χαροποῖς ὑπ' ἀκτῖσιν
φαίνεταί πως ἀθυμοῦντι καὶ δὴ θαυμάζοντι
ὁ καματώδης ἅπας βίος ἐν τοιῷδε
μόνον γ' ἐνεῖναι· τειχάριόν τι παρέρπειν
ὀστράκοις ἀκρόθι τραχύ.

Greek is a translation. Put it the other way and grant that it might, just might, be the original, and you have to admire Montale's skill in finding in the classical Italian sonnet (the sixteenth-century della Casan sonnet, surely, rather than the Petrarchan) a model that allowed him to capture something of the measured, even stately port of his mysterious original.

"For who knows? It was not long ago that the cartonnage wrapped about an Egyptian mummy revealed to our wondering eyes a new, perhaps almost complete work by the great Archilochus, a love poem of a kind unparalleled in ancient Greek. Has Egypt still stranger

Meriggiare pallido e assorto
presso un rovente muro d'orto,
ascoltare tra i pruni e gli sterpi
schiocchi di merli, frusci di serpi.

Nelle crepe del suolo o su la veccia
spiar le file di rosse formiche
ch' ora si rompono ed ora s'intrecciano
a sommo di minuscole biche.

Osservare tra frondi il palpitare
lontano di scaglie di mare
mentre si levano tremuli scricchi
di cicale dai calvi picchi.

E andando nel sole che abbaglia
sentire con triste meraviglia
com'è tutta la vita e il suo travaglio
in questo seguitare una muraglia
che ha in cima cocci aguzzi di bottiglia.

To laze at midday, pale and withdrawn, by a scorching garden wall, to listen to the blackbirds cackle and snakes rustling among the bushes and stubble.

To watch in the cracks in the ground or on the vetch the files of red ants, now breaking ranks, now interweaving on top of their miniature sheaves.

To observe through the leaves the far-off pulse of the sea while the quivering screech of the cicadas rises from the bald peaks.

And, walking in the dazzling sun, to feel with sad wonder how all life and its troubles is in this following along a high wall topped with spiky bits of bottle.

---

treasures to disclose? Can it be that these two Greek pieces *are really original poems, and that the translator is Montale?* Are they the survivors (perhaps not the only ones) of a body of Greek verse that has not come down to us? A very great deal of Greek literature has after all been lost, and it is not in itself improbable that the schoolmasterly persons responsible for our classical canon, finding this work too far from their notion of what classical literature should be, let it perish. Did it, however, not totally perish? Did a few manuscripts survive, jealously preserved from the eyes of the learned, a kind of poetic cache on which later poets could draw, letting them

Πτήσεῶν σκιὰς οὐ διασῴζει τὸ καπνῶδες
σφαίρας ἐρεμνῆς, οὐδ ἴχνος τῶν σῶν λέλειπται.
σπόγγος δ' ἀφάρκτους ἀκτῖνας ἐκ τοῦ κύκλου
τοῦ πρὶν χρυσηροῦς ἐξαλειψὰς ἤλασεν.
τὰ σὰ κοράλλια, σὰς λίθους, ἀρχὴν κραταιὸν
ἥτις σ' ἔμαρψεν, ἐνθένδ' ἐθήρων. φεύγω
τὴν σῶμ' ἐρημώσασαν θεᾶν· πόθοι δ' ἐμοὶ
μένοιεν ἔστ' ἂν σαῖς τήκωνται στεροπαῖς.
ἔξω δ' ἔλυτρα βομβεῖ, βομβεῖ χἠ παράφρων
ἐκφόρ', οὐδ' ἀριθμὸν ἔχουσί πώς τινες δύο.
στίλβης δ' ἐς ἄντυγα μαλθακαὶ πάλιν νέονται
ἑσπέριαι μέδουσαι. καὶ μὴν σὸς χαρακτὴρ
ἥξει κάτωθεν, οἵ χεῖρες ἀντείνουσ' αὐχμηραὶ
τοῖς σοῖς προσάπτειν ὠσὶ τὰ κοράλλια.

---

pass off as originals poems that in fact were translations from the Greek? Perhaps Yeats spoke more truly than he knew when he described Pound as a 'brilliant improvisator translating at sight from an unknown Greek masterpiece.'

"This possibility opens up exciting new fields of research: not, however, research of a kind that the learned world can be expected to welcome. Questioned about the authenticity of these two Greek compositions, a distinguished British Hellenist pronounced them to be 'an impudent fraud, obviously the work of some amateur Hellenist who would have been better employed studying ancient Greek grammar and metric.' Scholars in the field of modern literature are likely to adopt an even more unfavorable position, for should it prove that any sizable proportion of the writing they have won their spurs

Gli Orecchini

Non serba ombra di voli il nerofumo
della spera. (E del tuo non è piú traccia.)
È passata la spugna che i barlumi
indifesi dal cerchio d'oro scaccia.
Le tue pietre, i coralli, il forte imperio
che ti rapisce vi cercavo; fuggo
l'iddia che non s'incarna, i desiderî
porto fin che al tuo lampo non si struggono.
Ronzano èlitre fuori, ronza il folle
mortorio e sa che due vite non contano.
Nella cornice tornano le molli
meduse della sera. La tua impronta
verrà di giú: dove ai tuoi lobi squallide
mani, travolte, fermano i coralli.

No shadow of flights does the smokedark [i.e., lamp-black] of the
sphere retain. (And of yours there is no longer a trace.) The sponge has
passed that drives away the defenseless glitters from the gold circle.
Your precious stones, your corals, the strong mastery that ravished you
away, I was looking for there; I flee the disembodied goddess; I keep my
desires until they are dissolved by your lightning. The wing-cases drone
outside, the mad funeral drones and knows that two lives don't count.
Within the frame the soft medusas of the evening return. Your imprint
will come from below: where, at your lobes, squalid hands, turned up,
fasten the corals.

———————

professing owes its life-blood, its very existence, to Greek originals
they themselves are unable to read, their professional qualifications
are going to be severely called into question, and they (or their successors) will have to rewrite parts of the history of Western literature.
It might, for instance, turn out that Coleridge left *Kubla Khan* unfinished not because he was interrupted by the Person from Porlock,
but because the manuscript he was translating from broke off at that
point.

Ed."*

———————————————————————————————
*I am grateful to Mr. D. S. Carne-Ross for drawing my attention to these two Greek
translations—or original Greek poems, if that is what they prove to be—and to the
editor of the *Journal of Comparative Poetry* for allowing me to reprint them here,
together with the extract from his journal. R.W.

V
Vistas

Silence, the Devil, and Jabès

 ROSMARIE WALDROP

"THERE IS NO MUSE of translation," declared Walter Benjamin.[1] The Brazilian poet Haroldo de Campos (who otherwise follows Benjamin) counters with a fanfare: "If translation has no muse, one could however say that it has an angel."[2] The angel, we learn, is Lucifer, and a good translation should by rights be called a "transluciferation." I think Benjamin would have approved of the angel of light in this function since his highest claim for translation was that it allows "the light of pure language, as though reinforced by its own medium, to shine upon the original all the more fully" (p. 79). Although I have difficulties with the construct of "pure" language, I am happy to claim Lucifer for translation as bearer of light, as the father of lies, and as the one who says "no," who will not serve.

De Campos's *non serviam* is particularly directed against the "seemingly natural relationship postulated as dichotomy between form and content" in which the content is considered dominant in the way of an "inner presence" or spirit. Benjamin had already scoffed at this emphasis on translation as "inaccurate transmission of an inessential content," for "what does a literary work 'say'? . . . Its essential quality is not statement or the imparting of information" (pp. 69–70). I would add also the opposite danger, a mechanical understanding of form. We have all read translations of poems which boast of keeping rhyme and meter, but make it hard to believe that the poem was worth any attention to start with. Neither de Campos nor Benjamin considers this, and when they speak of translation as a "reproduction of form" their understanding of form is the intentionality of the work (Benjamin's *Art des Meinens*) rather than any rhyme scheme. De Campos translates Benjamin's word for reproduction, *Wiedergabe*, literally, a "re-giving" of form, and thus stresses in good Luciferian spirit that the original form has to be destroyed

225

first in order to be reshaped. He describes this process as a dionysiac orgy of signification which "dissolves the Apollonian crystallization of the original text back into a state of molten lava."

I wholeheartedly accept this, along with the more commonly remembered aspects of the devil image, because I have long held that translating involves envy, usurpation, and pleasure in destruction—vices and crimes, "negative," "satanic." I have often quoted this analogy:

> A psychoanalyst—dead now many years—showed to certain of his friends and patients photographs of ancient statues in perspectives that stressed the action of time: missing limbs, worn surfaces, features eaten by long erosion. His subjects—so he reports—were invariably uneasy, both attracted and repelled at the sight of these beautiful and ruined objects. Clearly, they felt themselves guilty, having in their hearts willed always death and torture and a slow grinding away of the human form.
>
> Now hard stone offered them mutilations in a dream of unchanging timeless flesh. Here an arm with perfect biceps, broken above the elbow. There a face, ideal, erased as if by sand. Nose, ear, nipple are particularly vulnerable, but chins, cheeks, everything goes, crumbled little by little or suddenly cracked. They stir in the unconscious, these damages—so the good doctor was convinced—not only guilt, the guilt of connivance, but also a longing for reparation, the restoration of destroyed beauty.

The passage is from a literary work, Keith Waldrop's *Quest for Mount Misery*,[3] but the reference is factual. The experiment took place.

Both phases of the viewers' feelings are found in the translation process. Only, my guilt is not just of connivance: I myself take over the action of time, grind away the form of the original work. Worse, I take pleasure in destroying it because it means making it mine[4] and perhaps simply because there is pleasure in destruction. But I assuage my guilt by promising to make reparation, by working to restore the destroyed beauty in my language.

The destruction is serious. Sound, sense, form, reference will never again stand in the same relation to each other. You have to break apart this seemingly natural fusion of elements, this seemingly natural presence. You have to break it apart no matter what your theory is. And unlike in writing, you must have a theory because you constantly have to make conscious decisions as to which elements of the original you will privilege. Even if the translator should not feel Luciferian, even if she *wants* to serve, she can only, in each instance, serve one element at the expense of another.[5] We must wrench apart. We must kill.

However, before I get too dramatic about the devilish side of translation, let us remember that a crucial "no" to what already exists is inherent in the urge to make, that destruction is part of the process of creation. There is always a whole range of structures which are undone. Artistic conventions, customary ways of perception, and, most basically, the structure of experience are transformed. The narrator in *The Book of Questions*[6] asks his protagonist: "Have I betrayed you, Yukel?" The answer has to be: "I have certainly betrayed you." Writing cannot help betraying experience.

> It is I who force you to walk. I sow your steps.
> And I think, I speak for you. I choose and cadence.
> For I am writing
> and you are the wound.
> Have I betrayed you, Yukel?
> I have certainly betrayed you.
>
> (p. 33)

I would therefore move to declare Lucifer the angel of all human creativity, not just of translation.

I would like to give two examples of "nose, ear, nipple" in Edmond Jabès's work, of the parts particularly vulnerable to the action of translation: wordplay, passages which develop from givens of the particular language, etc:

> Quelle différence y a-t-il entre l'amour et la mort? Une voyelle enlevée au premier vocable, une consonne ajoutée au second.
> J'ai perdu à jamais ma plus belle voyelle.
> J'ai reçu en échange la cruelle consonne.
>
> Edmond Jabès, *Le Livre des Questions* (p. 155)

> What difference is there between love and loss? A fricative taken away, two sibilants added.
> I've lost it forever, my lovely *v*
> I got in exchange the cruelest sound.
>
> *The Book of Questions* (p. 141)

In this passage as elsewhere, Jabès posits language (more precisely, the French language) as the basis of our thinking. Why does there seem to be a close relation between love and death? Not because of our evolutionary connection with the amoeba which literally dies into its offspring, as Bataille holds (though he may well be right), but because the two words (in French!) have a surprising number of letters in common. It was essential to find words in English which overlap at least somewhat in their letters, rather than keeping "love" and "death" which only share one "e" so that it is impossible to establish their connection on the basis of a linguistic closeness. I was fortunate to have "loss" available which shares at least half its letters with "love" and is close enough to the semantic field of "death." True, the description of the difference in English lacks the simplicity of the change from vowel to consonant that it has in the French. Operating with "fricative" and "sibilant" is both more technical and less precise because I shift to the level of pronunciation by ignoring the mute *e* in "love" (because it would complicate my description to the point of being cumbersome), but at the same time pay no attention to the fact that the *pronunciation* of the *o* is not the same in "love" and "loss." However, what makes up for this is that the text, within two pages, goes on to a passage about the Nazi S.S., indeed the cruelest letters, the cruelest sound in the context of a work which on one level is about the holocaust. A spectacular piece of translator's luck.

Less importantly, I also could not parallel the internal rhyme (*"belle, voyelle, cruelle"*) with which Jabès laments the loss of his vowel in the following couplet. I substituted a different kind of sound repetition (the assonance and consonance in "lost, forever, lovely, v"). I was pleased that I was able to make the repeated sounds the "l, o, v" of "love," and thus keep present through sound what is declared lost, as Jabès does.

The second example is one of failure. Here I had no luck at all. I could not even find an approximation and finally decided to leave the wordplay in French.

> "Sais-tu, dit-il, que le point final du livre est un oeil et qu'il est sans paupières?"
> *Dieu*, il écrivait *D'yeux*. "D pour désir, ajoutait-il. Désir de voir. Désir d'être vu."
> Trait pour trait, Dieu ressemble à son Nom et son Nom est la Loi.
> Edmond Jabès, *Aely* (p. 7)

> "Do you know that the final period of the book is an eye," he said, "and without lid?
> *Dieu*, "God," he spelled *D'yeux*, "of eyes." "The 'D' stands for desire," he added. "Desire to see. Desire to be seen."
> God resembles His Name to the letter, and His Name is the Law.
> *Yael, Elya, Aely* (p. 203)

Much discussion of translation focuses on this kind of salient problem. However, I think that their solution (which requires a combination of luck and ingenuity) is no measure of the quality of a translation. It is possible to have brilliant equivalents for puns and still produce a translation which misses the tone or rhythm of the work.

This brings me to my main point: What is the *unit* of translation? In contrast to Walter Benjamin, I am convinced that it is not the word, not even the line or sentence. I used to think it was the whole work, which is also what de Campos has in mind when he wants the original in a state of molten lava. The fluidity of this image comes close to the essential working of the process, although on the conscious level there are thousands of small decisions. Still, thinking in terms of the whole work, if you cannot do what the original does where it does it, you can at least do similar things in other places. You can rotate which aspect you privilege in each micro-decision and thus approximate the original at least as a whole.

I still hold with this. But I have recently come to think that the unit is even larger, that it includes what Hans-Georg Gadamer[7] calls the "third dimension" of a work of literature:

> Nothing that is said has its truth simply in itself, but refers instead backward and forward to what is unsaid. Every assertion is motivated, that is, one can sensibly ask of everything that is said, "Why do you say that?" And only when what is not said is understood along with what is said is an assertion understandable.

This resonates strongly with the work of Jabès, who has always stressed the importance of silence, philosophically as well as literally, in the white spaces in his text, the margins that let the words breathe. I was especially reminded of *The Book of Dialogue*:

> There is *pre-dialogue*, our slow or feverish preparation for dialogue. Without any idea of how it will proceed, which form it will take, without being able to explain it, we are convinced in advance that the dialogue has already begun: a silent dialogue with an absent partner.
>
> Then afterwards, there is *post-dialogue* or after-silence. For what we managed to say to the other in our exchange of words—says virtually nothing but this silence, silence on which we are thrown back by any unfathomable, self-centered word whose depth we vainly try to sound.
>
> Then finally there is what could have been the actual dialogue, vital, irreplaceable, but which, alas, does not take place: it begins the very moment we take leave of one another and return to our solitudes.

(p. 7)

Both Jabès and Gadamer take dialogue as *the* manifestation of language, not just a literal exchange between two persons. Gadamer accepts Plato's definition of thought as "the inner dialogue of the soul with itself." Writing and translating as dialogue are familiar metaphors, though I shall want to modify the assumptions about the partner: in writing, it is not so much the future reader as language itself, or, we could say, the potential work which in this process gradually assumes shape. In translating, it is more than just the original.

But there is a crucial difference between Jabès's "silence" and Gadamer's "unsaid." Jabès takes the silence which "we write on,"[8] with which we are lastly in dialogue, in an existential way. It is everything that is "other," non-human, everything that challenges us who are defined by language, by the word. But it also challenges us to assert ourselves in our definition. It is our ultimate motivation to use words. So when Jabès's *Livre du Partage* defines writing as a translation from silence ("the silence which has shaped the word") into more silence ("the silence of the book: a page being read"), we know he is also talking about our lives. But it takes words to make the silence visible: "Writing is an act of silence that makes it legible to us in its entirety" (pp. 45–46).

Here the translator is either struck by despair (how can we possibly translate silence?) or realizes that the problem is so large that it is not one of translation. Because, on this level, the crucial act is to engage, through the nearly infinite space of language, in a dialogue with its final limits, which are also ours: silence, death, the void, or, if you like, God. It is not very important whether we do this in the space of our own language or at one remove, in the space created by the tension between the limits of a piece of writing and two languages.

In contrast, I take Gadamer's "unsaid" not as this ultimate silence, but as what is potentially sayable within a language, but not articulated in a given utterance. It is a *space* for the utterance rather than an ultimate limit, a threat of non-space. This becomes clear in Gadamer's main example, a question which we cannot answer unless we understand why it is asked, what is intended by it:

> A question that we do not understand as motivated can also find no answer. For the motivational background of a question first opens up the realm out of which an answer can be brought and given. Hence there is in fact an infinite dialogue in questioning as well as answering, in whose space word and answer stand. Everything that is said stands in such space.

Curiously, Gadamer's example for the person who does not fully understand this silent, motivational background is the translator. So that in translations this space, this third dimension, becomes felt through its absence:

> Everybody knows how the translation makes what is said in the foreign
> language sound flat. It is reflected on one level, so that the word sense
> and sentence form of the translation follow the original, but the trans-
> lation, as it were, has no space. It lacks that third dimension from which
> the original is built up in its range of meaning. This is an unavoidable
> obstruction of all translation.

Well, not everybody knows this. On the contrary. "The" translation
exists even less than "the" poem or "the" story. Some translations
make what is said sound flat and some do not. But there remains
the interesting notion of the motivational background of the literary
work.

I like Gadamer's use of "space" here, partly because it has always
been my sense of language. Especially, changing my language from
German to English made me very aware of moving in a different
space or, rather, in and between two spaces. (I even wrote a poem
about being an amphibian.)[9] I have also had the sense that in translating I was letting another person's space invade me or that I in
turn was pushing into the author's space, trying to reach something
like its center, the point of conception of the work, though I had
not considered how much this involves another space beyond the
work.

But a space can be explored, even this space of the unsaid. If we
can translate Gadamer's statement into terms of practice, he seems
to be pleading that the translator have read as much as possible
around the work in order to get a feeling for the language as well
as for the literary and cultural context of the original and, most
importantly, for the relation in which the work stands to its linguistic
and cultural context. Not really a revolutionary demand,[10] but one
that Jabès might call a pre-dialogue with the work.

Nobody will be surprised that I found it helpful to read in the
Mishnah when I began translating Jabès's *Book of Questions* with
its texture of rabbinical commentary. I knew Jabès's earlier poems
that are in the wake of Surrealism of which I had read much and of
whose relation to language I had a pretty good sense. But the *Book
of Questions* fused this with an altogether different tradition. I felt
I needed to become at least somewhat familiar with the form in
which orthodox rabbinical commentary had been received into English. Herbert Danby's translation did not give me the language I
was looking for (I found its diction several notches too elevated),
but it gave me a sense of a rhythm of question and answer and
further question and commentary and commentary on the commentary which is behind the *Book of Questions*.[11]

But I would expand the requirement. I would not limit my reading to works explicitly or implicitly part of the tradition of the original. The whole *musée imaginaire* of literature may be involved in the "pre-dialogue" with the work. For instance, when I read Georges Limbour's *Les Vanilliers* I was strongly reminded of the tone of early John Hawkes novels. So, although there is no direct connection between the two writers, if I were to translate Limbour I would steep myself in Hawkes because there seems to be a similar relation to language. They seem to stand in a similar "motivational space." I would say the translator should be as well read as possible in *both* languages, should be conscious of the cultural "air" breathed by herself and by the original author, their differences and affinities. For I think that far from not having a space, translation stands in a very complex space which includes the "unsaid" potential of *both* languages and their relation (cf. Benjamin's "central kinship of languages" that makes translation possible at all) as well as what *was* said in the original work and has been rendered unsaid by the translation. For if there is anything certain it is that the original is part of the "motivational space" of its translation.

This would mean that the destructive phase of translating does not just break apart elements and melt them down to a state of lava still contained in a kettle as it were, but that it pushes the work out of the boundaries of the said, down into the tectonic stresses and heat of the volcano, if I want to follow out de Campos's metaphor, into the nucleus of creative energy where the work was conceived, where the author's dialogue with the infinite space of (a different) language took place. Only there can it take place again, as a more complex dialogue with the original and its space as well as with the space of the translator's language. Only there can the translator become "the one saying it again."

In order to achieve this, to come near recovering this "realm out of which an answer" or a translation "can be brought," the translator, says Gadamer, "must never copy what is said, but place himself in the direction of what is said (i.e., in its meaning) in order to carry over what is to be said into the direction of his own saying."

With the stress on "the *direction* of what is said," Gadamer rejoins Benjamin, whose definition of form is "mode of intention" and who sees the task of the translator as "finding that intended effect upon the language into which he is translating which produces in it the echo of the original" (p. 76).

The sense of transitiveness, of direction and intention, while not exactly a recipe, is a helpful *orientation* for the translator. It is a plea for a complex understanding of form as the *relation* in which the original stands to its language and traditions, its motivational space, as well as for finding a way of recreating, or at least echoing, this *relation* in the translator's language and tradition.

Jerome Rothenberg once argued in conversation that Japanese haiku should be translated in the idiom of Wordsworth because they occupy parallel cultural positions. An intriguing idea which at first sight seems to go in the direction of what I have been saying. But it does not. First of all, the translator would be working with *three* motivational spaces, two of which he does not naturally inhabit. But even without the problem of archaism, this argument privileges the relation to the historical cultural space over that to the language. This attitude makes for *too* smooth a transfer into the conventions of the target language and does away with the transitivity built into translation, the echo of another language. I agree with Benjamin that it is preferable to let the other language stretch and expand the possibilities of English (as the juxtapositions and extreme condensation of the haiku have done through the mediation of Waley and Pound).

I would like to end with an example of such a too smooth transfer, but one which confounds my theoretical convictions. It will be a reminder that translation is a creative act, that in spite of the need for theory its territory cannot be charted beyond a few rules of thumb, any more than that of other kinds of creation.

Here is the first stanza of poem 394 by Osip Mandelstam[12] in a literal version by Clarence Brown:

> Limping automatically [or involuntarily] on the empty earth
> with her irregular, sweet gait,
> she walks, slightly preceding
> [her] quick girlfriend and the youth one year older [or
> younger] than she.
> The straitened freedom of [her] animating affliction
> draws her on.
> And it seems that a lucid surmise
> wants to linger in her gait—
> [the surmise] that this spring weather
> is for us the first mother [i.e. Eve] of the grave's vault
> and [that] this will be forever going on.

W. S. Merwin:

Limping like a clock on her left leg,
at the beloved gait, over the empty earth,
she keeps a little ahead of the quick girl,
her friend, and the young man almost her age.
What's holding her back
drives her on.
What she must know is coming
drags at her foot. She must know
that under the air, this spring,
our mother earth is ready for us
and that it will go on like this forever.

The word-by-word rendering of Clarence Brown shows us that Mandelstam's stanza works exclusively with statement, with abstraction. Merwin changes the poem significantly by adding the image of the clock. Theoretically I disapprove. Adding is a bad idea to start with. Worse, adding an image to a stanza that avoids images and works with statement falsifies the original's relation to its language. The change assimilates Mandelstam into Merwin's own idiom and "cultural air," into a poetry dominated by images, which is still widely considered "mainstream" American poetry. On the other hand, when I read the stanza I am enchanted. The image is so apt, fitting both the limp and the sense of approaching death. The rhythm is so alive, the caesura of the line breaks between the forward and backward movement ("What's holding her back/ drives her on" and "what . . . is coming/ drags at her foot") so marvelous that I cannot help but surrender all theoretical opposition and enjoy the poem.

Still, I prefer a translation in the image of the mutilated statue. If a translation cannot avoid ravages ("chin, cheeks, everything goes"), it can through these ravages point beyond itself and suggest the lost beauty of the original. Thus it can approach Benjamin's ideal translation, a true "transluciferation," which "does not cover the original, does not block its light." And, to come back to Gadamer, if translation can reach such transitiveness, if it can point beyond the limits of what it says and, at its best, even beyond the limits of its language and traditions, it not only has a space to resonate in, but enriches this space, this third dimension, for all the literature in the target language. This may well be what Keith Waldrop's prose poem about the psychoanalyst calls the "beauty in the ruin as ruin."

NOTES

1. Walter Benjamin, "The Task of the Translator," in *Illuminations*,

ed. H. Arendt, tr. Harry Zohn (New York: Schocken, 1969), esp. 75, 79, 81. I have discussed some of my agreements and disagreements with this essay in "The Joy of the Demiurge," in *Translation*, ed. W. Frawley (Newark: University of Delaware Press, 1984), 41–49.

2. Haroldo de Campos, "Transluciferation," *Ex* 4 (1985), 10–14.

3. Keith Waldrop, *The Quest for Mount Misery* (Isla Vista: Turkey Press, 1983). The psychologist in question was John Rickman.

4. This is not quite as facetious as it sounds. Translation is never transparent. It will bear the mark of the translator and of his or her time. Stated extremely, the destruction of the original, a "parricidal" impulse, is necessary to provide the immense energy necessary to recreate, reengender the work.

5. This makes it evident that the whole concept of "fidelity" in translation is simple-minded, especially (though not only) when it means fidelity to the "content."

6. Edmond Jabès, *Le Livre des questions* (Paris: Gallimard, 1963); *The Book of Questions*, tr. R. Waldrop (Middletown, Conn.: Wesleyan University Press, 1976).

Other works of Jabès cited: *Aely* [*Le Livre des questions*, vol. 6], 1972; *Yael/Elya/Aely* [vols. 4–6], tr. R. Waldrop, 1983. *Le Livre du dialogue*, 1984; *The Book of Dialogue*, tr. Rosmarie Waldrop, 1987. *Le Livre du partage*, 1987.

On the closeness of writing and translating cf. Paul Valéry's *Variations sur les Bucoliques:* "*Ecrire quoi que ce soit . . . est un travail de traduction exactement comparable à celui qui opère la transmutation d'un texte d'une langue dans une autre,*" *Oeuvres* 1 (Paris, 1957), 211.

7. Hans-Georg Gadamer, *Philosophical Hermeneutics*, tr. David E. Linge (Berkeley: University of California Press, 1976), 67–68.

8. *The Book of Dialogue*, 39. Phrases like this abound throughout Jabès's work.

9. Cf. also the less abstract spatial metaphor of Wittgenstein:

> Our language can be seen as an old city: a maze of little streets and squares, of old and new houses, and of houses with additions from various periods; and this surrounded by a multitude of new boroughs with straight regular streets and uniform houses.

(*Philosophical Investigations*, tr. G. E. M. Anscombe (Oxford: Basil Blackwell, 1968), 83). Or Benjamin's forest:

> Translation does not find itself in the center of the language forest but on the outside facing the wooded ridge; it calls into it without entering, aiming at that single spot where the echo is able to give, in its own language, the reverberation of the work in the alien one. (76).

10. This is so basic it would hardly need to be mentioned if it were not for people like Robert Bly who presume that a smattering of grammar and a few consultations of a dictionary are ample preparation. The mutilation he has performed on Trakl, for instance, has nothing to do with the necessary

erosion I talked of, but only with ignorance, hubris, and contempt for the author he professes to admire.

11. If I had known about it at the time I would have consulted Arabic works like the *Wedding Nights* of 'Abd al-Rahmane al-Souyoûti, which has a similar structure of guests assembling on various occasions to tell stories, discuss, argue, quote poems or philosophers. A French translation by René R. Khawam was published by Albin Michel in 1972.

12. Osip Mandelstam, *Selected Poems*, tr. Clarence Brown and W. S. Merwin (Atheneum, 1974).

The Guest:
Second Thoughts on
Translating Hölderlin

 RICHARD SIEBURTH

BY SECOND THOUGHTS, I mean that particular mode of revisionary, retrospective reflection akin to what the French call *l'esprit de l'escalier*. That is, the withering repartee that suddenly leaps to mind as you find yourself on the stairway, making your exit from some social gathering where, just a few minutes before, to your utter discomfiture and humiliation, you had proved miserably unable to devise an appropriate comeback to some witty conversational challenge, but instead had just stood there, taken aback, tongue-tied, publicly exposed as incapable of rising to the linguistic or dialectical occasion at hand. Now, as you retreat from the scene of your defeat and make your way up the privacy of the darkened stairs, you are suddenly illuminated with hindsight. A miraculous flush of fluency suddenly overwhelms you as you come to realize, in delayed epiphany, what it was you should have said back there and then. But of course the words have come too *late*. You cannot go back and rectify your failure. All you can do is mull your way home, replaying the incident over and over in freeze frame or slow motion.

I offer this as a metaphor for one of the most disquieting episodes in the life of a translator—the moment at which he or she queasily thinks back on an encounter that, in retrospect, seems to cry out for revision or rectification, and yet whose deficiencies, now graven on the public printed page, lie there for all and sundry to inspect and dissect. How few of us, as translators, are ever given a second chance to correct all the errors that seem to multiply in hindsight—the typos, the dropped lines, the *mot* that still refuses to be *juste*, the downright misreadings, the infelicities of rhythm or phase? How few of us, given the Darwinian economics of publishing, are ever allowed the luxury of revised editions of our efforts? With a few, very rare exceptions, we translators tend to be stuck with our shortcomings. Once published, our versions become in an odd sense *irreversible*. What was initially apprehended as a series of provisional decisions has now strangely acquired the status of something definitive. Or to put it in slightly different terms: what was originally experienced as a *verb*, that is, as an ongoing activity or process or dialogue or encounter or event, has now been transformed into a *noun*—a reified text or object that sits there on the page, facing both its original and its translator like some ironic stillbirth or abortion.

It may be that I am simply evoking the postpartum melancholia that afflicts any author—the euphoria of gestatory expectation giving way to the despondency that attends one's awareness of the sheer irrevocability of the small, helpless textual thing that has thus finally emerged. But I think that the situation I am describing—and I am basing it on my own second thoughts about translating Hölderlin's late Hymns and Fragments—involves a *tristitia* peculiar to translators: given the inevitably "secondary" or "derivative" nature of their enterprise (if one wanted another obstetric metaphor, one might say that a translation is merely an "afterbirth" of the original), the awareness they engage in is always belated, always provisional, always contingent. To me at least, the most interesting translations (among them Hölderlin's Sophocles or Pindar) are not those that fix or ground their originals, but that somehow manage to leave them "up in the air," to suspend them, as it were, for that precarious and precious instant in which original and translation miraculously collide and come asunder, converge and take on distance—I am deliberately borrowing this figure of unstable encounter from Hölderlin's own meditations on the paradoxical measure (or *Maass*) that defines the space in which the human and the divine are simultaneously conjoined and divorced: *"Nah ist, / Und schwer zu fassen."* Near and / Hard to grasp. In "The Task of the Translator" Walter Benjamin explores a similar figure in his celebrated simile of the tangent: "Just as a tangent touches a circle fleetingly and at but a single point, and this touch rather than the point prescribes the law it is to follow on its straight path to infinity, so a translation touches upon the original fleetingly and only at the infinitely small point of sense [*Sinn*] in order to pursue its own private course, observing the laws of fidelity in the freedom of linguistic flux."

Benjamin's image of translation as a vector that tangentially grazes the "sense" of the original only to pursue its own independent path brings me to another area of postmortem reflection. If, on the one hand, I have been describing the kind of retrospective alienation a translator might feel vis-à-vis his or her all-too-finished product—a kind of nostalgia for that period of innocence when everything still seemed virtual, when nothing was yet "definitive," when every decision still lay open to revision, in short, a period in which the very *process* of translation, of discovery, of experiment, seemed to matter far more than its eventual completion (in my case this lasted some seven years)—on the other hand, I also now find myself reacting in exactly the opposite fashion, that is, I look back on what I have done and, far from seeing it as irrevocably fixed in some final printed form, I watch it unravel in front of my very eyes. I suppose if one wanted metaphors for these two complementary predicaments, in the former case the translator assumes the position of Lot's wife: to look back is to experience petrification, immobilization; the living tissue of the text now reads in retrospect like so much dead letter. But in the latter case, the experience more resembles that of Orpheus: you look back only to discover that your loving translation has vanished. And in its place—uncannily—now stands the original.

Let me explain. Anyone who has engaged in translation has probably experienced that particular phase of the process (it is one of the stages in what George Steiner terms "the hermeneutic motion") in which one's translation seems to have more or less completely "covered" the original. I use the term "cover" here in a number of senses, all involving various implications of protection, concealment, and mastery. One displays one's mastery of a subject or field by covering it. Stallion covers mare. Text covers text in a palimpsest. A book in turn may or may not be told by its cover. To cover for someone is to substitute one's presence for another's absence or act as an accomplice in dissimulation. In rock 'n' roll parlance, a cover is a recording made by one performer or aimed at one market of a tune originally recorded by a different performer and aimed at a different market (as in, say, a Rolling Stones "cover" of an earlier Chuck Berry hit). All of which I think very nicely covers a number of different dimensions of translation. To return to my own personal encounter with Hölderlin's late Hymns and Fragments, I felt as I completed my translation (but is a translation ever "complete"?) that I had more or less succeeded in covering the texts I had chosen (or that had chosen me). Indeed, so absorbed was I in getting my versions just right that in the end I could no longer see or hear the original: Hölderlin's German had been completely obscured, blocked out, covered by the English that I had so labored to put in its place. The translator as Narcissus, so entranced by the reflection he has crafted that he remains blissfully oblivious to the beckonings of Echo.

Little by little, however, after the initial exhilaration of publication had passed and I returned to what I had done (whether in classroom teaching of Hölderlin or in private rereading), a strange and marvelous thing began to happen. The originals that I had so triumphantly thought I had laid to rest now began to stir into life again—and so insistently that they seemed to be gradually erasing or obscuring the versions I had created in their stead. Or, more precisely (and this is one of the virtues and perils of an *en face* edition), the originals were once again reasserting their place *alongside* my translations to such an extent that the light emitted by Hölderlin's German on the left page was now blinding my parallel English versions on the right. Or, to use a slightly different metaphor, it was as if the original, now come back to life, had returned to haunt the translation like some uncanny revenant or doppelgänger. A psychoanalysis of translation might well conclude that the situation I am here evoking involves a kind of return of the repressed, a salutary reminder that the original (especially an original of the power of Hölderlin) can be mastered or surmounted only *à ses propres risques et périls*. Hölderlin's own translations of Pindar and Sophocles are perhaps the most eloquent examples we have of such tragic hubris: reaching out to appropriate the fire of Hellas, he gets burned in the process, and yet it is precisely the intensity of this conflagration that accounts for the dark, charred radiance of his versions. As he writes in one of his late fragments: "*Verwegner! möchst von Angesicht zu Angesicht / Die Seele sehn / Du gehest in Flammen unter.*" Reckless! wanting to see the soul / Face to face / You go down in flames.

I certainly do not want to give the impression I am comparing my own experience as a translator to Hölderlin's—that would be grotesquely hubristic. I am merely trying to explore the basic provisionality or instability of the relation between the original and translation by underscoring how, in my case at least, Hölderlin's text seemed to recoup itself, to uncover itself (Heideggerian *aletheia?*) only *after* having been silenced or occluded by my translation. In other words, although I had initially set out with the intent of rendering Hölderlin's late work more "accessible" to the English-speaking reader, this enterprise had paradoxically blocked my own access to the originals. Only in hindsight, only in retrospective distance, only by having watched my own translations fall apart and fade in the face of the original, could I now begin to read (or reread) Hölderlin's German afresh. Without wanting to overly Hegelianize it, I suppose the model of translation I am describing here is closely linked to the metaphors of sacrifice that inform so much of Hölderlin's own work: the original is sacrificed (or canceled or "sublated") in the translation, just as the translation is in turn sacrificed back to the original so that the latter, now renewed and transformed, may continue on its course.

Walter Benjamin's "The Task of the Translator" (which is in itself a "translation" of Hölderlin) speaks of this process in terms of the essential historicity of literary works—their *Fortleben* or *Ueberleben* or *Nachleben*, that is, the way in which works of the past, despite (or precisely because of) the fact that they are no more, continue to survive or pursue an afterlife. Translations, Benjamin argues, are the crucial vehicles of this posthumous survival, for in them "the life of the originals attains its ever-renewed, latest and most abundant unfolding [*Entfaltung*]." "In its afterlife," Benjamin continues, "the original undergoes a change. Even words with fixed meanings can undergo a process of maturation or decomposition. What once sounded fresh may later come to sound hackneyed; what was once modern may someday sound archaic." In short, Benjamin insists that the original is in no way *fixed*; as it moves through the various avatars of its afterlife, it is subject to any number of ramifications. And the same holds true of translations. Benjamin notes: "While a poet's words endure in his own language, even the greatest translation is destined to become part of the growth of its own language and destined to be absorbed by its renewal [Benjamin's German here plays on the verbs *eingehen* and *untergehen*: a translation both *goes in* to its own language and *goes under* in it]. Translation is so far removed from being the sterile equation of two dead languages that of all literary forms it is the one charged with the special mission of watching over the maturing process of the original language and the birthpangs [or deathpangs] of its own." That is, not only does translation as *Fortleben* reveal the death (or deconstruction) of the original, but it also watches over its own inevitable demise, mournfully aware that its encounter with the original can never be definitive.

Benjamin underlines the lability that characterizes the life (or afterlife) of both the original and its translations. If the original is conceived as a historical process moving through time, the translation in turn becomes merely a momentary point of convergence along this posthumous path, a point that will soon be left behind in the dust—just as Hölderlin's German has now passed through my English with a jolt to pursue its slightly deflected course into future readings, future versions. Benjamin's profoundly temporal or historical approach to translation makes him, I believe, the first theorist of translation to break with the dominant tradition of viewing translations as having an essentially *metaphorical* relation to their originals—that is, as being somehow analogous or similar or equivalent to their originals. True, he rhetorically deploys metaphors throughout his essay, but only in order to insist that translation is something very different from the theory or practice of imitation. Translation, he argues, should not be confused with such concepts as similarity, substitutability, copying, or reproduction [*Wiedergabe*]—all species of metaphor. Instead, the figures he privileges are *synecdoche* (i.e., a translation is "part" of the ongoing afterlife of the original) or *metonymy* (i.e., a translation is an effect whose cause is the original or, in slightly different terms, a translation exists as a contiguous extension of or supplement [*Ergänzung*] to the original). For Benjamin, the privileged form of this metonymic adjacency is the targum or interlinear version of the Scriptures, the translation that does not so much resemble its original as lie in between its lines, both languages dovetailed together as the fractured parts of some greater "pure Language" [*reine Sprache*]—the two broken shards of a *symbolon* momentarily brought together as a sign of shared promise or contract.

Benjamin rejects the traditional view of translation as a mode of representation, reproduction, or mimesis in favor of a more "figural" approach (hence his attractiveness to such theorists as de Man and Derrida). Despite his apparent espousal of radical literalism or *Wörtlichkeit* ("For if the sentence is the wall before the language of the original, literalness is the arcade"), Benjamin by no means recommends this "wordliness" on the grounds that it permits a greater resemblance or equivalence between translation and original, but rather because it allows both to enter into a *relation* or participate in an *exchange* that, ideally, will serve to liberate the space (or Language) that lies in between the two—much as Mallarmé insists that it is the blanks, the intervals, the margins, the silences, that constitute the true armature of a poem.

As I now look back on my translations of Hölderlin, it is above all the space *between* my English and his German that occupies me. If I take up the published book, it is no longer the right-hand page that automatically draws my eye, but rather the entire space to the left of it—the intervening whiteness between the *en face* texts, and, further to the left, of course Hölderlin's originals in which, from time to time, I can occasionally see the faint traces of my own words reaching through the palimpsest. I suppose I originally undertook my versions in the naive belief that some metaphorical condition of resemblance might emerge: I was going to produce texts that would somehow read "like" Hölderlin to the American eye and ear. In hindsight, however, I now realize that something altogether different was really at issue all the while: to offer temporary hospitality to Hölderlin's errant original, to have it over as a guest for a while, to experience the communion of simple adjacency, one language sharing a moment of silence with another. Oddly enough, this was the subject of the very first Hölderlin fragment I ever translated, the fragment that led me to undertake the entire enterprise in the first place. Only now in retrospect, filled with second thoughts, am I beginning to grasp the point it makes about translation:

> *Bauen möcht*
> I want to build
>
> *und neu errichten*
> and raise anew
> *des Theseus Tempel und die Stadien*
> the temples of Theseus and the stadiums
> *und wo Perikles gewohnet*
> and where Perikles lived
>
> *Es fehlet aber das Geld, denn zu viel*
> But there's no money, too much
> *is ausgegeben heute. Zu Gaste nemlich hatt*
> spent today. I had a guest
> *ich geladen und wir sassen beieinander*
> over and we sat together

BACKGROUND READINGS

Jacques Derrida, "*Des Tours de Babel*," in Joseph F. Graham, ed., *Difference in Translation* (Ithaca: Cornell University Press, 1985).

Paul de Man, "Conclusions: Walter Benjamin's 'The Task of the Translator,'" in *The Resistance to Theory* (Minneapolis: University of Minnesota Press, 1986).

Translation in Theory and
in a Certain Practice

 DENIS DONOGHUE

I

I CHOOSE FOR COMMENTARY an anonymous love-poem written in Irish, probably in the first half of the seventeenth century; it is readily available in *An Duanaire 1600–1900: Poems of the Dispossessed*, edited by Sean O'Tuama and translated into English by Thomas Kinsella (Dolmen Press, 1981) and in *The New Oxford Book of Irish Verse*, edited with translations by Kinsella (Oxford University Press, 1986.) In *An Duanaire* it is given as one of a class "of elegant occasional poems in loose syllabic meters dating from the seventeenth century—love poems, satires, religious poems and others." In the *Oxford Book* the date is revised to fifteenth/sixteenth century. As O'Tuama notes in *An Duanaire*, the common form of such poems is syllabic, each stanza of four lines, seven syllables in each line; there are rhyming linkages between the end words of the second and fourth lines, between the final syllable of the first line and an internal syllable in the second, and between the final syllable of the third line and an internal syllable of the fourth. In the second stanza, for instance—see the text below—internal rhyming in the first two lines links *Créad, d'éag, bhéal,* and *déad.* In the third line, internal rhyming links *míolla* with *aol,* and *crobh* with *t-ucht;* in the fourth, *dáibh* with *bás.*

Here is the poem:

Ní Bhfuighe Mise Bás Duit
Ní bhfuighe mise bás duit,
  a bhean úd an chuirp mar ghéis;
daoine leamha ar mharbhais riamh,
  ní hionann iad is mé féin.

Créad uma rachainn-se d'éag 5
   don bhéal dearg, don déad mar bhláth?
An crobh míolla, an t-ucht mar aol,
   an dáibh do-gheabhainn féin bás?

Do mhéin aobhdha, th'aigneadh saor,
   a bhas thana, a thaobh mar chuip, 10
a rosc gorm, a bhráighe bhán.
   ní bhfuighe mise bás duit.

Do chiocha corra, a chneas úr,
   do ghruaidh chorcra, do chúl fiar—
go deimhin ní bhfuighead bás 15
   dóibh sin go madh háil le Dia.

Do mhala chaol, t'fholt mar ór,
   do rún geanmnaidh, do ghlór leasc,
do shál chruinn, do cholpa réigh—
   ní mhuirbhfeadh siad acht duine leamh. 20

A bhean úd an chuirp mar ghéis,
   do hoileadh mé ag duine glic;
aithne dhamh mar bhíd na mná—
   ní bhfuighe mise bás duit!

In the introduction to *An Duanaire* O'Tuama and Kinsella said
that their primary aim in the translations was to secure "the greatest
possible fidelity of content": the translations "are as close to the
original Irish as we could make them." More specifically: "All images
and ideas occurring in the Irish are conveyed in translation and
images or ideas not occurring in the Irish are not employed."

Here is the translation (I shall refer to it as Kinsella's, since he
gives it again without change in his *Oxford Book*):

I Will Not Die for You
I will not die for you,
   lady with swanlike body.
Meagre men you have killed so far,
   and not the likes of me.

For what would make me die? 5
   Lips of red, or teeth like blooms?
A gentle hand, a lime-white breast?
   Should I die for these?

Your cheerful mood, your noble mind?
   O slender palm and flank like foam, 10
eye of blue and throat of white,
   I will not die for you.

Your rounded breasts, O skin refined,
   your flushed cheeks, your waving hair
—certainly I will not die   15
   on their account unless God will.

Your narrow brows, your hair like gold,
   your chaste intent, your languid voice,
your smooth calf, your curved heel
   —only meagre men they kill.   20

Lady with swanlike body,
   I was reared by a cunning hand!
I know well how women are.
   I will not die for you.

A few comments on meaning, emphasis, and tone. Line 1: *mise*
is the emphatic form of the first person singular, so it is more insis-
tent than Kinsella's "I will not die for you." Still in line 1: *duit* does
not quite mean "for you," if "die for you" is construed as implying
sacrifice. Not "for your sake," but "on account of you." I will not,
like weaker men, die because of you. Line 2: *Úd* means "yonder,"
a distancing word. *Bean* means woman, but Kinsella's "lady" is all
right, and it gets the distance; the speaker is not talking to her
directly but across barriers of caste and class. *An chuirp mar ghéis*
is a genitive, therefore more constitutive than Kinsella's merely
dative and adjectival "with swanlike body." You, yonder woman, of
body like a swan. Line 3: *daoine leamha* means empty-headed,
foolish people. Line 5: *rachainn-se* is more emphatic again than
Kinsella's "me": what would make (a fine fellow like me) go off to
die? Line 6: *déad* means the whole tooth-plate, not the individual
teeth. Line 7: *an t-ucht mar aol*, the breast like lime. Lime was used
in the Big House as whitewash and disinfectant, so it has associations
with majesty. Line 8: *féin* keeps the insistence going: I myself. Line
9: *saor* means "free," but Kinsella's "noble" is close enough, since
only noble ladies could have free minds. Line 10: *thaobh* means
"side." Kinsella's "flank" is a bit Audenesque. Line 13: *Úr* means
"fresh," alive-looking, not (or not necessarily) Kinsella's "refined."
Line 14: Kinsella reverses the phrases: *do ghruaidh chorcra* means
"your waving hair," *do chúl fiar* is "your purple cheeks," but Kinsella's "flushed" meets the case pretty well. Line 17: *Do mhala
chaol* means "your narrow brow" (singular) or temple, narrow probably because of the veil, hood, or wimple she wears. Line 18: *leasc*
means "modest" rather than Kinsella's "languid." Line 19: Kinsella
again reverses the phrases. *Do cholpa réigh* means "your ready (or

fine) calf." It is a bit livelier than Kinsella's "smooth." Line 22: Kinsella's "by a cunning hand" is not in the Irish. *Duine* means "person": I was taught by a clever one. Line 23: *aithne* is one of the three forms of knowledge discriminated in Irish: it means what I have learnt about people, or about one person, as distinct from *eolas*, which is general information, and from *fios*, which means wisdom. Curiously, *aithne* also means commandment, as in the Ten Commandments, but I do not suppose that comes into the poem.

When the *Oxford Book* came out, I argued that Kinsella was ill-advised in preferring his own translation, in every case, to earlier ones, because this preference suppressed the entire history of the reception of these Irish poems. In the period from about 1885 to 1940, English translations of the Irish sagas and lyrics were the only means by which most of the modern Irish poets and their readers gained access to the lore upon which the ideology of the Irish Literary Revival was based. Yeats and most of his contemporaries did not know enough Irish to read the original poems. Kinsella's decision to use only his own translations had the effect of transcending the experience of several generations. His gifts as a translator are formidable, but it is hardly surprising that every poem he translates sounds as if he had written it. His compacted, laconic style takes charge; as in the fifth stanza:

> Your narrow brows, your hair like gold,
>   your chaste intent, your languid voice,
> your smooth calf, your curved heel
>   —only meagre men they kill.

The last line is far more abrupt than the Irish: *ni mhuirbhfeadh siad acht duine leamh.* I agree that earlier translations have sinned by taking freedoms. Frank O'Connor's translation of that stanza reads:

> The devil take the golden hair!
>   That maiden look, that voice so gay,
> That delicate heel and pillared thigh
>   Only some foolish man would slay.

In the Irish the devil does not take anything, and his intervention not only ignores the woman's narrow brow but ruins the symmetry of the two companionable phrases in each of the first three lines, and therefore the change of tone in the last one.

It may be thought the highest praise to say that Kinsella's translations make the poems sound as if he had written them. But this is a disputed matter, and I want to rehearse a little of the dispute.

II

There would be no dispute if the translation were offered as a new poem, inspired indeed or at least prompted by the original but now an independent work. The simplest analogies for this procedure come from painting and music. Brahms's *Variations on a Theme by Haydn* pays tribute to an original theme, alludes to it, but does not undertake any representative duty toward it. Nor does Picasso's *Les Demoiselles d'Avignon* propose to speak on behalf of its sources—various *Baigneuses* by Cézanne, bits of Iberian and African sculpture. Allusion is not translation; its relation to the original is opportunistic rather than representative. In one respect, the translator is a modest fellow; he wants to walk by placing his feet in the footprints left by someone else. In another respect, he is a braggart, he claims to carry over—I need a different metaphor—someone else's meaning from that someone's language. Kinsella's translation—I revert to the first metaphor—follows the anonymous Irish poem step by step, and pretends that the differences between Irish and English do not nullify the effort, that the content of the Irish speaker's imagined feeling for the woman may still be recovered. But there is a limit to Kinsella's modesty, and that limit is the settled character of his style: he insists on always sounding like himself.

In *The Sense of an Ending* Frank Kermode discusses the practice of treating the past as a special case of the present. In translation, we do this when we make the original submit to our modern style, disappearing into it. If we regarded the original as absolutely alien, we would have to deem it untranslatable, an instance of the sentiment in which we regard our "fictions of accord"—to use Kermode's phrase in another context—as specious. In practice, no translator is so severly principled. If a translation is attempted, it is assumed to be at least reasonably possible. The original, upon being addressed, says: "Change me, into yourself; even if you fail and your failure is foredoomed." Upon that invitation, a relation of some kind ensues between the original and the emerging translation.

But there is a scrupulous device, employed in Stanley Burnshaw's *The Poem Itself:* that is, you do not offer to transpose one structure— say, Mallarmé's *"Don du poème"* into another, a poem in English. Burnshaw has argued that the only way we can experience the poetry of a language we do not understand is "by learning to hear and pronounce (if only approximately) the sounds of the originals and 'simultaneously' reading literal renditions." In Burnshaw's practice, the reader is held within the sounds and sense of the original language, and is aided by literal rendering and by judicious commentary; in the commentary, the translator points to acoustic and semantic properties of the original. The advantage of Burnshaw's method over a crib is that the original poem is not replaced by something else, it is not reduced to a meaning or an action in another language. For the duration of the reading the reader stays in the ambience of the foreign language, an experience so valuable, in Burnshaw's eyes, that even its limitedness is preferable to any English substitute.

There are further possibilities, of course. Pound's theory and practice of translation are predicated on two assumptions: one, that certain foreign poems have perceptions which English lacks; two, that these perceptions testify to a road not taken, a development which English should have pursued. In his major essay on Cavalcanti Pound argues that English poetry since Shakespeare has lost much by resorting to Petrarch rather than to Cavalcanti:

> We appear to have lost the radiant world where one thought cuts through another with clean edge, a world of moving energies *"mezzo oscuro rade," "risplende in se perpetuale effecto,"* magnetisms that take form, that are seen, or that border the visible, the matter of Dante's paradiso, the glass under water, the form that seems a form seen in a mirror, these realities perceptible to the sense. . . .
>
> (Literary Essays, p. 154)

Pound's way, in his several translations of Cavalcanti—starting with *The Sonnets and Ballate of Guido Cavalcanti* (1911), then the long essay in *The Dial*, 1928 and 1929, finally canto 36—is to go back to a pre-Shakespearean English for which Campion and Henry Lawes provide clearest warrant; and to write as if Wyatt, Surrey, and Shakespeare had not dominated English in Petrarchan modes. The results have been examined by many critics, notably by Donald Davie in *Ezra Pound: Poet as Sculptor* (1965); Hugh Kenner in his brief introduction to *The Translations of Ezra Pound* (1953) and in a recent essay, "Ezra Pound and Modernism," *The World and I*, June 1988, pp. 559–70; and by John Hollander in his *Vision and Resonance* (1975; 1985).

Some aspects of the procedure are clear, starting with Kenner's insistence that Pound "never translates 'into' something already existing in English." When Pound translates Cavalcanti, he shows what English might have become if it had taken a different tack at a crucial moment, roughly 1600; if it had retained rather than forgotten Chaucer; if it had taken its character from Elizabethan music rather than Elizabethan theater. But Kenner's further argument is more questionable; that Pound "doesn't translate the words," that he goes behind or through the words to "the thing he expresses: desolate seafaring, or the cult of the plum-blossoms, or the structure of sensibility that attended the Tuscan anatomy of love." It follows— or it would follow, if Kenner were right—that what Pound is translating is "a modus of thought or feeling" which happened to have been "crystallized," once before, by Cavalcanti or Rihaku or someone else. I do not think anyone would now accept Kenner's easy separation of "the words" from the thoughts and feelings supposedly lying silent behind them. It might be wiser to avoid that problem by holding every issue within language; as Hollander does in his commentary on Pound's deliberate archaism in the Cavalcanti translations and the *Cantos*.

Quoting and analyzing Rossetti's translation of Dante's so-called "Story Sestina"—"A while ago, I saw her dress'd in green"—Hollander shows that there were indeed available to Pound non-Miltonic instances of translation into English, and he goes on to say that "the archaizing element" in Pound's translation of Cavalcanti's "*Donna mi Prega*"—"In memory's locus taketh he his state" "may be a rather profound matter, part of a deep attitude toward style and a self-consciousness about it":

> Perhaps it is more like a Chattertonian style of pastiche than we have been able heretofore to think. The matter of Romance was not only an alternative to the mythopoetic world of the American Romantic tradition—the dialectic of landscape and selfhood and their mutual intrusions. An emphatic and intense show of coping with it became for a while as authentic a way to "drink, and be whole again beyond confusion" as, for example, E. A. Robinson's deep draught of English literature, even to the point of his reconsecrating society verse to real poetic purposes.
>
> (*Vision and Resonance*, second edition, p. 243)

Romance as an alternative to Emerson; "an emphatic and intense show of coping with it": I take these as indicating Pound's attempt to posit for English a different destiny. The archaism is his insistence that he knows what he is doing, and that it is only because English has taken another road that his translations sound archaic. As Kenner notes in "Ezra Pound and Modernism":

> The radical novelty of "The Seafarer" is that instead of adapting the original to a set of metrical and syntactic conventions we're prepared to recognize as a normal English poem, it adapts the norms of English poetry to the original. That's a Trojan-horse approach to the translator's

art; once admitted, some harmless-seeming alien entity proceeds to take possession, modify, conquer.

(P. 563)

The analogy is in one respect misleading: whatever combination of syllables, phonemes, words, and syntactical procedures Pound made in "The Seafarer," these were already "there," in English, waiting to be activated. Kenner's references to Victorian poetry make it seem far more circumscribed than it was—it included Hopkins, Whitman, Clough, and Dickinson—and therefore make Pound's translations seem even more daring than they were. However, he is right to speak up for them. Indeed, there is no reason why we should be more hostile to Pound's deliberate archaism than we are to the efforts of other writers, notably Barnes, Hopkins, and Joyce, to give English a different destiny. In any case, Pound's theory of translation is clear enough: try to recover what we have lost, carry over from earlier poets of a better tradition something of what they have and we need. The process is what Hollander calls "the internalization of other prior models, that they may be incorporated into the new poetic being."

But "internalization" does not quite meet the case: its spatial figure is entirely assimilative, it does not allow sufficiently for one of the richest options available, a translator's resistance to his own process, a scruple darkening the decision. When I said that Kinsella's translations make the original poems sound as if he had written them, I had such resistance in mind. It is not merely an excess of nationalism which prompts me to think that Kinsella might have made the Irish poem offer more recalcitrance, a principled resistance to the destiny he proposed for it. I am not entirely resigned to the implication that an Irish poem goes into the English language so amiably; or, otherwise put, that Kinsella's English, in which one hears not only Kinsella but Eliot and Auden and the Joyce of *Dubliners* and much besides, so winningly smooths over the differences between a seventeenth-century Irish poem and a twentieth-century English one. I would like to find that the Irish poem has retained a mind of its own.

So I want to look at two theories of translation, Walter Benjamin's and Paul de Man's, which in their different styles propose a more arduous relation between translation and original.

Benjamin's essay is "The Task of the Translator: An Introduction to the Translation of Baudelaire's *Tableaux parisiens*" (*Illuminations*, ed. Hannah Arendt, tr. Harry Zohn, 1968). It is a difficult work, mainly because it implies a theology of pure *Logos* which may be intuited but only with great inadequacy discussed. So far as the essay may be summarized, it emphasizes that a translation isssues from an original, not so much from its life as from its afterlife; it marks a certain stage in the continued life of the original. But the merit of a translation does not consist in transmitting the information, content, or meaning of the original: such an aim would be trivial. Ultimately, the purpose of a translation is to express "the central reciprocal relationship between languages." This relationship is not one of likeness, but of kinship: the kinship is one of intentionality, "an intention, however, which no single language can attain by itself but which is realized only by the totality of their intentions supplementing each other: pure language." Pure language, in Benjamin's context, seems to be the utterance of a primordial *Logos*:

> In this pure language—which no longer means or expresses anything but is, as expressionless and creative Word, that which is meant in all languages—all information, all sense, and all intention finally encounter a stratum in which they are destined to be extinguished.

It is the translator's task "to release in his own language that pure language which is under the spell of another, to liberate the language imprisoned in a work in his re-creation of that work."

I repeat that Benjamin's essay is more a tone poem than a paraphrasable essay. At various points he seems to say that in at least one respect a translation has a worthier purpose than the original. Every consideration that causes other translators to despair of their mission—inevitable failure; disjunction between the connotations of one language and another; the unyieldingness of their own language—is welcomed by Benjamin. I think the reason is that he welcomes every occasion on which unity is demonstrably impossible; just as he makes out a stronger ethical case for allegory than for symbol. He is not dismayed, for instance, to remark that "while content and language form a certain unity in the original, like a fruit and its skin, the language of the translation envelops its content like a royal robe with ample folds: for it signifies a more exalted language than its own and thus remains unsuited to its content, overpowering and alien." Hence "it is not the highest praise of a translation to say that it reads as if it had originally been written in that language." Poet and translator are different beings, the difference is vested in their different intentions. "The intention of the poet is spontaneous, primary, graphic": that is, the poet wants to write a poem, wants to express something-or-other, wants to incarnate a feeling, a desire, a passion real or imagined. The intention of the translator "is derivative, ultimate, ideational"; that is, it makes no claim upon the original intention or intuition, does not pretend that it is his own or otherwise accessible beyond words. Benjamin's reason seems to be that it is the translation, not the original, which points beyond itself toward pure language. Evidently, the way up and the way down are the same: down, plunging from abyss to abyss: up, coming to rest in Holy Writ. The particular merit of a translation, Benjamin appears to say, is that it knows it speaks a fallen tongue, it knows that abjection is the condition of its existing at all.

It follows that the relation between a translation and its original, so far as the sense of the original is in question, is comparable to that between a tangent and the circle it touches:

> Just as a tangent touches a circle lightly and at but one point, with this touch rather than with the point setting the law according to which it is to continue on its straight path to infinity, a translation touches the original lightly and only at the infinitely small point of the sense, thereupon pursuing its own course according to the laws of fidelity in the freedom of linguistic flux.

By "fidelity" in that passage Benjamin does not mean the conventional "fidelity to the original"; he means fidelity to the ideal of pure language, and freedom in its pursuit.

The difficulty with Benjamin's essay is that it veers between intuitions of sublime silence, language as Pure Act, and—on occasion—fairly straightforward recommendations; such as the advice offered by Rudolf Pannwitz in *The Crisis of European Culture* that a translator should allow his own language to be powerfully affected by the foreign language of the original, rather than insist on keeping his own language in the state in which he finds it. (This advice, by the way, would support Pound in his dealings with Cavalcanti.) It remains to be said, of Benjamin's theory of translation, that it is a theory of allegory and at the same time a theory of the sublime; of the linguistic intention of meaning, willing to see itself abject at every point and persisting in its abjection. Translations are precious in this context because they emphasize that the translation, in this sole respect like the original, consists of broken fragments of a once putatively intact vessel. Benjamin's theory is also post-Hegelian, inasmuch as it is a theory of translation as the necessarily fallen recognition of Absolute Spirit.

Paul de Man's essay, a commentary on Benjamin's, was delivered as the last of his Messenger Lectures at Cornell on March 4, 1983;

it is most conveniently available in *The Lesson of Paul de Man*, *Yale French Studies* no. 69 (1985). Almost as difficult to summarize as Benjamin's, it begins by setting aside the messianic or what I might call the "logological" element in Benjamin. Benjamin's *reine Sprache*—pure language—is an embarrassment to de Man, who hastens to declare that there never was such a thing: "There was no vessel in the first place, or we have no knowledge of this vessel, or no awareness, no access to it, so for all intents and purposes there has never been one." The assertion is gruff, indeed positivistic. Benjamin never claimed that a *reine Sprache* exists or has existed as an accessible form of speech; any more than a Christian claims access to the primordial Logos, except inasmuch as the imitation of Christ as mediator gives one a partial glimpse of it. The mode of being of Logos is in principle, not in particle. But de Man will have none of this talk of *reine Sprache*; if we are exiles, most of all in our native language, we are exiled from a homeland we have never had.

Glossing Benjamin's essay, de Man insists on the differences between poet and translator:

> The poet has some relationship to meaning, to a statement that is not purely within the realm of language. That is the naiveté of the poet, that he has to say something, that he has to convey a meaning which does not necessarily relate to language. The relationship of the translator to the original is the relationship between language and language, wherein the problem of meaning or the desire to say something, the need to make a statement, is entirely absent. Translation is a relation from language to language, not a relation to an extralinguistic meaning that could be copied, paraphrased, or imitated.

Translation, therefore, is concerned with "what in the original belongs to language." It is by definition belated.

Like Benjamin, de Man turns this necessity into a virtue, though not one susceptible to pleasure. The categorical belatedness of a translation allows it to exist in a critical or ironic relation to the original. Like critical theory or, presumably, like Deconstruction, translation acts precisely by not imitating or reproducing the original, and by this refusal it shows in the original "a mobility, an instability, which at first one did not notice." The translation can put the original "in motion" and question its claim to canonical authority by showing that it, too, is merely an afterlife, therefore an absence, a death. De Man values translation—or at least respects it—for the shadow of death it casts upon an original which was naive enough to think itself buoyantly articulate. Translations, de Man takes a certain grim pleasure in reporting, "kill the original, by discovering that the original was already dead."

At the end of his essay, commenting on Benjamin's distinction between *das Gemeinte* and the *Art des Meinen*—between what is meant and the way in which language means—de Man argues that the first is indeed intentional, but the second is not; or at least that "whereas the meaning-function is certainly intentional, it is not a priori certain at all that the mode of meaning, the way by which I mean, is intentional in any way."

> The way in which I can try to mean is dependent upon linguistic properties that are not only not made by me, because I depend on the language as it exists for the devices which I will be using; it is as such not made by us as historical beings, it is perhaps not even made by humans at all.

Who made the English language seems to me a fairly ascertainable question. Who made language "as such" is not at all interesting, even as a conceit. Paul de Man's version of Deconstruction was always the sinister side of angelism. But in any case he was unduly restrictive in his sense of "the language as it exists." It is one of the purposes of translation to show us that the language as it exists is far more diverse than we had thought. Kenner, too, as I have indicated, thinks he knows the lineaments of the language as it exists. Quoting Pound's "Cino,"

> Lips, words, and you snare them,
> Dreams, words, and they are as jewels,
> Strange spells of old deity,
> Ravens, nights, allurement:
> And they are not;
> Having become the souls of song

he remarks, "This isn't the English soul of 1908." Perhaps not, but I do not see how he could know what "the English soul" could possibly be, in 1908 or at any other time. That there are and have been English souls, I am ready to concede, but "the English soul" is a mere notion. Besides, the English language in 1908 contained at least *in potentia* the possibilities enacted by E. P. in that year. And more. We may indeed be imprisoned in our language as it exists in our time, but there is no merit in complaining that the space is intolerably restricted and the conditions otherwise disgusting.

III

It is clear that Benjamin and, even more insistently, de Man think of translation not as transmission of meaning but as the exposure of a text to a more explicit stage of its doom. De Man regards the afterlife of a poem as proof not of its continuance but of its death. Translation is a coroner's report: the body is pronounced dead, and the cause of its death is disclosed. The merit de Man claims for translation, as for the deconstructive form of hermeneutics, is the removal of what is deemed to be mystification. The particularly guilty form of mystification is the acquired and reiterated sentiment of unity, unity of apprehension, unity of being.

In common practice, few translators see their job in these terms: the trope of *translatio,* transmission, "bringing over," is still in place. If failure in translation is by definition inevitable, so that the only question is one of degree, most translators put up with this disability, they do not take skeptical pleasure in it.

Kinsella assumes, for instance, that a certain recognizable feeling went into the Irish poem, took that form without visible residue. His aim as translator is to suggest the quality of that feeling; on the assumption that the feeling is common to all, a manifestation of love, desire, need, lack, resentment, barriers of class and station in a particular constellation of sentiment. He shows no serious misgiving about language as such, or the capacity of language to apprehend a certain structure of sentiment. The main problem arises from the structural and other differences between Irish and English. A different translation would testify to a different sense of these factors. If I were to translate the first stanza as

> I shall not die on your account,
> Lady, body of a swan,
> Puny men you have ever killed
> But not the likes of me

I would claim, with whatever justice, that my first line comes closer than Kinsella's to the tone, the stance, of the original, the degree of emphasis in the speaker's pride; that my second line is more correctly sensuous than Kinsella's, that it observes the constitutive or genitive intimacy of the description; that my third line is a little more accurate—*riamh* meaning "ever"; that my fourth line is more idiomatically correct—"but" rather than "and"—and that we are both at about the same remove from literalness, the literal translation of the line being, "They are not the same as I." But there are no ideological differences, so far as I can see, between Kinsella's translation and mine. My theory is grumpier than Kinsella's, I suppose, because I want the differences between Irish and English to remain visible, unelided. But my practice, if I had one, would observe what Jacques Derrida has called the "twice one" concept of translation, "the operation of passing from one language into another, each of them forming an organism or a system the rigorous integrity of which remains at the level of supposition, like that of a body proper." (Jacques Derrida, "Two Words for Joyce," in Derek Attridge and Daniel Ferrer, eds., *Post-Structuralist Joyce* (Cambridge: Cambridge University Press, 1984, pp. 155–56).

As for Benjamin's theory of translation, and Paul de Man's more lucid version of it: they seem to me to belong, like Deconstruction, to the history of irony. A translator might indeed proceed in that spirit, but it is clear that most translators continue, like Kinsella, to live among words in the conviction of a more accommodating possibility.

The Presence of Translation:
A View of English Poetry

 CHARLES TOMLINSON

I PROPOSE TO DISCUSS some of the preferences displayed in editing *The Oxford Book of Verse in English Translation*, and also to note regretfully one or two poems that got away and that I would have liked to include. My initial choice brought home to me how centrally the art of translation has mattered in the history of English poetry, though its history has never been fully written from that point of view. The presence of translation changes, or should change, our vision of the whole. Its presence in the *oeuvre* of a number of major poets should change our all-over view of *them* and of the riches they have to offer to present and future heirs. This is a long story, and I shall confine myself to a handful of protagonists in it, chiefly between the early sixteenth and mid-eighteenth centuries. My argument will have to contain, besides an account of the translators, *some* account—however foreshortened and simplified— of English poetry also.

A twentieth-century Hungarian poet, when asked to name the most beautiful Hungarian poem, replied, "Shelley's 'Ode to the West Wind' in the translation of Árpád Tóth." I have sometimes dreamed of being asked "What is the *greatest* English poem of the eighteenth century?" and of replying, "Homer's *Iliad* in the translation of Alexander Pope." And this comes close to what Pope's contemporaries thought: in the eighteenth-century Houbracken print of Pope's portrait, in a little scene inset on a stone structure halfway between an altar and a sarcophagus, it is Homer who leads Pope up to Apollo and the Muses to receive his poet's laurels.

Dr. Johnson in his life of the poet refers to Pope's *Iliad* as "that poetical wonder . . . , a performance which no age or nation can pretend to equal," and he looks at the prospect of poetry after its

258

publication in the light of what Pope had achieved and made available to other poets: "His version," writes Johnson, "may be said to have tuned the English tongue, for since its appearance no writer, however deficient in other powers, has wanted melody." In Johnson's nutshell here, in this "[tuning] of the English tongue," there is a short history of eighteenth-century poetry through Gray, Collins, Smart, Goldsmith, Johnson himself, even early Wordsworth, not to mention the beautiful hymns of Wesley.

Our received view of English poetry is characterized by the absence of any prolonged mention of translation and its effects. We do not immediately associate it with Apollo, though there are groups of specialists, like the Boston University Translation Seminar, who know that this must be wrong. It is usual, for example, to ignore the fact that young Mr. Pope matured his comic vision through his dealings with the deviousness of Homer's gods and goddesses, and his sense of potential catastrophe (I am thinking of the climax of *Dunciad*, book 4) by his contemplation of the fall of Troy. A poet who, from his twentieth to his thirty-eighth year, has spent a sizable portion of his life in the company of Homer, going on from the *Iliad* to complete the *Odyssey* with the help of assistants, can hardly have been unaffected by the experience. It might, in addition to the comic and the catastrophic, have also impressed upon him a sense of human grandeur in the presence of which that satire he is justly famous for must of necessity rise above the merely destructive. Pope without his Homer is—well, not Hamlet without the prince—but by ignoring the presence of Pope's major translation in the rest of his work and in the history of English poetry, we write defective history and partial criticism. And the same could be said of the accounts we have of other poets and their translations. Who, for example, is the first important American poet? Anne Bradstreet seems to have been engineered into that position. But why not George Sandys with his translation of Ovid's *Metamorphoses*, completed while he was treasurer of the Virginia Company between 1621 and 1626? Why do we demote our translations, while the Hungarians (say) are so grateful for theirs?

The simple answer, I suppose, is the sheer variety, the long-standing copiousness and continuity of English poetry—now English-and-American poetry. If one were a Russian, the history of one's poetry begins effectively in the eighteenth century. In the case of German—a literature which had dwindled into provinciality after the Middle Ages—we find Goethe, virtually single-handed, restoring its poetry to the center of the European scene at the end of the eighteenth century. With no Elizabethan Renaissance behind him, no *grand siècle*, and no Augustan Age, he is technically in a situation far different from that of the English or French poets of his own era or the previous era. In the late 1780s, he confides to the notebook which became his *Italian Journey:* "The main reason why, for several years, I have preferred to write prose is that our prosody is in a state of great uncertainty. . . . What has been lacking is any prosodic principle." Dryden, a hundred years before, could hardly have expressed himself thus, as he reached back to free Chaucer, via translation, from the prosodic uncertainty *he* imagined Chaucer suffered. Though Dryden, of course, was not just correcting Chaucer: he was learning from him in astonishing ways. He thought of this poet three centuries back in his own tradition as a great forerunner and master, as the equal in his *Knight's Tale* of Homer and Virgil. Indeed, poets and certain key translators, as if sensing some vitamin deficiency in our literature, have intuitively gone back to Chaucer in an attempt to cure it. But this is to anticipate a theme to which I shall be returning in a moment.

We arrived at Chaucer down the vista of the long-standing copiousness of English literature—something the Russians and the Germans do not have in the same proportion. And it was that theme which had brought us to Goethe. Now, one of Goethe's most readable modern translators, Michael Hamburger, supplies a thought which has some bearing on this topic. He is underlining the literalness of his own translations and says with a disarming modesty: "I am not offering 'English poems in their own right' here, but pointers to the original texts, inductions to them for persons with little or no German. If one or two of my versions also stand up as poems in English, that is a bonus, a stroke of luck." And he concludes: "English poetry is so rich as to have little need or room for additions in the guise of translations."

One feels obliged to respond to this conclusion by saying that English poetry happens to *be* so rich because of what it managed to incorporate into itself "in the guise of translations," and that the creative translations of men like Oldham, Dryden, Pope, and, in our own century, Pound, helped English shed its provincialisms. Furthermore, these men, whose translation work is a meaningful part of the richness of English poetry, were seldom content to offer merely "pointers to the original texts"; for the texts they were incorporating into English demanded an extension and enrichment of English itself if they were to be adequately and imaginatively embodied. Can it really be supposed, to borrow Hamburger's phrase, that "persons with little or no German"—or Greek or Latin or Chinese—can be inducted into those poetries simply with the aid of "pointers"? Dryden, on the other hand, out of a prolonged contemplation of Latin poetry and through his versions of Ovid, Homer, Chaucer, Lucretius, Juvenal, and Virgil, permanently changed the scope of English poetry itself, and his originals, seen from the vantage of what he did with them, can never appear quite the same either. The phase of Dryden's greatest verse translations seems to have coincided with a spiritual crisis when he was actively seeking to confront and reembody the spiritual values of classical poetry. Perhaps something of this nature—a serious and profound need brought to bear on a foreign text and by a great writer—is what accounts for the compelling power of some of our finest translators. Along with Dryden, his young contemporary John Oldham comes to mind, and Oldham's extraordinary re-creations of Horace, Boileau, and Juvenal. Yet Oldham is hardly read, and only very slowly has the full story of Dryden's genius as a translator come to be told. To others than Michael Hamburger, English poetry has appeared "so rich as to have little need or room for additions in the guise of translations," and so the real news, in Pound's phrase, has been a long time in arriving.

Reflecting on this thought, I found myself wondering what my own generation was actually taught about such matters. The answer is: not much. At Cambridge the full glory of the English Renaissance was unquestionably felt to inhere in the Elizabethan-Jacobean drama. Erik Satie, asked why Beethoven was so famous, replied, "Because he had such a good business manager"—meaning, of course, Beethoven himself. The business manager for Elizabethan-Jacobean drama was undoubtedly Shakespeare, and his great prestige seems to have reflected back and also forward over the whole era and fallen upon several lesser talents. "Our" renaissance—that is, the renaissance of us students up at Cambridge in my day—took a broad look at Wyatt and Surrey, both translators, though this fact was never dwelt upon, and Surrey's partial translation of the *Aeneid* was evaluated less for its actual quality than for its having brought blank verse into English—blank verse with which others, principally the dramatists, were to do things of greater importance. One of the first essays I did at Cambridge was on Christopher Marlowe, which meant I read every bit of what he wrote, including such dramatic scraps as his *Massacre at Paris* and *Tragedy of Dido*. We were even persuaded that the scrambled and poorly written scenes in the middle of his *Doctor Faustus* were somehow gauged to show us the rather trite choices Faustus made when, having sold his soul to the devil, those choices could have been unlimited. No one told us to read Marlowe's splendid translation of Ovid's *Amores*. My copy contained these, and a curious fight went on in my own mind between the implanted idea that they "were only translations" and the sense that I *liked* these poems—read rather hastily, because one's energies had to be invested elsewhere, in the dramas. It did not occur to me then that Marlowe's Ovid translations offered a quite alternative rhetoric to that of some of his most famous plays—something that might be said of other major Elizabethan translators in relation to the drama. (I am thinking of Golding's *Metamorphoses*, the Sidney Psalter, and Fairfax's Tasso, all represented in the *Oxford Book*.) Just how trans- lation could offer an alternative rhetoric, and thus another possibility for English poetry, did not become fully articulate for me for a number of years. This happened when, on November 22, 1956, Hugh Kenner delivered, at the Royal Society of Literature, a remarkable paper with the title "Words in the Dark" (*Essays by Divers Hands*, 1958, New Series, vol. 29). Kenner's dealings with Marlowe in that paper catalyzed worries which had long jostled among my thoughts and which had to do with the sort of poetry I was at that time trying to write. The story is, once more, the relation between original poetry and what translated poetry has to teach the poet—in this instance myself, as I shall explain.

Kenner comments on two passages from Christopher Marlowe. Both of these passages were old friends to me, but I realized, as one sometimes does when brought up sharp by a perceptive critic, that I had never quite earned my right to those two bits of mental furniture which I could even quote. The first was half a dozen lines from Marlowe's translation of Ovid's *Amores*. The lover is addressing the coming day:

> Now in her tender arms I sweetlie bide,
> If ever, now well lies she by my side,
> The ayre is colde and sleep is sweetest now,
> And byrdes send forth shrill notes from every bow.
> Whither runst thou, that men and women love not?
> Hold in thy rosie horses that they move not!

Kenner is contending that "there are potentialities in Chaucer that have never been developed since, because the Elizabethan drama had no use for them, and brought modern English to a working maturity without them." He quotes Marlowe's Ovid to show how a poet, not serving a theatrical purpose and audience, could still tap those Chaucerian potentialities—namely a close fit between the word and its object and a certain plainness and clarity of sense and definition in the refusal to let every phrase run almost unbidden into metaphor. Kenner puts over against Marlowe the translator, Marlowe the dramatist—the famous passage in which Faustus gets his wish to see Helen of Troy and exclaims,

> Was this the face that launch'd a thousand ships,
> And burnt the topless towers of Ilium?—
> . . . O, thou art fairer than the evening air
> Clad in the beauty of a thousand stars;
> Brighter art thou than flaming Jupiter
> When he appear'd to hapless Semele;
> More lovely than the monarch of the sky
> In wanton Arethusa's azur'd arms;
> And none but thou shalt be my paramour!

Kenner's comment on this, with its "bright halo of imprecision" around the incantatory words, establishes its fundamental difference from the more Chaucerian rendering of Ovid.

> These words . . . are a verbal substitute for the vision. . . . What the audience *saw* was the costumed and painted boy; the words however don't encourage it to examine what can be seen, but to dream away from the visible. We are not told by what extent the face of the authentic Helen . . . would transcend what is shown: we are encouraged to ignore what is shown:
>
>> O, thou art fairer than the evening air
>> Clad in the beauty of a thousand stars—
>
> fairer than the evening air, not the evening sky; and that air not adorned with stars but clad in their beauty. These lines more than any others in the speech appeal to remembered delights of the senses, yet even their appeal to the senses is refined into ethereal abstraction by the operation of the words "air" and "beauty." A "face" is mentioned, but it is not shown. . . . And while the words evoke hapless Semele and wanton Arethusa, Helen is not compared to either of them but to a brightness and a loveliness: the loveliness of the monarch of the sky and the brightness of flaming Jupiter.

Matthew Arnold, reflecting on the difficulties of a poet of the nineteenth century in achieving a unified style, complains about "those damn'd Elizabethans" and the influence of "their purple patches" on subsequent verse. Kenner is less belligerent than this as he goes on to trace the persistence of a rhetoric, an attitude to words and metaphors, evolved by the Elizabethan dramatists, continuing right through the romantics—he does not mention Wordsworth, who might have provided an interesting exception—on to Tennyson and ultimately even Eliot. "These dramatists," Kenner says, "virtually invented the procedures of nineteenth and twentieth century English poetry. Their tradition was slow in establishing itself—Dryden's *All for Love* may be noted as an episode of resistance—but by Coleridge's generation they were firmly established . . . as seminal poets."

What of the role of the business manager, Shakespeare himself, in Kenner's version of the history of English poetry? Shakespeare figures in this version as the author of the lines from *Antony and Cleopatra*:

> She looks like sleep
> As she would catch another Antony
> In her strong toil of grace.

Amid the magical suggestiveness of this, "grace," says Kenner, "is neither the theologian's grace nor the hostess's nor the dancer's but mingles the prestige of all three." And he contrasts this calculated imprecision rich in connotations with the definition and de-notation of Ben Jonson's

> Underneath this stone doth lie
> As much beauty as could die.

A great translator, Ben Jonson invented a style that takes on something of the chiseled demarcation of his Latin originals. Suffice it to say of Shakespeare that *his* Latinity was not the Latinity of Jonson but often a glamorous over-plus, something magically produced in the words as another language transforms itself into our own:

> Nay, this my hand will rather
> The multitudinous seas incarnadine . . .

Shakespeare's style left open many options—a fact Kenner does not dwell upon—including the reincarnation of the Chaucerian Duke Theseus from the *Knight's Tale* in *A Midsummer Night's Dream*, but these options did not prevent the development of English verse from Marlowe through Shelley, Tennyson, and Eliot along other lines—lines sometimes resistant (as in the case of Marlowe's dramatic verse) to what translation had to offer.

I can now say why Kenner's account struck me with such particular force in 1956 and how it then came to be borne out and even amplified by my dealings with translation and as editor of *The Oxford*

Book of Verse in English Translation. In the first place, Kenner's lecture spoke to me principally as a poet. I had been writing poems that were influenced by Marianne Moore and were beginning to be influenced by William Carlos Williams, as I tried to blot out the golden voice of Dylan Thomas and the "halo of imprecision" around *his* words as he intoned:

> Altarwise by owl-light in the halfway house
> The gentleman lay graveward with his furies; . . .

The result of my own American-prompted reaction as a poet to that was a general incomprehension from English publishers and an unplaceable manuscript that lay around for several years and was finally published in New York. You can perhaps imagine the warmth with which I responded to Kenner's concluding peroration where he brought on to the scene the names of both Marianne Moore and William Carlos Williams, suggesting that British readers might find them "bare and astringent to the point of incompetence" because of British preconceptions about poetic resonance. "They write," he explained, "out of the logic of their real world, in which the Elizabethans in fact did not really exist." If I was right in sensing the decadence of much of Thomas—a kind of fluent manipulator of the imprecise, a last inheritor of Tudorbethanry rather than a new direction—how heartening to be told from the podium of the Royal Society of Literature that British ears were still imprisoned by a tradition of stage rhetoric going back three and a half centuries, and that one had allies elsewhere.

Kenner's initial distinctions were drawn by placing side by side those two passages—Marlowe as dramatist and Marlowe as translator—and finding in the latter Chaucerian potentialities "that have never been developed since." "Never" is perhaps to overstate the case, as a glance at Dryden and Pope will readily show. In going on now to speak more undividedly of the presence of translation in English poetry, I wish to touch on that persistence of the Chaucerian. Chaucer himself was no stranger to translation, although he was chiefly concerned with completely transforming what he took from others—most magisterially from Boccaccio—into his own thing. One of his most sustained passages of poetic translation is to be found in *The Legend of Good Women*, the episode from the first book of the *Aeneid* where Aeneas, along with Achates, meets his mother Venus in disguise:

So long he walketh in this wildernesse,
Til at the laste he mette an hunteresse.
A bowe in hande and arwes hadde she;
Hire clothes cutted were unto the kne.
But she was yit the fayreste creature
That evere was yformed by Nature;
And Eneas and Achates she grette
And thus she to hem spak, whan she hem mette;
"Saw ye," quod she, "as ye han walked wyde,
Any of my sustren walke yow besyde
With any wilde bor or other best,
That they han hunted to, in this forest . . . ?"

That couplet tune is taken up again by Gavin Douglas in his complete translation of the *Aeneid*, finished "apon the fest of Mary Magdalen," July 22, 1513. Gavin Douglas speaks of "my mastir Chaucer," and one both sees and hears what he means when one reads this same passage in his version. It seemed only just to begin the *Oxford Book* with Douglas as the initiator of its Renaissance section—after all, Surrey knew his version and echoes it and still gets most of the credit because of his use of blank verse. Another piquant reason—culture is like this!—for beginning with Douglas is that his Virgil is not strictly speaking in English but Scots, a literature which through Henryson, Dunbar, and Lyndsay, from the later fifteenth century onward, deeply imbibed Chaucer's influence just when the English seemed not to know what to do with Chaucer. Thus the Scottish incorporation of Chaucer into another tongue becomes in essence an act of translation, across a divide as great almost as that between German and Dutch. Chaucer's couplet melody in Douglas's Scots now sounds like this:

Venus, eftir the gise and maneir thair,
An active bow apon hir schuldir bair
As scho had bene ane wild hunteres,
With wynd waving hir haris lowsit of tres,
Her skirt kiltit till hir bair kne,
And, first of other unto thame spak sche:
How, say me, yonkeris, saw ye walkand heir,
By aventure ony of my sisters deir,
The cace of arrowis taucht by hir syde,
And cled into the spottit linx hyde. . . ?

Ezra Pound, in his *ABC of Reading*, goes so far as to claim that "Gavin Douglas . . . with his mind full of Latin quantitative metre, attains a robuster versification than you are likely to find in Chaucer." Pound is, of course, a great and vocal admirer of Chaucer— he thinks Chaucer's culture "wider than Dante's"—and yet he repeats, "the texture of Gavin's verse is stronger, the resilience greater than Chaucer's." Be that as it may, here we have a twofold translation—of the lesson of Chaucer and the poetry of Virgil into Scottish verse. Douglas's achievement was noted by Surrey when the latter did his partial *Aeneid*, but Surrey made of Douglas a lesser thing, taking over echoes into a more refined and yet ultimately less expressive English. Douglas stands then on the threshold of the *Oxford Book* as something for the specifically *English* Renaissance to measure up to. His particular challenge was not met. His *Aeneid* disappeared from view—there was no edition between 1553 and 1710. When Dryden came to translate Virgil's poem in the late seventeenth century, an edition of Douglas was hard to come by. Dryden may, however, have laid his hands on a copy, as William Frost in *Comparative Literature* 36 (1984) has recently suggested, also quoting there from a periodical of 1693, the *Athenian Mercury:* "Gawen Douglas's Aeneads (if you can get it) the best version that ever was, or we believe ever will be of that incomparable poem." So once more, it does seem from this quotation that the generally supposed neo-classical abhorrence of works of more barbarous times has been exaggerated. And in saying that, while thinking about translation, one is already tentatively sketching out an alternative picture of seventeenth-century poetry itself.

If Douglas, via translation, carries to the brink of the Tudor era— indeed, as far as the *Athenian Mercury* in 1693—a fundamentally Chaucerian possibility, a similar possibility crops up once more in the Elizabethan era itself with the publication of Golding's translation of Ovid's *Metamorphoses*. (This is the book that Shakespeare virtually quotes from in *The Tempest*, in Prospero's invocation of the spirits of act 5—Ovid's passage is given in the *Oxford Book*.) I find it hard to go along with Pound in claiming that Golding's *Metamorphoses* is "the most beautiful book in the language"—Dryden seems to me, by and large, a finer translator of Ovid than Golding. But Golding is a fascinating example of a poet in touch with Chaucer's simplicity, clarity, and narrative verve, while suffering sporadic attacks of that logorrhea which afflicted the Elizabethans— as it does Chapman in his translation of Homer's *Iliad*. Yet there exists in the best passages of Golding's ambitious translation something like an antidote to that same logorrhea, as when the giant Polyphemus woos the nymph Galatea:

More whyght thou art then Primrose leaf my Lady Galatee,
More fresh than meade, more tall and streyght than lofty Aldertree,
More bright than glasse, more wanton than the tender kid forsooth,
Than Cockleshelles continually with water worne, more smoothe . . .
More cleere than frozen yce, more sweete than Grape though ripe ywis,
More soft than butter newly made, or downe of Cygnet is . . .

One might well, faced with passages like this or with the sheer spryness of Golding's best narrations, ask with Ezra Pound, "Is Golding's Ovid a mirror of Chaucer?" and concur in the spirit of Pound's next question: "is a fine poet ever translated until another his equal invents a new style in a later language?" Golding is hardly Ovid's equal, but in passages like this, he *is* the inventor of a new style—a new style rooted in an intelligent awareness of earlier English poetry. As Pound concludes, in his "Notes on Elizabethan Classicists":

> . . . Golding was endeavouring to convey the sense of the original to his readers. He names the thing of his original author, by the name most germane, familiar, homely to his hearers. And I hold that the real poet is sufficiently absorbed in his content to care more for the content than the rumble [Pound is fighting against Milton here]; and also that Chaucer and Golding are more likely to find the *mot juste* than were for some centuries their successors, saving the author of *Hamlet.*

If what Pound says is true of Golding, then the discipline of translation has brought to focus something that was rare enough in so-called "original verse."

Pound's tendency to measure later poets and translators against Chaucer—as he does in the case of Golding and Douglas—has an interesting bearing on our theme of alternatives to the rhetoric of Elizabethan drama—alternatives supplied during the Elizabethan age in (say) Marlowe's Ovid or the Sidney Psalter. As Pound writes of Chaucer in the *ABC of Reading*:

> Intending writers can read him with fair safety, in so far as no one can now possibly use an imitation of Chaucer's manners or the details of his speech. Whereas horrible examples of people wearing Elizabethan old clothes, project from whole decades of later English and American writing.

To Kenner's comment that "Dryden's *All for Love* may be noted as an episode of resistance" to a given type of Elizabethan rhetoric, one might add that it was Dryden's own enthusiasm for Chaucer— "Here is God's plenty," as he famously said—that enabled him in his later translations of that poet to touch ground and bedrock in a quite new way. He thought Chaucer's language "followed Nature more closely" than Ovid's characteristic "turn of words." He thought Chaucer's *Knight's Tale* and Duke Theseus' vein of pity were superior in conception even to Homer because "Homer can move rage better than he can move pity." And he had a certain rather English dislike of heroic conceptions where pity is at a low premium, as when he spoke of "those Athletick Brutes whom undeservedly we call heroes" and again of "a mere Ajax, a Man-killing Ideot." I do not believe there are enough of Dryden's translations of Chaucer in my anthology. The problem was chiefly one of space. You cannot demonstrate everything at once, and I had my eye on Dryden's Ovid, but perhaps an ideal anthology of Dryden could underline the fact that, practically simultaneously, he is doing two things—Dryden, an Anglican Christian and later a Catholic, is entering into a serious dialogue with paganism via his translation of Lucretius and Ovid, and is making re-available to a reading public that found the idiom and meter out of reach a large body of Chaucer's work: all of the massive *Knight's Tale, The Flower and the Leaf*, which was supposed to be by Chaucer, *The Character of a Good Parson, The Nun's Priest's Tale*, and *The Wife of Bath's Tale* (these last two, incomparable masterpieces of translation that would have to be printed complete in our imaginary ideal anthology). That both these tales are concerned with sex and sexual morality and that Venus should get special treatment (a more extended one than Chaucer's) in Dryden's version of *The Knight's Tale*, points to the way that Dryden in translating the pagans, in his dealings with Lucretius and Ovid, takes the power of Venus as seriously as that other "neo-classical" author, Racine in *Phèdre*. The positive aspect of Venus appears in the *Oxford Book* in that lovely evocation from Lucretius rendered by Dryden before he came to do Chaucer:

> Delight of Humane kind and gods above;
> Parent of Rome; Propitious Queen of Love; . . .
> All Nature is thy Gift; Earth, Air, and Sea:
> Of all that breaths, the various progeny,
> Stung with delight, is goaded on by thee.
> O'er barren Mountains, o'er the flowry Plain,
> The leavy Forest, and the liquid Main
> Extends thy uncontroul'd and boundless reign.
> Through all the living Regions, dost thou move,
> And scatter'st, where thou goest, the kindly seeds of Love . . .

The "Seeds of Love" may be "kindly," but other words from this fragment of Dryden's Lucretius hint at the less amenable forces of Venus: "stung," "goaded," "uncontroul'd," "boundless." "Uncon-

troul'd" is what Myrrha's incestuous passion for her father is in
Ovid's story from the *Metamorphoses*, which Dryden went on to
translate in one of his supreme versions, where the fluctuations of
the woman's mind and feelings in thrall to obsessive and forbidden
love irresistibly remind one, in Dryden's rendering, of Racine's por-
trayal of the combined incandescence and shocked resistance in the
mind of Phèdre. This is the Dryden Matthew Arnold and the Victorians preferred to forget, but the Dryden of whom Doctor Johnson
said that he was "not one of the *gentle bosoms*. . . . He hardly
conceived [love] but in its turbulent effervescence with some other
desires; where it was inflamed by rivalry, or obstructed by difficulties. . . ." Sir Walter Scott, in similar vein, speaks of Dryden's
knowledge of "the stronger feelings of the heart, in all its dark or
violent workings. . . ." Johnson's phrase "obstructed by difficulties" describes well the love of Palamon and Arcite for the same girl
in Chaucer's *Knight's Tale*. Palamon, the worshiper of Venus, gets
the girl: all's well that ends well, but in Dryden's temple of Venus
(unlike Chaucer's) there are "issuing sighs that smoked along the
wall," and Dryden tops up Chaucer's list of those "by love undone"
by extending Chaucer's "Th'enchantementz of . . . Circes" to
"Circean feasts / With bowls that turned enamoured youths to
beasts." Venus' worshiper, Palamon, having lost the tournament but
won the girl because of a rather blatant divine intervention by Venus
and Saturn, the goddess puts in an extended appearance in Dryden.
She is there by implication in the great concluding speech of Duke
Theseus, much reinforced by Dryden:

> The Cause and Spring of motion from above
> Hung down on earth the golden chain of Love.

And she comes on at the end in a passage of Dryden's devising
(though it is devised in Chaucerian mode with its mixture of irony
and sexual frankness):

> Smil'd Venus, to behold her own true Knight
> Obtain the Conquest, though he lost the Fight,
> And bless'd with Nuptial Bliss the sweet laborious Night.
> Eros, and Anteros [Cupid's brother], on either Side,
> One fir'd the Bridegroom, and one warm'd the Bride;
> And long attending Hymen from above,
> Showr'd on the Bed the whole Idalian Grove.

I have spoken of Dryden's serious dialogue with paganism, and
it seems to me that his engagement with Venus (powers, passions,

ironies, and all), extending from his superb evocation of her in *Aeneid* book 8, from Lucretius to Ovid and Chaucer, is as deeply responsive as his re-creation of Lucretius' rather bracing atheism in *Against the Fear of Death*. This atheism, in Dryden's imaginative contemplation of it, while it abolishes any possible hope of an after-life, yet argues that since there is only one life, we should live it fully without bemoaning our lot. This optimistic atheism, as one might call it, finds an answering echo in the pagan philosophy of Duke Theseus, as previously imagined by Chaucer and now reincarnated in Dryden's words:

> What makes all this, but Jupiter the king,
> At whose Command we perish, and we spring?
> Then 'tis our best, since thus ordain'd to die,
> To make a Vertue of Necessity . . .
> Enjoying while we live the present Hour,
> And dying in our Excellence and Flow'r. . . .
> What then remains, but after past Annoy,
> To take the good Vicissitude of Joy?
> To thank the gracious Gods for what they give,
> Possess our Souls, and while we live, to live?

Here we have one of those moments of creative translation, when in the hands of a great writer, the text comes to speak his deepest feelings and convictions for him. It is comparable to that scene in Pound's version of Sophocles' *Women of Trachis* when Herakles, suffering the effects of the shirt of Nessus and about to die, sees suddenly (for himself and for the translating poet) the logic and consequence of his life and cries out:

> SPLENDOUR,
>   IT ALL COHERES.

With all their differences, both passages—Dryden's Duke Theseus and Pound's Herakles—speak for the poets and yet speak for more than the poets, because these translators are, in their however freely adaptive way, finding and extending something which is demonstrably present in the original text. I feel myself that Dryden achieves this with far greater security than Pound: *Women of Trachis*, with its uneasy hodge-podge of diction, does not really "all cohere," as Dryden's *Knight's Tale*, and Duke Theseus' speech there do. What is interesting, though, is that Pound, Chaucer, and Dryden are trying to imagine how it could "all cohere" for a pagan Greek. And that is what I mean by saying that the Catholic Dryden enters into a serious dialogue with paganism.

Dryden's Duke Theseus speech is translation, but it is also late seventeenth-century poetry at its full height, returning us to our initial theme that the story of English poetry cannot be truly told without seeing translation as an unavoidable part of that story. The editor of the recently published *New Oxford Book of Eighteenth-Century Verse*, with a most courteous nod toward my own volume, resolves to avoid the translations of the age, preferring to stick to its "original verse," though admitting "imitations" whereby an old source is updated as in Johnson's use of Juvenal in *The Vanity of Human Wishes*. The trouble with this is that so much of the poetic vigor of the age went into great translations. Ignore them, and you get the whole picture out of proportion. And with this thought in mind, I come to my last major illustration of that theme—the work of another Chaucerian, Alexander Pope. I shall be touching on two aspects of Pope—his Chaucer translations and his *Iliad*.

Prompted by Dryden's example, the sixteen-year-old Alexander Pope turned to translating Chaucer. We hear much of the prodigy of a Rimbaud, with his marvelous visionary fireworks—for which he had, of course, to pay an early price, realizing that his systematic derangement of the senses was costing too dear in human terms, so that he abandons art as precociously as he began to practice it. There is a lot more good old-fashioned common sense about our other sixteen-year-old prodigy—indeed, it is as if Pope went to two of Chaucer's creations that could tell him most directly what common sense was—*The Merchant's Tale*, with its clear-eyed view of what happens when the elderly marry the young, and *The Wife of Bath's Prologue*, where one of the unforgettable characters of literature tells us what marriage is like—or, at any rate, *her* conception of marriage.

Kenner, you will recall, spoke of certain Chaucerian potentialities "that have never been developed since." Yet one of the miraculous things is to hear Chaucer's couplet music still there in the translations of these two Augustans, Dryden and Pope. It helped tune *their* tongues, to borrow Doctor Johnson's phrase. As you well know, the imitation of the form and sound of a foreign text is often impossible and frequently unadvisable, yet in reaching back to English at an earlier stage in its development, Dryden and Pope were able to bring over something of Chaucer's music into their own contemporary idiom, and they were, after all, using the same basic form as Chaucer, the couplet. They "made it new" (in Pound's slogan) in a way altogether more radical and convincing than those modern efforts to translate Chaucer—from Coghill's dreary versions downward, that we saw in the 1940s, 1950s, and 1960s, and that were written in a

sort of no-man's-English. If we want to complain that the idiom of
Dryden and Pope is much more four-square and balanced than that
of Chaucer or that it lacks the freshness of Douglas or Golding, we
should pause, with Coghill's example in mind, to consider the fact
that it is a genuine idiom, consistent with its time, and not an
attempt to cobble together medievalisms with coyly self-conscious
modern turns of phrase.

In terms of tune and diction, what Dryden's modernization had
to offer Pope shows clearly enough in the way Dryden appropriates
Chaucer's Chanticleer. Chanticleer enters Chaucer's text with a lyric
clarity such as Golding was to inherit. Here is Chaucer's cockerel that

> In al the land of crowyng nas his peer . . .
> His coomb was redder than the fyn coral,
> And batailled as it were a castel wal;
> His byle was blak, and as the jet it shoon;
> Lyk asure were his legges and his toon;
> His nayles whitter than the lylye flour,
> And lyk the burned gold was his colour.
> This gentil cok hadde in his governaunce
> Sevene hennes for to doon al his pleasaunce,
> Which were his sustres and his paramours,
> And wonder lyk to hym, as of colours. . . .

And here is Dryden—the countrified and the courtly less intimately
at one perhaps, and yet why make excuses for what bids so undividedly for the ear's attention, discovering so infallibly its own substitutes where the vocabulary, word order, stress, and actual pace of
English have altered over the years:

> High was his comb and coral red withal,
> In dents embattled like a Castle-Wall;
> His Bill was Raven-black, and shon like Jet,
> Blue were his Legs, and Orient were his Feet:
> White were his Nails, like Silver to behold,
> His Body glitt'ring like the burnish'd Gold.

> This gentle Cock for solace of his Life,
> Six Misses had beside his lawful Wife;
> Scandal that spares no King, tho' ne'er so good,
> Says, they were all of his own Flesh and Blood. . . .

As Marvin Mudrick put it many years ago in "Chaucer as Libret-
tist" (*Philological Quarterly* 38, 1): "The moral seems to be that the
Augustans were the last English poets who had a sufficiently large
command of technique and decorum, and sufficient trust in the

versatility of their idiom, to be capable of turning Chaucer into a contemporary." "Into a contemporary"—that is the point. What twentieth-century poet has been able to reincarnate the Wife of Bath as the sixteen-year-old Pope did when she turns on her husband who is reading her, in bed, a book on the weaknesses of women?

> When still he read, and laugh'd and read again,
> And half the Night was thus consum'd in vain;
> Provok'd to Vengeance, three large Leaves I tore,
> And with one Buffet fell'd him on the Floor.
> With that my Husband in a Fury rose,
> And down he settled me with hearty Blows:
> I groan'd, and lay extended on my Side;
> Oh thou has slain me for my Wealth (I cry'd),
> Yet I forgive thee—Take my last Embrace,
> He wept, kind Soul! and stoop'd to kiss my Face;
> I took him such a Box as turn'd him blue,
> Then sigh'd and cry'd *Adieu my Dear, adieu!*
>
> But after many a hearty Struggle past,
> I condescended to be pleas'd at last . . .

and she goes on to coax out of him mastery over both his person and his wealth:

> —As for the Volume that revil'd the Dames,
> 'Twas torn to Fragments and condemn'd to Flames.

If we were Hungarians (so to speak), a poem like this would be among our acknowledged masterpieces, and if we knew *our Iliad* (our greatest eighteenth-century poem, as I suggested), we might even catch an echo of Chaucer's comic vigor in the marital set-to's of Jupiter and Juno. True enough, in the first book of his *Iliad*, Pope—still the *young* Pope, he is now twenty-five—was perhaps too awèd by his task to allow himself the full comic freedom of Dryden's dealings with the royal couple, or to risk calling their lame son, Vulcan, "the rude Skinker" or barman. However, Pope's *Iliad* continually takes fire and increases in daring as it progresses. I wonder if those who have written on it have not perhaps underestimated just how comically devious the gods are shown to be. Jupiter (it has been said) stands too close to Milton's God the Father, yet his awful majesty is surely often qualified in a manner Milton would never have dreamed of for the supreme deity. There are many instances of this, including the tone of massive threat in which Jupiter reminds the restive Juno of how he had once had to hang her up in a golden chain from the ceiling of heaven. This (from book 15) follows on her deception of him in book 14, leading to the biggest family row in the whole poem. In an ideal anthology one would need both of these books, and if one could not have them both, then all of the marital comedy in 14.

In the *Oxford Book* I have tried to substantiate some of my claims for Pope's Homer. It seems to me that the array of epic similes there, the separate incidents—particularly the marvelous episode where the River Scamander attacks and fights with Achilles—and the whole sequence of the forging by Vulcan of Achilles' shield, go a long way to support Doctor Johnson's estimate with which I began: "that poetical wonder . . . a performance which no age or nation can pretend to equal." But one thing *is* lacking in my *Oxford* choice (space precluded it)—namely, the high comedy of the interventions of the gods in the Trojan war and the sense of how this comedy—in Shakespearean fashion—is so mingled with and accentuates the tragic waste in the poem, reinforcing, as it does, our awareness of how that is just the way things interact in the daily texture of life. In conclusion let me say a few words about books 14 and 15.

In his notes—a brilliant and unique addition to the translation—Pope has theological difficulties. He is worried that the Almighty (as he calls Jupiter) carries on the way he does in book 14. Pope's text, however, feels itself free to accept the power game and the marital scuffles of Jupiter and Juno and portrays them as not much more complex than the power game and marital scuffles of the Wife of Bath. What really upset Pope is Jupiter's sexual passion for Juno (she's borrowed Venus' girdle to distract him while her brother Neptune helps the Greeks; Jupiter, of course, is favorable to the Trojans). The poem doesn't in the least reveal the embarrassment of its notes at this point, but splendidly pursues its course through Jupiter's almost operatic and self-blinding catalogue of Juno's charms to the consummation of his desire until

> At length with Love and Sleep's soft Pow'r opprest,
> The panting Thund'rer nods and sinks to rest.

Jupiter's famous nod, usually indicating his power, has become something else. We go from here to the horrors of battle and then we go back again to the marital quarrel once Jupiter wakes up to what is happening. You would imagine from certain critics that Pope's *Iliad* sounds all the same—the homogenizer of the heroic couplets blandly absorbing all those mightly hexameters and (to change the metaphor) making them come out like links of sausages. I suppose some such feeling as this was what prevented Ezra Pound from warming to

Pope's *Iliad*, along with the evident influence of the detested Milton
on Pope. It must be said, however, that the swiftness of Pope's couplets makes much lighter what he derived from Milton. He takes
Milton's freight on board and yet manages to carry it at his own
speed, which is often amazingly rapid. Books 14 and 15 are proof, if
it were needed, of Pope's variety and of his ability to keep changing
tone and focus in following his original. This ability—the context
need not always be comic—is one that is shared by Homer, Virgil,
Lucretius, and Ovid, as they move from close-up to long shot—an
effect as of poetic montage, immersing themselves and then standing
back and letting things re-group into perspective. It is a capacity the
twentieth-century poet could learn from. Pope's rendering of one of
Homer's great images in book 15 points the way. Here a child playing
with sand and the wrecking of the Grecian wall by Apollo are accom-
modated side by side in (to keep up our cinematic image) three shots:

> Then with his Hand he shook the mighty wall;
> And lo! the Turrets nod, the Bulwarks fall.
> Easy, as when ashore an Infant stands,
> And draws imagin'd Houses in the sands;
> The sportive Wanton, pleased with some new Play,
> Sweeps the slight Works and fashion'd Domes away.
> Thus vanish'd, at thy touch, the Tow'rs and Walls;
> The Toil of thousands in a Moment Falls.

Had we but world enough and time, our story of the presence of
translation would not end with the Great Augustans. It would need
to be taken up again with Ezra Pound. That, in turn, would necessi-
tate a leap across romanticism where the primacy of poetic translation begins to flag—with one important exception, Shelley. Shelley,
who could write with all the ethereality of Marlowe's "O, thou art
fairer than the evening air," was marshaling, before his death, a
suppler and intellectually more intricate style, much influenced by
his own direct experience as a translator—of Euripides, Dante, Calde-
rón, and Goethe. But all that—a little of it is told in the *Oxford
Book*—would be an essay in itself.

Contributors

FREDERICK AHL is professor of classics at Cornell University, author of *Metaformations: Soundplay and Wordplay in Ovid and Other Classical Poets* (Cornell University Press, 1985); *Seneca: Three Tragedies* (Cornell University Press, 1986); and *Lucan: An Introduction* (Cornell University Press, 1976). He has forthcoming books on Sophocles and Vergil.

DONALD CARNE-ROSS is University Professor of classics and modern languages at Boston University. His works include *Instaurations: Essays In and Out of Literature* (University of California Press, 1979); and *Pindar* (Yale University Press, 1985). He is a founding editor of the journals *Arion* and *Delos*.

DENIS DONOGHUE holds the Henry James Chair of Letters at New York University. His most recent books are: *We Irish* (Knopf, 1986); *Reading America* (Knopf, 1987); and *England, Their England* (Knopf, 1988).

MICHAEL EWANS teaches in the departments of drama and classics at the University of Newcastle, New South Wales, Australia. He has published two books, the award-winning *Janáček's Tragic Operas* (Indiana University Press, 1977), and *Wagner and Aeschylus: The "Ring" and the "Oresteia"* (Cambridge University Press, 1983), as well as numerous articles on Greek tragedy and modern opera. He has translated Büchner's *Woyzeck* and Aischylos' *Oresteia* for performance, and has recently completed a theatrical commentary, based on his productions, to be published together with the Oresteia script. A similar commentary to accompany the *Woyzeck* translation will appear in 1990 from Peter Lang Publishers, and a book on neo-classical and modern "re-creations" of Greek tragedy, by Racine, Goethe, and Hofmannsthal/Strauss, is planned.

AGNES MONCY GULLÓN is associate professor of Spanish at Temple University. She is the author of *La creacion del personaje en las novelas de Unamuno* (Santander, Spain: Isla de los ratones, 1963); and *La novela experimental de Miguel Delibes* (Madrid: Taurus, 1981). She has published numerous articles and essays on Spanish literature, and her translation of Galdós's *Fortunata and Jacinta* appeared in 1986 from the University of Georgia Press.

TONY HARRISON was born in Leeds in 1937. He has published several books of poetry, including *The Loiners*, which won the Geoffrey Faber Memorial Prize in 1972, and *Continuous*. He has written much dramatic verse in the form of libretti for the Metropolitan Opera, New York, and for collaborations with several leading modern composers, including *Yan Tan Tethera* (with Harrison Birtwistle). He has written verse texts for the National Theatre, including *The Misanthrope* (1973); *Phaedra Brittannica* (1975); *Bow Down* (1977); *The Oresteia* (1981) (which was performed at the ancient Greek theater of Epidaurus and was awarded the European Poetry Translation Prize in 1983); and the much-acclaimed *Mysteries* (1985). He is the author of *Theatre Works 1973–85* (Penguin, 1986); and two long poems, *v.* and *The Fire-Gap*, both published in 1985. His *Selected Poems* are published in the United States by Random House. His new play, *The Trackers of Oxyrhynchus*, had its world premiere in the ancient stadium of Delphi in July 1988.

SEAMUS HEANEY, born in Northern Ireland, now makes his home in Dublin, in the Republic of Ireland, and since 1982 has taught one semester annually at Harvard. *Sweeney Astray* was published originally in Ireland in 1983. His most recent volumes of poetry have been *Station Island* (1984) and *The Haw Lantern* (1987). A volume of critical essays, *The Government of the Tongue*, was published by Faber in 1988, with U.S. publication by Farrar, Straus & Giroux early the following year.

PARKER PO-FEI HUANG was born in 1914 in Canton, China, where he was a journalist. After World War II he served as editor-in-chief of Chinese newspapers in Hong Kong and the U.S.A. From 1952 until his retirement in 1985, he taught Chinese at Yale University. Besides his many books on written and spoken Chinese and Cantonese, including a Cantonese dictionary, he has published four volumes of Chinese poems in Taiwan and Hong Kong. His English poems have appeared in the *New York Times*, *New York Herald*

Tribune, The Yale Review, Hudson Review, and other publications. In addition to writing poems he also gives performances in which he chants ancient Chinese poetry in Mandarin, Cantonese, and Toishanese. He has performed at the Guggenheim Museum and the Library of Congress, among other places.

J. JORGE KLOR DE ALVA is associate professor of anthropology and Latin American studies, and director of the Institute of Mesoamerican Studies, State University of New York, Albany. He has been a fellow of the John Simon Guggenheim Memorial Foundation, translated various works in Nahuatl, Spanish, and English, and is the author of numerous articles and monographs on cultural contact and change among Nahuatl speakers in colonial Mexico and among contemporary Hispanics in the United States.

SUZANNE JILL LEVINE, professor of Latin American literature at the University of California at Santa Barbara, is currently writing a book on the artistic and critical process of translation, titled *The Subversive Scribe.* Her translations include the works of Adolfo Bioy Casares, Jorge Luis Borges, Guillermo Cabrera Infante, Julio Cortazar, Jose Donoso, Carlos Fuentes, and Manuel Puig. She has twice been the recipient of the NEA fellowship grant for literary translation.

CHRISTOPHER MIDDLETON is an English poet and translator, living in Austin, Texas, since 1966. He has published nine books of poems and short prose, two books of critical essays, and numerous translations from German. His most recent book of poems is *Two Horse Wagon Going By* (Carcanet Press, 1986). Carcanet will publish his *Selected Writings* in 1989 (paperback edition from Paladin Books, London). For his translations of Robert Walser he was awarded in 1987 the Max Geilinger Stiftung Prize (Zurich).

A. K. RAMANUJAN is professor in the Department of South Asian Languages and Civilizations, the Department of Linguistics, and the Committee on Social Thought at the University of Chicago. His translations include *Speaking of Siva* (Penguin, 1973); *The Interior Landscape* (Indiana University Press, 1967); and *Poems of Love and War* (Columbia University Press, 1985). He has published many volumes of poetry as well, including *The Striders* (1966), a Poetry Society recommendation; *Hokkulalli Huvilla* (1969); *Relations* (1971); and *Selected Poems* (Oxford, 1976).

RICHARD SIEBURTH, professor of French and comparative literature at New York University, has recently published translations of
Walter Benjamin's *Moscow Diary* (Harvard University Press, 1986);
and Michel Leiris's *Nights as Day, Days as Night* (Eridanos Press,
1988). His translation of Hölderlin's late *Hymns and Fragments* was
published by Princeton University Press in 1984.

DENNIS TEDLOCK is McNulty Professor of English in the Program
in Folklore, Mythology and Film Studies at the University of New
York at Buffalo. His translations include *Finding the Center: Narrative Poetry of the Zuni Indians* (University of Nebraska Press, 1978);
and *Popol Vuh: The Maya Book of the Dawn of Life* (Simon &
Schuster, 1985). For the latter book he won the PEN Translation
Prize in Poetry.

CHARLES TOMLINSON is professor of English at the University
of Bristol. His books include *Collected Poems* (Oxford University
Press, 1987); *The Return* (Oxford University Press, 1987); *Some
Americans* (University of California Press, Berkeley, 1981); *Poetry
and Metamorphosis* (Cambridge University Press, 1983); and a volume of his graphics, *Eden* (Redcliffe, 1985).

ROSMARIE WALDROP has translated *The Book of Questions* by
Edmond Jabès (Wesleyan University Press, 1984); Paul Celan's *Col-
lected Prose* (Carcanet, 1986); and *The Vienna Group: Six Major
Austrian Poets* (Station Hill Press, 1985) (with Harriet Watts). Her
own most recent books are a novel, *The Hanky of Pippin's Daughter*
(Station Hill Press, 1987), and poems, *The Reproduction of Profiles*
(New Directions, 1987).

ROSANNA WARREN is coordinator of the Translation Seminars at
Boston University, and assistant professor in the University Profes-
sors Program and the departments of English and Modern Languages.
She has translated selected prose of André Derain and Alfred de
Vigny, selected poetry and prose of Gérard de Nerval, and poems of
Max Jacob and Pierre Reverdy. A translation of Euripides' *Suppliant
Women*, in collaboration with Stephen Scully, is forthcoming from
Oxford University Press. Her most recent book of poems is *Each
Leaf Shines Separate* (Norton, 1984).

Index